**Brown Rice for Better Health** | **GENMAI**

Eiwan Ishida

# GENMAI

## Brown Rice
## for Better Health

Japan Publications, Inc.

Published by JAPAN PUBLICATIONS, INC., Tokyo and New York

*Distributors:*
UNITED STATES: *Kodansha International/USA, Ltd., through Harper & Row, Publishers, Inc., 10 East 53rd Street, New York, N. Y. 10022.* SOUTH AMERICA: *Harper & Row, Publishers, Inc., International Department.* CANADA: *Fitzhenry & Whiteside Ltd., 195 Allstate Parkway, Markham, Ontario, L3R 4T8.* MEXICO AND CENTRAL AMERICA: *HARLA S. A. de C. V., Apartado 30–546, Mexico 4, D. F.* BRITISH ISLES: *Premier Book Marketing Ltd., 1 Gower Street, London WCIE 6HA.* EUROPEAN CONTINENT: *European Book Service PBD, Strijkviertel 63, 3454 PK De Meern, The Netherlands.* AUSTRALIA AND NEW ZEALAND: *Bookwise International, 54 Crittenden Road, Findon, South Australia 5007.* THE FAR EAST AND JAPAN: *Japan Publications Trading Co., Ltd., 1–2–1, Sarugaku-cho, Chiyoda-ku, Tokyo 101.*

First edition: March 1989

LCCC No. 88–080453
ISBN 0–87040–781–3

Printed in U.S.A.

# Foreword

Brown rice, known as *genmai* in Japan, cures illnesses, promotes health, and strengthens one's vitality. But most people are unaware of this. Mankind has remained largely ignorant of the powers of *genmai* throughout the millennia that he has been eating rice. People have preferred to fill their empty stomachs, tantalize their taste buds, and satisfy the other cravings of their senses while overlooking the importance of achieving happiness by raising the level of their existence through the use of rice in association with life, health, treatment, and renewal.

The view by modern science of food as a mere fuel to be measured in calories of available energy presents a far greater impediment than can be imagined to an understanding of the proper relationship between rice and humanity. This casts our thought and knowledge into a materialistic mold that regards food as nothing more than an object, a "thing." We have no patience for approaches to life and philosophies that treat food as life-giving. Modern man sees food as merely something to fill his belly—a fuel as it were, like coal or gasoline. This is hardly surprising, for we even think of the human body as an object, much as we would a piece of machinery such as a locomotive or car.

I too was just such a person. Never in my wildest dreams did it occur to me that I could recover from my illnesses and achieve happiness through food. I thought that doctors and drugs cure illness, and that happiness is brought by money. I was firmly convinced that drugs are far more important and useful than food. I don't know how often I ignored my daily diet, prizing instead the food supplements and medication that I took. For well over ten years my faith in drugs remained unshaken, and my faith in doctors persisted even longer. In spite of this, my health did not show even the slightest improvement. To the contrary, with every passing year my body grew weaker and my mental vigor ebbed to such an extent that my doctors were telling me that I would probably live only to about thirty-five. It was a mystery to me why I, faithful as I was in observing the enjoinments of modern medicine, should be so wracked with illness and grow constantly weaker. This experience was not limited to me alone. I found it incomprehensible that, in spite of the constant development of new drugs, the steady advances in medical technology, and the continuous improvements being made in the living environment and standard of living, the number of diseases and sick people failed to decline.

This puzzle has been completely resolved through genmai and genmai macrobiotics. Had I not had the fortune of stumbling upon a correct way of eating genmai, I would surely have been done in by now through my inborn frailty or through drug poisoning. I was saved by genmai and macrobiotics.

Genmai has a vitality and healing and therapeutic powers that are not even a consideration in synthetic drugs. Genmai is an incredible food that is precious to man.

6

It never ceases to amaze me that although the majority of the world's peoples and population have eaten rice for thousands of years, they fail to have a correct understanding of the merits of brown rice.

I pray that more people will come to a proper understanding of genmai and genmai macrobiotics, even if for no other reason than to:

(1)  cure modern illnesses, promote health, and strengthen vitality;

(2)  eliminate the biological, physiological, economic, social, cultural and other ill effects, as well as the waste and extravagance, of meat-eating (animal-based food products);

(3)  preserve and revive the earth's resources;

(4)  enable the supply of enough food for preserving peace and maintaining the health of all people at a required minimum level or above; and

(5)  restore the rising world population to a natural order in keeping with the natural ecosystems of the earth.

Today, the incredible power of genmai spurs me on to a "Campaign for Eating Rice Properly." Merely practicing a diet in which rice is correctly eaten could enable at least one in every three sick people to regain their health, while genmai macrobiotics would make it possible for even more sick people to recover and would help to resolve other difficult problems as well. It is not enough, however, to merely adopt genmai or rice as one's food staple. One must practice a macrobiotic genmai diet that is based on proper dietary principles and is in keeping with the order of life and physiology.

The earth, nature, humanity, organisms, and our modern age are all suffering. The chief culprit is man. Unless we change the way we live and bring our lifestyles into harmony with the universal order, it will be impossible to cure our modern malaise.

I am deeply grateful to Iwao Yoshizaki, President of Japan Publications, who, having noticed an earlier book of mine written from the above perspective (*Seikatsu kakumei=Genmai seishokuho* [Life Revolution=Macrobiotics], perceived the importance of spreading a correct understanding of genmai and macrobiotics. Without his constant encouragement, this book may never have been written. I am fortunate also in that the translator of the Japanese manuscript, Frederic Metreaud, himself practices a genmai diet and has a keen appreciation for the benefits of brown rice. I wish in addition to express my heartfelt thanks to Tatsundo Hayashi, Yotsuko Watanabe, and the many other individuals who gave me their assistance.

EIWAN ISHIDA
*June 1988*

# Contents

# Introduction:
# Words that Sustain Me

"In the beginning was the Word, and the Word was with God, and the Word was God." This is the famous line from the first chapter of the Gospel according to John.

"In the beginning was the Word"—this world does indeed begin with words. It began with words.

For me it began with words, and for you as well it is beginning with words. I would thus like to quote below those words—of the many that have brought me forth, raised me, and today animate and sustain me—with which I have an especially profound association.

My health and fortunes were revived through the indirect guidance of George Ohsawa. For this reason, I cannot help quoting from Ohsawa with the deepest sense of gratitude. Time after time, I have read and reread these words of his. I imagine that you too have your own selection of favorite quotes and phrases, but I ask you to carefully consider the words that I quote below. I am convinced that these will become a great source of strength for you when you set out to clear a better path towards personal health and fortune.

## Words of George Ohsawa

"All people are happy. But one's spiritual soundness (virtue) and physical soundness (health) are directly proportional both to the depth of discovery, self-enlightenment, and understanding of the basic universal principles—the basic principles of life, human existence, and nature—and to the direction of personal experience. Hence, if a person is not happy, the reason for this is his own vice, ignorance, and lack of understanding. The *I Ching* (the *Book of Changes*) teaches us the basic universal principles in the simplest and clearest of words (or symbols), Yin and Yang."

> "Happiness is the view of the world of the heart given only to those who know that world and strive of themselves to become citizens of it."

> "Disease is a sin. Unhappiness is a decoration bestowed upon scoundrels and evildoers."

> "Only those people without a sense of guilt become ill or unhappy.

> "Happiness is the infinite realization of dreams."

"Diet is correct knowledge concerning all things that create human life; nourishment is the process of properly applying the correct knowledge of food to living."

"Salt  —Up to 6 grams, a tonic;
        In a dose of up to 20 grams, a laxative;
        At 60–70 grams, death.
Sesame—When eaten raw, strong constipation;
        When eaten appropriately, an elixir of eternal youth;
        When taken raw in quantity as an oil, diarrhea, of course."

"For Shame! To have heard even once of macrobiotics, and to have fallen ill again!"

"Die! Those of you who still are not saved by macrobiotics! And you who refuse the knowledge and practice of macrobiotics are mere refuse that has already lost the capacity to live."

"God has no need for money. Life and health are themselves God and the order of the universe. That is why moving away from God is the only sin and the greatest unhappiness. This is my absolute immunological approach to all disease."

"The sole unhappiness of mankind is to trample upon the universal order without knowing it. This is man's greatest sin. Unhappy people first commit this greatest of sins in their diet. From this ensues sickness and agony. All disputes and misfortunes arise from sickness and agony. The universal order is the true principle of life, and is the one and only road—albeit a wide road— to health and freedom, happiness and peace."

"It is true that the difficulty of a deed becomes increasingly clear the more one carries it out. And you shall gradually come to see that the smaller the order the more important the results it brings."

"As long as we take care only to avoid upsetting the order of the universe, then we have nothing to fear."

"God is the ancient name of Truth itself that science is searching for at such a heavy cost."

"I affirm that all illnesses arise from ignorance of God."

Next, I must cite Mahatma Gandhi. There is no need for me to describe Gandhi. The reason I quote him here is that his words serve as a vital force in the mastery of Ohsawa's teachings by helping to light the way for us. Of his many writings, I shall quote only those words of his which are particularly dear to me.

# Gandhi's Words and Way of Life

"There are various keys to health, each of them important, but that which is particularly indispensable is self-restraint."

"A person capable of controlling his appetite is easily able to control his other senses."

"Our bodies must inevitably suffer in accordance with the extent to which we eat for the sake of pleasing our palate.

"Three pillars:
  (1) *brahmacharya* (autolysis)
  (2) *ahimsa* ("non-injury" or "non-killing")
  (3) *satyagraha* ("truth-grasping")
Continued and unbroken autolysis leads to absolute non-violence."

I should add here several more quotations which continue even today to encourage me each day. Let me include just two more.

"Should you be refused a cup of water, repay this with the choicest delicacies
   of the land and sea.
Should you fail to be greeted in a friendly manner, kneel down with a sincere
   heart and receive this.
Should a single penny be denied you, return this with gold.
Should a life not be saved, do not lament it.
Pay back the smallest service tenfold.
The truly noble-hearted know all people as one, reward evil with good, and
   take delight in this."—(a poem of the Gujarat region of India)

And now I present a favorite poem of mine, a powerful poem that guides effort to success. Difficult problems and matters, worthwhile work, lofty aspirations, grand dreams and adventures, great enterprises—these are not things that are easily realized in a day. Yet, it is a fact that dreams and hopes can indeed be realized and achieved. All that is required is that one master the principle of success. This poem teaches us one element of that principle.


Hickson


Try over, and over, and over again;
This is the lesson that will protect you.
Even if at first you do not succeed,
Try over, and over, and over again.
In so doing, courage will surely arise.
If you do not give in, if you do not quit,
Then in the end you shall prevail.

Do not be afraid.
Try over, and over, and over again.
—Adaptation of poem by Edward Whymper

I am a great fan of George Ohsawa's. Maybe such a frank admission of affection
is impertinent and even impolite to this great teacher, but it is the only way I know
how to honestly express my true feelings.

No matter how short our lives may be, each one of us has various encounters
and contacts with others. Yet, no matter how long one may live, it is impossible
to meet everyone. And encountering those pioneers and forerunners no longer with
us is certainly out of the question. The only way we have of meeting the great
pioneers of the past is through their writings, calligraphy, music, paintings, pottery,
statues, recorded voices, and such other remains as may exist. Even those things
which we are able to come into contact with represent but a small part of the
individuals that we venerate. Nor does it necessarily follow that one will like and
revere everything that one does come into contact with. People like or love, respect
or worship others because of various deep motives and associations; each holds
these dear to himself.

It is in just such a sense that I wish to introduce to everyone the George Ohsawa
that I so dearly treasure. The words of Ohsawa that I have quoted above are but
a very small sampling of his very prolific writings. These are just a few quotes that
I happen to have recorded, a few words that I have kept as constant companions.

What impressions do you have upon reading the above quotations? Although
you may not care for them all, if there is even one that burns in your memory,
then I suggest that you too try climbing this mountain called George Ohsawa and
further enrich your life.

Next to Ohsawa, I am but a foolish midget. Yet even I am able to state today
with unalterable conviction and to demonstrate that, as Ohsawa says, "all diseases
arise from ignorance of God." If you or someone in your family or home is ill or
unhappy, then this is certainly because you have not yet had the opportunity to
come into contact with macrobiotics and the Unifying Principle.

Rice (by which I always mean *genmai*, or brown rice) can change your health
and fortune. *Genmai* has amazing powers. In this book, I will describe the things
that I have learned and personally experienced in my own way through eating
*genmai*. It is my hope that what I have set down here will prove to be of some
use to you too, however small.

# A Definition of Macrobiotics

According to my understanding of it, macrobiotics consists of both proper diet and the Unifying Principle:

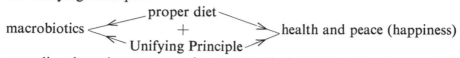

Proper diet alone does not constitute macrobiotics; nor does the Unifying Principle. Only when these are combined do they form what we know as macrobiotics. This is my interpretation based on my own experiences. The reason I point this out here at the beginning of the book is that proper diet is practiced in different ways in different lands throughout the world. The manner in which proper diet is practiced differs with climate and other local conditions. The Unifying Principle distinguishes accurately between these differences and determines what form proper diet should take. In a sense, the Unifying Principle could be called a "second instinct."

Today, we are destroying nature on this precious earth of ours. If man were living together with nature in the manner dictated by the ecosystem, the most proper thing for us to do would be to live and act according to our own instincts like all other living things on this planet. However, human intelligence has persistently abused our earth, destroying and ravaging the terrestrial ecosystem and in the process disrupting the instincts of living things. Mankind has developed intelligence and reaped the fruit of madness. It could even be said that humanity has developed intelligence in order to create insanity.

This is unacceptable. We as humans do not seek a world of chaos; it is not our desire to ravage the earth. Determining how to reintegrate this overdeveloped intelligence of mankind into the natural ecosystem, the cosmic ecosystem, and the original universal order (instinct) will require our greatest powers of judgment. The Unifying Principle is an instinctive power of judgment that will serve as what I call here our "second instinct."

The key ingredient that awakens this second instinct and nurtures it into a supreme power of judgment is none other than proper diet. Thus, proper diet and the Unifying Principle are the two essential components that together make up macrobiotics. This is the conclusion I draw from my own limited experiences.

Proper diet revived and restored my body and spirit which had been totally overrun by disease and insanity. The Unifying Principle served as a great doctor that examined the course of my madness and prescribed a proper diet.

Through brown rice and the Principle of Yin and Yang, I was able to learn that proper diet and the Unifying Principle (by which I mean macrobiotics) is a unique way for man to live in harmony with the order of the universe.

I shall now relate my own experiences in the hope that these will be of some benefit to you.

# 1

## Starting Out
## on a Brown Rice Diet

# My Daughter and Brown Rice

My family and I began eating brown rice with the birth of our first daughter. Had our daughter not been born, I doubt whether we would ever have come across brown rice. Brown rice saved her life, and she saved the lives of me and my family.

Our oldest daughter was born in November 1964, two years after the birth of our first child. At the time, I knew absolutely nothing about nutritional therapy or brown rice diets. Not only was I totally ignorant of these, I was a firm believer in the modern science of nutrition and every day ate nutritious food at each meal. For instance, I ate meat or fish at least once a day without fail. I made certain to eat eggs, milk, cheese, and butter on a daily basis, and meals were always followed by fruit. Moreover, because even this somehow seemed inadequate, I took also food supplements such as vitamins and minerals, as well as various medications. Because I was always in poor physical shape, I became an increasingly strong devotee of dietetics, which enjoins us to consume high-nutrition food.

Then, about three months after our daughter was born, for some unknown reason she began losing her appetite. At the same time, she started regurgitating everything that she was fed.

Being such a strong believer in nutritional science, I was also, quite naturally, a firm believer in modern medicine. Whenever someone wasn't feeling well, it had always been our wont to rush right over to the doctor's. So when we realized that something was wrong with our daughter, we took her at once to our pediatric clinic.

Her symptoms weren't acute—there was no high fever, no diarrhea or constipation, no respiratory distress. She had simply lost her appetite and would spit up whatever she drank, so at first we didn't think that what she had was too serious. The pediatrician took the matter lightly, apparently thinking like us that she would soon recover after taking medication for a while.

But that's not quite the way things turned out. When we began giving her the medicine prescribed by the doctor, the baby's symptoms got worse; the vomiting intensified and the amount of fluid she was spitting up increased.

Both the doctor and I thought that the medicine simply didn't agree with her, and so he tried other preparations. But instead of relieving the baby's symptoms, these only seemed to make them worse; as the vomiting became more severe, she began losing strength.

Unable to bear this any more, along with changing her medication, I decided also to try changing doctors as well. So began our "pilgrimage" from hospital to hospital.

A pilgrimage is supposed to be an act that strengthens our life forces and expresses gratitude to whatever helps us strengthen those forces. Indeed, such feelings were very much a part of our wanderings. We went from hospital to hospital and clinic to clinic, hoping in this way to help speed the recovery of our daughter. If hospital A could do nothing for us, then we set off for hospital B; if hospital B fared no better, then it was on to hospital C; and if hospital C was just as disappointing, we went to hospital D. And all the while, our feelings of dependence on hospitals and physicians grew ever stronger.

But, for whatever reason, whether because they had no idea what our daughter was afflicted with or they simply didn't know how to treat it, none of the physicians we saw were successful in remedying her condition. Eventually, after all of this, we found ourselves going to the Gunma University Hospital, a modern and well-equipped facility, for a close examination.

We were in awe of doctors and hospitals. Because the physician represented to us a supreme being and the hospital was a place where miracles were worked, when we were told that we ought to do this or that, we always followed our instructions to the letter. Even when this entailed expenses for medication that almost sent us reeling, we managed somehow or other to pay up. Strange as it may seem, however, the higher the cost of the medication, the more violently our little daughter threw up. By this time, she had begun having convulsive fits.

At the Gunma University Hospital, she underwent extensive examinations that were like placing her under torture. We were told that a cure would be impossible unless her condition were properly diagnosed through a battery of tests, so I stood by the entire time, silently imploring her over and over not to cry: "Come on, little one, please don't cry. It'll be over soon."

This infant, still less than four months old, desperately fought those painful tests. She cried with all the strength her little body could muster, and with all her strength she resisted the blood collection needle and the instruments thrust down her throat and esophagus.

Already greatly weakened as she was, no matter how much the nurses looked for blood vessels in her arms, legs, and thighs, no blood was forthcoming. Yet, they kept right on searching, repeatedly thrusting in that needle with a motion that seemed to tear into the flesh.

She was suffering and in pain, but there wasn't a thing we could do. We could only try to encourage her to "do as the doctor says." How heartless, how devoid of self-respect, how base we were as parents. Here we had taken the liberty of bringing a child into this world and not only were we unable to raise her strong and healthy, but, after having put her through pain and suffering, we were subjecting her to a torture-like agony and unable even now to help her in any way, had placed her entirely in the power of a doctor—a total stranger. We were parents without qualifications for parenthood; parents far worse than any animal—parents in name only who were unable to raise and nurture the children we had ourselves given birth to.

"The test results will be out in a week," we were told. "Come back in a week's time at the appointed hour."

It was a very long week for us. During that time, the condition of our daughter just got worse and worse. She was unable to keep anything down at all. Whatever we gave her, whether it was medication, coarse tea, milk (we tried powdered milk, nonfat dried milk, condensed milk, whole milk, and soy milk), juice, soup, or even the little mother's milk that flowed, she would invariably spit out at once in three to five times the quantity that entered her mouth. And the pain and agony that racked her little body when she did this were unbearable to watch. I don't know how many times I thought she was about to die of suffocation.

Needless to say, this considerably weakened our daughter even more. Her body became flabby like a balloon that has lost air, and her skin took on a sallow, grayish color.

With all this, my wife had become a little neurotic. As for me, whenever I found time between our hospital visits, I went to the specialty food stores in Tokyo and searched among the foreign dairy products and infant formulas for something that might be good for our daughter, something that might help to nourish her. I believed that this was the least I could do as a parent, that it was an expression of my love for my daughter.

The week following the tests was spent in this way. Both my wife and I waited anxiously for the week to pass, convinced that once we knew the results, our baby would be saved.

When the day finally arrived, my wife gathered up our frail little daughter in her arms and went to the Gunma University Hospital. Upon arriving, she learned that a reliable report could not be made that day and was told to return the next day with me.

The following day, my wife and I went to the hospital as early as possible and received an announcement from the physician handling our daughter's case that totally stunned us. Here is what he said: "I'm very sorry to have to tell you this, but we have no idea what the cause of your baby's symptoms are. Since we are unable to determine what the cause is, we have no idea how to treat her and so there is nothing we can do for her under the present circumstances."

"What?!"

I was unable to suppress a cry of surprise. With my unquestioning faith in Japan's modern medical and therapeutic technology, it had never even crossed my mind that there might not be a method of treatment. I was so startled that I even went so far as to ask, "You mean even with Japan's superb medical technology, there is nothing you can do?"

"Yes, unfortunately. I'm very sorry. Please try to resign yourselves to this."

"Huh?"

My wife and I felt as if we had just been pushed off a cliff. For a while we were at a total loss for words. We failed to grasp at first what he had meant by "resigning ourselves."

"You can't be serious!" I muttered unintentionally. Having thought medicine in Japan to be at the forefront of Western medical technology, I had believed that some cure would surely be found. But that turned out to be just a great illusion. Even if the level of medicine in Japan were the highest in the world, medicine itself was not all-powerful. The uncritical attitude with which I had lived my life entrusting my own body to doctors and drugs had made me a blind believer in the omnipotence of modern medicine; we had failed to notice this delusion of ours.

Still, in retrospect, we are indebted to that honest, conscientious doctor. Had the doctor in charge of our daughter been someone who was even a little concerned with his honor and appearance as a physician, he might not have been so forthright. Had he tried instead one thing then another, and continued handling the case without any prospect of recovery until our daughter's life expired, that would have been that. We would have had no cause for complaint, even had he been unable to save our daughter; not only that, in the modern medical system, there would have been no grounds for reproach of the doctor's actions. Fortunately for us, the doctor admitted his inability to treat our daughter without attempting to save face. I hate to think how things would have turned out had he been less frank with us.

So, abandoned by the hospital and doctor that we had so strongly believed in, we wearily returned home. I began searching desperately for what we should do next.

Then it occurred to me that there existed a method of treating illness with food. Since we had tried everything possible through modern medicine and had been forsaken by it, we no longer cared to rely on Western medicine. It was only natural then that we should wonder whether some other way existed. The following turn of events led us to realize that therapeutic methods based on the use of food existed.

This happened exactly one year before my daughter was born. The firm I was working for was making arrangements to begin sales of a new product to a company in Osaka, and it so happened that the managing director of the Osaka company, someone by the name of Kozo Yamamoto, had come to take a tour of our plant. Since I was in charge of new product sales, the task of receiving and entertaining Yamamoto fell to me. He had brought with him a magazine called *Health and Peace* (the former name of *Seishoku*, a Japanese macrobiotics journal) to read on the train.

When we had dinner together during his visit, he had talked of brown rice diets and nutritional therapy. But, being a firm believer in the modern science of nutrition, what he told me had sounded like so much gibberish; instead of paying attention, I had discounted what he was saying as absurd. "What? Curing illnesses through food? Of all the dumb notions," I had chuckled to myself. All I had was just a faint recollection of that scornful laugh of mine. After talking about this therapy, he returned to Osaka, leaving me the copy of the magazine that he had brought with him.

At a loss as to what to do about my daughter's illness, I remembered for the first time that discussion about curing illnesses with food and I recalled also that I had a copy of *Health and Peace* lying somewhere on our bookshelves. Upon returning home from the hospital, I searched everywhere for that magazine.

I suppose that in times of desperate need, we find a way; or, as it is said, "Ask and you shall receive." That recollection of my meeting with Yamamoto was a gift from heaven. I found the copy of *Health and Peace*.

At once, I phoned the World Macrobiotic Association in Osaka. Shuzo Okada, current chairman of the Association, answered.

I have absolutely no recollection of what exactly I said and how my query was received in that phone call. I must have blurted out what was on my mind, oblivious to all else. Okada explained to me in simple terms how to prepare powdered brown rice milk and suggested that we feed this to our baby.

My wife immediately went out to buy brown rice from the local rice merchant. She prepared a gruel of brown rice and, after diluting this even more, strained it to give a milky preparation. She put the fluid in a baby's bottle and placed the nipple in our daughter's mouth. Now, at the time, whenever we brought the nipple to her mouth, perhaps in response to the odor of the bottle's contents, our daughter would screw up her mouth and absolutely refuse to admit the nipple.

When my wife apprehensively brought that nipple full of brown rice milk close to our daughter's mouth, to our surprise, the expression of displeasure and agony that the baby always had at such times and which so filled us with dread did not appear. Not only did that expression not appear, but after waiting a little to see what happened, she even began moving her mouth to suck on the nipple herself. Our daughter did not have that hearty, gluttonous appetite that strong, healthy babies have. She had lost the strength to drink herself and had to be force fed. But whatever she was fed, she would immediately spit up the next instant with a strength we didn't know she still had in her.

But what about the brown rice milk? Although she was unable to drink more than a few drops, ten minutes, twenty minutes, thirty minutes passed and she still hadn't regurgitated. I cannot properly express with words the delight we felt when we saw this. I suppose "ecstasy" would come close. It was joy mixed with profound relief. At the same time, a doubt soon arose in our minds: "Why didn't she spit up the brown rice milk?"

For the first three days, the baby took only a very small amount, but even so she didn't regurgitate a single time. We were so very thankful for this.

Once brown rice milk had settled in our daughter's stomach, she gradually drank more and more. We were able to sense the life returning to our baby's body and face. Brown rice milk with just a touch of salt added—that's what saved our daughter's life.

Back then, we knew nothing whatsoever of brown rice cooking, macrobiotics, or nutritional therapy. As we watched our daughter become healthy at long last, we hurried to learn whatever we could about eating brown rice. Naturally, under the circumstances, we could hardly have been expected to know the ins and outs of how much of what to employ in nutritional therapy and the appropriate and skillful use of first-aid. Eager as we were to see our daughter gain full health as soon as possible, we added a bit more salt to the brown rice milk than we had been instructed to. It wasn't even necessary to add salt each time. A very tiny pinch added from time to time, just enough to slightly flavor the milk, was all that was needed. Over-flavoring with salt was our only mistake.

In any case, our daughter was saved thanks to brown rice. Although she was always on the small side due to the addition of a bit too much salt to the brown rice milk when she was an infant, she grew up to be an energetic adolescent active in school clubs and sports.

In pediatric medicine, an increase has been noted lately in the birth of infants with congenital metabolic anomalies. Since I am not a physician myself, I am unable to discuss this in the language of the specialist, but it is my understanding that "congenital metabolic anomalies" refers to a lack in the neonate's normal ability to live due to abnormalities in its metabolic functions. Perhaps my daughter was among the first infants with such metabolic anomalies. Although this happened more than twenty years ago, such cases may still have been rare in the medical world back then. Perhaps this was why nothing was known about both the cause and the cure. When I hear the expression "congenital metabolic anomalies" that has begun to catch so much public attention of late, I recall the experience of my daughter. Although I cannot be sure that this was what she had, the description seems to fit.

I have reflected somewhat on why such a condition should arise. I myself had a feeble physical constitution, so I was a big fan of drugs. I had been constantly taking one medication or another ever since the latter half of my junior high school years. My wife, on the other hand, had a strong, healthy body and had rarely taken drugs in her youth. But she had been brought up to be very careful about nutrition, so when we married, this represented a coming together of Western pharmacology and Western dietetics.

After our marriage, in addition to partaking generously of high-nutrition food, I took food supplements. Meanwhile, my wife, in addition to the nutritious meals to which she was accustomed, also took from time to time food supplements. We thought that this was modern, Western-style living at its best.

Our daughter laid her life on the line to show us the error of our ways. The way I see it, congenital metabolic anomalies in a newborn infant are a manifestation of the parents' mistaken lifestyle.

Although my wife had always detested drugs and medications and had had nothing to do with them, when she became pregnant with our daughter, through my influence she began taking vitamins. The effects of these vitamins were especially strong on account of the very healthiness of her constitution. The vitamin C and other pills that she took to prevent morning sickness and facial blemishes clearly were directly responsible for upsetting the health of the fetus she carried. Now, my wife did not routinely take synthetic drugs, which is probably why the effects on our daughter were no worse than I have described. Had she taken the supplements she took in larger doses along with other drugs as well, our daughter may well have ended up being among the twenty percent of Japanese infants that the American environmental health scientist Gordon Park has said are malformed at birth.*

Because I took drugs on a regular basis for so many years, the hardening of my joints and neck muscles is considerably more advanced than in other people of my age. It seems that chemicals such as those in drugs tend to deposit preferentially in the neck and joint areas; because the body tries to avoid the entry of foreign substances into the brain cells, it prevents ingress at the neck. In people with a long-standing habit of ingesting medications and other chemical products on a regular basis, the neck muscles eventually become as rigid and hard as a board.

Thanks to brown rice, however, both my daughter and I have been able to eliminate most of the impurities that cause hardening of the neck muscles. The power of brown rice never ceases to amaze me.

Nowadays one often hears warnings that women should avoid taking medications when pregnant. Not only do drugs create deformed infants, they also are a cause for the birth of mentally retarded infants and infants with various birth defects. Caution in regard to drugs and medications should not begin with pregnancy, however, but long before pregnancy. One could even say that young men and women should prepare for marriage by living a life free of all contacts with medicines.

What led our little three-month-old daughter to risk her life and continue time

---

* T. Tamura. *Kikeiji wa naze* [Why are some children born malformed?].

and time again to regurgitate and reject medications and chemical preparations even to the point of having convulsive fits was that sublime instinctive reflex that eliminates and rejects artificial impurities.

Although there was plenty of mother's milk for our first-born, very litte milk flowed for our daughter. She wasn't thriving as a baby should, so it is hard to describe just how awful we felt at the poor flow of milk when we realized that if only we were able to give her enough milk she would probably be okay. But there were reasons why the milk was not flowing properly.

It is commonly thought today that the mother must receive ample nutrition in order for enough milk to flow. Hospitals and physicians instruct and encourage not only pregnant women but virtually all patients to get adequate nutrition, and should a patient complain of certain symptoms, then he or she is inevitably given some synthetic drugs and supplements. This is what has hampered the flow of milk.

After we became aware of the errors in our way of eating, we adopted a plain and simple brown rice diet and my wife's milk started flowing normally again. This appears strange in a way. Yet the only reason it seems strange and incredible is that the commonly accepted notions that we have are all wrong. George Ohsawa, the great teacher of macrobiotics, once wrote, "There is no greater sin than ignorance." What he meant was that no greater sin exists than ignorance of the truth and the order of the universe; but our conviction had been that it is this very modern life which is so at odds with the natural laws and the universal order that is the solitary truth.

Some time ago, a Dr. Maremitsu Izumitani (associated with the Nutrition and Food Research Institute at Kyoritsu Women's University) offered the hypothesis that excessive nutrition hampers the secretion of mother's milk. Although this was just a tentative report stating that excessive nutrition may be an important factor in the decline of lactation in women, I found myself in total agreement.

When the secretion of milk eventually stops, as is natural, in a mother who has only her all-important milk to give her infant, this is in accord with the natural order. It is maternal instinct. Hence, as long as one lives in accordance with the natural laws and the universal order, both the fetus and, later, the infant will grow and develop normally, and the mother's milk will flow normally.

Well then, just what does it mean to live in accordance with the natural laws and the universal order? I'd like to describe what I have learned about living this way from my own, albeit limited, personal experiences.

## Initial Doubts

What in the world is this brown rice, or *genmai*?

I asked myself this question countless times as I watched my daughter begin at last to thrive and grow on brown rice milk and a brown rice diet.

Our pediatrician, whom we had counted on so highly, had essentially told us, "There is no longer any hope of saving the life of your child. Please try to resign yourself to this." And how had it all turned out? When we cut out all the expensive medications and injections, and placed our entire faith instead in treatment through a brown rice diet, not only did this completely alter our way of living up until then, our baby daughter began to recover. There can be no doubt about it—the perfect timing of this change in our lives was a gift of God. Had the change come at a different time, the outcome might have been different.

My wife and I are responsible for bringing our daughter to the brink of death, and the real burden of responsibility lay with me, because of my total dependence on medicines and doctors. To fully explain what this change in our lifestyle has done for us, I must return to the days when I was in poor physical health and describe the condition of my body back then as well as the changes that I underwent upon turning to a brown rice diet.

As a small boy, I enjoyed normal health. But, under cover of this normal state of health, there lurked the seeds of an abnormal craving for food. I was an uncommon glutton who always sneaked out food and ate it when no one was looking. Yellow snot constantly dribbled from my nose and I always had cuts at the corners of my mouth; although I suffered for it, still I was unable to stop my constant eating. I would make short work of a box of caramels or a bag of sweetened adzuki beans, would down in a twinkling a whole can of condensed milk or other sweet canned foods, and never was satisfied with just two or three rice crackers or biscuits. My mother brought us up fairly strictly, but when she distributed sweets among us, I would later search out the spot where she had put the rest away and gobble up everything that was left when I found it.

This greedy disposition as a small boy later reflected itself in my poor physical condition as an adolescent and a young man.

To begin with, I had gastrointestinal disorders. When I had problems with my stomach or bowels, I took a digestive and bicarbonate of soda. When I had stomach cramps, I took the bitter, red Toyama pills that were a standard household medicine. I took my medicine and continued my gluttonous ways. At the time I had no idea that when the gastrointestinal system is out of sorts, eating little or nothing at all is far better for the body than any medicine. And even had I known this, it is very likely that I couldn't have curbed my gluttonous ways.

The stomach and intestines are the root of our health. When these are weak, the other internal organs gradually become affected. Because I was unable to hold my greedy impulses at bay, the poor condition of my gastrointestinal system grew worse, resulting in gastroptosis. As for my nose, the greenish-yellow snivel oppressively weighed down the front part of my head. This was empyema. Once I learned I had empyema, I began making frequent visits to an otorhinolaryngologist.

In time, I started getting tonsillitis. This was triggered very easily and my tonsils would soon redden and swell up. I never received surgery for the empyema because it wasn't clear whether this would really cure it, but since the doctor told me that getting my tonsils removed would keep me from ever getting tonsillitis again, I had them taken out in the spring of my first year in high school. There is no sense in regretting that decision now. After all, at the time, I thought that removing them was the best solution. Ever since then, I've been constantly afflicted with bronchitis.

The common cold is said to be the cause of all diseases, yet the reason we catch colds in the first place has to do with the weakening and disorder of the gastrointestinal system. Since I did not know that the stomach and intestines were the source of all disease, when I caught a cold or the flu, I tried everything I could to cure just the symptoms of the cold.

Whenever I thought I was a little tired or felt a chill wind blowing, I soon came down with bronchitis. The back of my throat would swell and turn red, my throat would feel irritated and sore, and I would get a high fever. Colds like this continued throughout the years of my youth.

As soon as I thought I might be coming down with something, I was no longer able to stay on my feet. I believed that the bug had got me because I wasn't physically fit enough to resist it, I would at once start swallowing whatever foods I thought would help give me strength: meat, eggs, milk and other dairy products, fruit, and so on and so forth. In addition, I took also my indispensable medications and food supplements.

If I really made an effort, I'm certain that I could remember dozens of drugs that I took on a regular basis back then: Panvitan, Tioctan, Mastigen, Alinamin, Popon-S, Vitahealth, Double-Health, Jubelon, Aspara, Guronsan, Chocola, Hicee, Glycyron, etc. In addition, I took various gastrointestinal medications such as stomach powder, Taka-Diastase, Wakamoto, Ebios, and Wakamatsu. Many other drugs were also occasionally prescribed to me at the hospital, the names of which I no longer recall. Writing all these out, I get the feeling that I was some sort of guinea pig for drug manufacturers. Whenever I saw an ad for a new drug company product, it seemed to me that this was the newest, most effective drug around and I would soon run out to buy it. Having taken as many different kinds of medication as I did, it seems a bit amazing that I never was afflicted with a disorder such as SMON disease. Yet, although I was fortunate enough not to have fallen victim to a strange and unusual drug-induced malady, the fact is that my physical condition did suffer as a result of my constant association with medications.

Thus, I continued to use food supplements and drugs with even greater regularity than I did food. There is an old saying that goes, "Too much of something is as bad as too little." This certainly was true of my persistent use of drugs. Although there is the consolation that I suffered no extreme damage or side reactions from my excessive use of pharmaceutical drugs, I did spend an enormous amount of money on these. The only reason I continued to fork out so much money and swallow this endless stream of pills and capsules was because I so desperately wished to become healthy and strong.

However, contrary to my expectations, I never got any healthier. At every change in the seasons, I would invariably get a feeling of general discomfort. With each small change in my habits or the environment—a change in the weather, a cold wind blowing, staying out under the blazing sun a bit too long, a little physical overexertion, working at night, an anxiety weighing on my mind—the oppressive feeling that felt as if a sheet of lead had been slung over my back and pelvis just got worse, my throat started to ache, and I could no longer stay up. I would place two *futons* under me, throw I don't know how many quilts over me, and would be unable to get up again until I had drained as much sweat as possible out of myself. Once I was laid up in bed, I would have to take a week to ten days off from work, and since this went on throughout the year, everyone would resign themselves in dismay to wait out the days until I was back on my feet again. To think of how much I must have inconvenienced my family, those around me, the company at which I worked, and my customers. But when I had a cold I just couldn't stay on my feet, so there was nothing to be done about it. After a week or so, and after repeatedly sweating so copiously that the futons on which I lay were drenched, I would at last start feeling refreshed. But my illness had not run its course, for it took more than just a bit of sweating to cure me of a cold. Once I had shaken off those first signs of illness, my nose, mouth, and the border of my lips started tingling and feeling itchy; soon after this, the most unpleasant cold sores—filled with a clear, light yellow fluid—emerged all over at once. I never shook a cold without my face first breaking out like this. These blisters and the accompanying stomatitis swelled red, eventually breaking open, then drying. Another ten days to two weeks passed before these symptoms receded at last.

It was very unpleasant afterwards to have to face other people with all these scabs on my face. They would remark, "Oh, cold sores again, huh?" Seeing as this was a year-round thing with me, they got fed up with it all and gave it little thought.

As this went on recurring, I wondered why I should be so susceptible to colds. Yet no matter how much I thought about it, since I was living a life estranged from truth, I was unable to find any clue to resolve this. So I decided to eat as nourishing a diet as I could, take food supplements, and get an appropriate amount of exercise. I immediately applied myself to this program I had set up for myself. However, before the scabs had completely fallen off, I would inevitably feel as if I was coming down with something again, at which point I would go at once to see my doctor. This sequence of events was repeated countless times.

While the doctor was giving me a shot in the arm at the clinic, I would always ask him, "Doc, even though I do exactly as you say and make sure to get proper nourishment, plenty of exercise whenever I can, and live as regular a life as possible, why is it that I keep getting sick like this all the time? Why can't I become healthy and strong like other people?"

"Well, you've got a weak physical constitution. You may have been born that way." The doctor too was used to this exchange. He always gave me more or less the same answer.

"If I'm frail as you say, then what should I do to make myself stronger?"

"Like I always tell you, what you've got to do is eat plenty of nourishing food and make sure to get enough exercise and plenty of rest. The idea is to make your body stronger and more resistant. That's the only way."

"But I'm trying as hard as I can to do exactly as you say, and still I'm not getting any better. Why not?"

"Well, you can't expect things to improve overnight. You've got to keep at it and gradually strengthen your body."

Apart from my poor physical condition, I wondered if there wasn't some way to at least avoid the stomatitis that I got so often and those unpleasant sores that always broke out just as I was getting over a cold. I asked my doctor about this countless times: "Doc, what are these itchy blisters anyway? Why do I get them all the time?"

His answer never varied: "Lots of people get fever blisters. That's a consequence of your physical makeup. It's quite common among people who tend to be allergic."

When questioning the doctor, I never ceased to be amazed. Here I would bring my miserable self, sores and all, before the doctor's very eyes and ask him questions about what I didn't know. For example, I had asked him countless times what these blisters were and why they arose in the first place. Even supposing he didn't know the first time I questioned him, if a physician didn't clearly understand himself, then he should at least collect a sample of the fluid from these blisters, analyze what this unpleasant fluid was, and study the problem. Wasn't the failure to do so negligence on the part of the doctor? If he were to do some research and arrive at a solution, wouldn't this be a great service to both doctors and patients? Such thoughts constantly ran through my mind. This was one large doubt I had. But my doctor appeared to have no interest whatsoever in resolving this and always gave me the same answer: "Those cold sores are viral; that's why they itch and tingle like that. Allergens, which cause allergic reactions, also cause the same sort of reaction."

When the doctor gave me a pat answer like this, I would always wonder: "Well, if it's a virus, then what kind of a virus is it and how can it be destroyed? And if it's an allergen, then there must be some way to take care of it. Don't tell me that in this day and age, medical scholars and physicians are unable to fully understand the cause of cold sores and how to treat them properly."

Doubtful as to how seriously my doctor concerned himself with my illness and health, I changed physicians and clinics countless times, hoping for the best as I went in to be examined. However, none of the doctors could give me a straight answer. Whether it was because they were unable to respond to every question posed by a high-strung patient or they simply had no clear solution to the cause of an illness, I continued to harbor doubts and suspicions towards all the doctors I met. Even so, I thought of the doctor as the highest teacher of sickness and health.

Later on when I observed physicians, I found that they too catch colds and get fever blisters, they too suffer from diseases such as diabetes, and some doctors even fall dead suddenly from cerebral hemorrhages. Newspaper articles reporting the deaths of successive directors of the Cancer Institute of Japan and of famous physicians and heads of major hospitals succumbing one after another to cancer and cerebral hemorrhage never cease to amaze me.

With this unbearable suspicion I had of doctors, I felt as if I had to do something, and so I began searching for medications myself.

Now that I think of it, I realize that the treatment of someone who is ill by a physician is far more difficult than the average layman may imagine. This is because the doctor usually knows little or nothing about the patient's lifestyle. Although the physical condition of the patient and the symptoms of the disease are generally apparent after a physical examination, the doctor has no deeper and more detailed knowledge of the patient. If the doctor and the patient were to live together for many years, the doctor would certainly be able to provide more appropriate and reliable treatment and guidance. However, it's plainly impossible for a physician to share the daily life of all sick people and patients. Yet the doctor tries, in spite of this lack of familiarity with the patient, to cure the illness he sees before him. So it is indeed a difficult task.

Moreover, it is no surprise if a doctor has a hard time understanding etiological factors arising from those aspects of a patient's life unseen to him, especially when the patient is unable to place his entire faith in the doctor's treatment and incessantly conducts a search of his own for this or that new patent medicine. Unless a sick person's overall lifestyle, life history, lineage, and upbringing are clearly understood, deciding on an appropriate method of treatment is impossible. And even supposing for a moment that these things should be understood, it would be a mistake to expect the treatment dictated by modern medicine, which addresses only the symptoms of the disease, to be fundamental. The very expectation of fundamental therapy today is asking for too much.

In any case, I came down with the same sort of illness time after time, and was nothing but trouble to my family, my friends, and my fellow workers. Quite naturally, everyone thought of me as sickly and weak, about which there was nothing to be done.

The opinion of others aside, I myself experienced great discomfort. Not only was I always catching colds, the food I ate would sit heavy on my stomach, I would get heartburn and stitches in my side, and I would always have a dull, heavy feeling at the back of my stomach; towards evening, I would feel weary all over. My stomach would splash around, sounding like a balloon filled with water.

As I persisted in taking several kinds of internal medicine on a regular basis, my belly became rigid to the point where the doctor would cock his head to one side in perplexity while palpating. Then he would tell me that my kidneys would go bad, that I would contract liver diseases, that I would suffer a nervous breakdown, and so on and so forth. I was a veritable repository of disease.

Because some part of me was always hurting or unwell, I would take a drug for this and a drug for that. But I failed to notice that the general weakening and decline in my internal organs was precisely on account of this habit of constantly taking medication in the fervent hope of curing my illnesses.

This was where things stood with medications. As for nutrition, let me give here one example of the efforts I expended to ensure that I ate well.

After graduating from high school, I joined a construction-related firm. Shortly after starting my job, I was assigned to an outlying branch office and began living and cooking for myself in a company dormitory. Since I was already troubled at the time by the poor condition of my body, along with medication, tonics, and food supplements, I devoted a great deal of attention and funds to nutrition, as the doctor had advised me. The thought that I must get sufficient nutrition constantly weighed on my mind. I was convinced that by lunching at restaurants, I could compensate for any nutrition that I might be missing by cooking my evening meals myself.

For example, day after day, I would eat thick pork cutlets dripping with pork sauce or would order a large hamburger steak topped with two eggs along with a side order of rice covered with meat sauce. Or I might wish to try something different and, imagining that *sushi* prepared with fish and other fresh ingredients would provide me with the nourishment that I needed, I would settle on sushi for lunch and eat sushi many days running. Or if I got together with the other young guys in the office after work for a drink, dedicated as I was to the idea of good nutrition, I thought that roasted giblets was just about the best nutrition one could get and so we would often go out to eat liver, gallbladder, chicken fat, or the like.

While being constantly attentive to nutrition in this way, I also took great care in the cooking I did for myself. I spent almost my entire salary on eating out, the tonics and supplements I was always buying, and an occasional book. And yet, in spite of all that I did, instead of getting any better, my physical condition only deteriorated further and the frequency with which I was laid up sick in bed just increased.

"Why is it impossible to prevent those awful, itchy sores that form just as I'm getting over a cold? And why is it that even though I'm doing my utmost to follow the doctor's instructions, my health isn't improving?"

These two questions continued to plague me throughout my adolescence and early adulthood. I had also many other doubts and concerns over my health, but these two were constantly on my mind.

And when I saw just how quickly these concerns of mine were resolved and how easily the causes underlying my problems were explained by a brown rice diet, I could not help but be amazed.

## The First Week on Brown Rice

Although my family's brown rice diet began with our daughter's illness, it took a good while for all the members of the family to get accustomed to life based on a brown rice diet. My daughter and I started out on three legs, so to speak. As I closely observed my daughter finally regain her health, it occurred to me that something which had such a powerful effect on her would certainly be good as well for me as her father. This was my original reason for venturing out on a brown rice diet.

Free at last of any association with medications, injections, and infant formulas, our little daughter began thriving on a diet composed almost entirely of brown rice milk or gruel with a little vegetable soup added to it. Seeing this, I decided that I too would begin a brown rice diet and resolved at the same time to abandon the nutriments and medicines that I had used continuously up until then; I intended as well to abandon the notions I had of modern nutritional science. I gathered up the many bottles of medication I always kept around me and threw them all away. I was uneasy about parting with this medication, but my reason for taking such a drastic action was to free myself of the compulsion to take them.

The first problem we encountered was where to get our brown rice. In our case, we bought it from the local rice shop. Of course, at the time, rice shops did not sell brown rice and so we got some strange looks; the rice merchants were no doubt wondering why in the world we should suddenly want brown rice when everyone else ate white rice. This tended to make us an object of local curiosity, which was an embarrassment since we were not really prepared yet to describe to others the merits of a brown rice diet. However, general interest in eating brown rice has grown recently, and an increasing number of rice dealers are aware today of what a brown rice diet is. Getting hold of brown rice is no longer the problem that it used to be.

The second problem was how to cook brown rice so that it is tasty. We use a pressure cooker, although automatic rice cookers that cook brown rice have been developed recently. The first step in adopting a brown rice diet consists of making certain to cook brown rice properly. Let me describe how this is done with a pressure cooker.

Brown rice is softened by applying a higher pressure than for white rice, and so it is necessary for the person cooking the rice to get the knack of how much water to add, how much heat to apply, how long to cook the rice, and so forth. Whether using an electric or gas stove, those who are unaccustomed to using pressure cookers will at first be fearful of approaching the cooker when the rice is boiling and sending out spurts of vapor through the pressure control valve. Until we got used to our pressure cooker, we were always wary of it. And it took us longer than we expected to learn how to properly cook our rice. I'd say that it took a good week of serious effort and the inevitable failures—undercooking, overcooking, burnt rice—before we got the hang of it. The recent advent in Japan of automatic rice cookers which can cook brown rice has made it much easier to adopt brown rice as the staple of one's diet. However, I am not so sure that making everything convenient and automatic is in the best interest of people.

When my family ate white rice, we too used an automatic rice cooker; we accepted the automatic rice cooker as doing the job of cooking rice for us. All we had to do to cook rice was measure out the correct amounts of rice and water, and press the switch on the cooker. But I have strong doubts as to whether this should be the extent of our knowledge and effort when it comes to cooking rice.

Things changed completely when we adopted a brown rice diet. This was long before automatic rice cookers for brown rice appeared on the market. With an automatic rice cooker, as long as you set the timer at night, the rice cooks even if you oversleep in the morning, so you have freshly cooked hot rice for breakfast. Or, even in the absence of a timer, you can get up early and flip the switch in the morning then go back to sleep for a while. All this is impossible, however, with a pressure cooker. Not only that, the proper amount of water that must be added varies with the variety of brown rice. You also have to consider the strength of the flame (the stove setting), the timing involved both in applying pressure and in releasing the pressure and allowing the steam to escape, as well as the length of time the rice is allowed to steam after cooking. Careful attention must be paid to each of these important points in order to properly cook the rice. What a big difference between this and simply flipping a switch and going back to bed. My wife was no longer able to sleep late in the morning.

There is good- and bad-tasting white rice, but the difference between these extremes is even greater in the case of brown rice. That is why when we went to buy brown rice at the rice dealer's, we acquired the habit of placing a few grains of the rice in the palm of one hand and examining it for quality. We actually became able to distinguish between different types of rice based on the form and shape of the kernels, luster, and other characteristics. In fact, we were even able to determine when one type of rice needed to be cooked with a little more water, and another with a little less. Eventually, you even reach the point where, when the rich, pleasant aroma of brown rice starts to emanate as the rice begins boiling and giving off steam, you have a good idea of the taste of that rice and of its final cooked state. Rice that has been grown using pesticides retains an odor of pesticides. Force-dried rice and naturally dried rice differ in aroma and taste. One learns a lot also by observing the strength of the flame used to cook the rice. In adopting a brown rice diet, we started to learn many things that we never would have been able to experience merely by cooking white rice with an automatic rice cooker. One cannot cook brown rice well if one doesn't really have one's heart in it.

I cannot help feeling that a well-prepared meal is a work of art. My wife says that whenever a brown rice meal is deliciously cooked it has invariably been cooked with wholehearted enthusiasm and care; she claims that when a meal is not delicious, this is because the cook was distracted or not feeling well. Frankly, it does seem as if one must put one's whole heart into it in order to cook good brown rice deliciously. George Ohsawa, our brown rice mentor, wrote that, "The tastiness of a meal is a barometer of the cook's affection." What I imagine he meant was that the deliciousness of a meal is a barometer of the care devoted to cooking delicious rice, and also of love and affection for one's family and for those people who are to eat the meal one prepares, as well as gratitude for the meal itself.

One learns nothing from a lifestyle in which rice is easily cooked with an automatic rice cooker. I have come to believe that taking great pains to cook brown rice with a pressure cooker represents a very precious way of life. The very act of doing all one can to cook good rice greatly enhances the savoriness of the rice and one's appreciation for that rice. However, because white rice today is so very easy to prepare, people today have completely lost their sense of gratitude for rice and treat it carelessly.

My wife threw herself wholeheartedly into the task of curing the illnesses of her daughter and husband with brown rice cooking. As with anything else, if a task is approached reluctantly, little can be expected in the way of results or gratitude. Cooking, in particular, when done unwillingly and without a bright, joyful feeling, will end up tasting bad. I have found it best that whatever one does be done with dedication and enthusiasm.

I got a copy of George Ohsawa's *Shin shokuyo ryoho* [A New Theory of Nutrition and Its Therapeutic Effects] and began with one of the basic principles of brown rice diet described there:

*Stage One Regimens of New Diet (daily amount)*

A.  Roasted brown rice (prepare by sprinkling about 10% of concentrated salt water onto freshly roasted brown rice); 10–20 grams of *takuan* (pickled daikon) or other pickled vegetables (not colored or flavored with artificial dyes or sweeteners).

B.  Buckwheat flour (prepare with cold or hot water as buckwheat dumplings; season with salt and garnish with about 20 grams of raw scallion or grated daikon).

C.  Buckwheat bread (knead together 6 parts of buckwheat flour, 2 parts of *udon* (wheat noodle) flour, and 2 parts of wheat or rice bran; add 1 or 2 parts of scallion, dropwort, honewort, burdock, lotus root, and other ingredients, and bake).

D.  Brown rice (add at least a pinch of salt and cook) and one bowl of miso soup (the miso should be old-fashioned, country-style miso made without rice *koji*; as the ingredients, add a little sautéed scallion, dropwort, leek or seasonal herbs).

E.  Brown rice (same as in D) and vegetables in one-third to one-fifth the amount of rice (any vegetable is okay; this may be boiled down with soy sauce or seasoned with salt. Adding a little oil is even better.

34

These are all simple meals, but any one of them may be taken for several consecutive days. It is essential, however, that the staple food here be chewed at least 100 times (the more times the better, 200 or 300 times being even more preferable). After taking a new mouthful, place your chopsticks and bowl on the table. Do not pick up your chopsticks again until you have finished chewing.

Tea and hot or cold water must all be kept to an absolute minimum (such that males urinate no more than 4 times a day, and females no more than 3 times; this may be five or six times daily in the case of those who are at least fifty years old).

People who are restless and unable to chew slowly may eat while they work. Three meals a day is acceptable, as is also two, or even one daily meal. One may eat at any time when hungry, and in any amount.

*Foods to Stay Away From:* Those attempting to establish a health body and mind through a proper way of life should decide on one of the above five regimens during the "training period" and take no other foods. The following are especially forbidden: all animal-based foods (including milk, eggs, butter, etc.), potatoes and sweet potatoes, all fruits, sweets (including candies and all products containing sugar, honey, saccharin, Dulcin), vinegar, all alcoholic beverages, commercial miso and soy sauce (it is okay to smoke cigarettes).

Follow the above regimen for at least one month and up to about 6 months. Do not take the forbidden foods mentioned above until you have established the fullest confidence in your health.

I started with regimen D. The first week passed. I did not always follow this regimen strictly every single day, yet something strange began to happen to me. Both my hands, from the wrists to the fingertips, turned purple in color, just as if ink had been injected into my blood. It was not exactly pleasant to watch this happening in myself. I couldn't help thinking that my hands looked just like those of a dead man. These purplish-black hands of mine were ice-cold. Black-and-blue blotches the size of quarters appeared on my knees and calves. The same symptoms later reappeared many times. While this was going on, the overall condition of my body improved so much that I began to feel better than I ever remember having felt before. I felt refreshed and invigorated. My body was warm.

I at once attended a brown rice diet workshop, where I asked about the changes that had taken place in my body upon starting a brown rice diet. I learned that these are some of the initial reactions to a brown rice diet, and that there may also be many other reactions. In my case, the predominating reactions were sores and skin eruptions. Time after time, sores arose about my nose and mouth. People all experience different reactions, but in the first couple of weeks after starting a brown rice diet, everyone is beset by anxieties due to the arisal of various reactions. Because one is beginning a diet entirely different from that which one is accustomed to, it is only natural that there should be changes and reactions of some sort. Some people vomit, become diarrhetic or constipated, extremely listless or anemic; some, like me, undergo changes in the color of the blood, the emergence of eruptions and sores, increases in dandruff, mucus, eye and nasal discharges; through illness, they may suffer another round of fever, aches and pains, coughing, and other symptoms. Yet, in spite of such changes and reactions, the body overall feels somehow refreshed. Apparently, these may be thought of as reactions signaling the onset of the body's recovery to a normal condition.

## Three Months Later

After being on a brown rice diet for about three months, I began to understand many things. The more faithfully I adhered to this diet, the clearer everything became to me. I basically followed regimen D, but because in many respects I chose to observe this in my own way, I did not go strictly by Ohsawa's book. There were still too many things I didn't know about macrobiotics at the time and, no matter how highly I thought of it, my former notions about life and diet remained deep-rooted; I continued to have misgivings about a brown rice diet. Yet, by my third month on this diet, I had begun to learn a great many things. First of all, I noticed to my surprise a sharp decline in my level of fatigue. This may sound like an exaggeration, but I virtually lost all sense of fatigue. Up until that time, over a period of three months I would normally have come down with symptoms such as stomatitis, laryngitis, or bronchitis and been laid up in bed two or three times. Yet nothing of the sort had happened and I was able to apply myself to my job without interruption. For me to be able to go on working like everyone else without coming down with a cold or the flu and having to stay home in bed was a new and welcome experience. To one whose existence had for so long been inextricably tied to nutrition, shots, tonics, and doctors, getting along without any of these after just three months on a brown rice diet was a very major event, a revolution of sorts. Nor was stoic endurance necessary to begin a brown rice diet. Before I knew it, I had grown accustomed to it. And what was particularly amazing was my invigorated sense of body and mind. Where before I had always felt weary and in poor physical condition, now I felt light and energetic; my physical carriage improved tremendously and in the morning I awoke easily and refreshed.

I was overjoyed by these changes and became convinced that I should apply myself with even greater earnestness. Yet I had taken just the first step in the door; I knew nothing more about this new diet and way of life. Intent on learning whatever I could about brown rice and macrobiotics, I began reading one after another of George Ohsawa's writings and other related books.

It was only much later after I had begun eating brown rice that I learned of the existence of several schools of brown rice diet, so it was just pure luck that I came into contact with Ohsawa's ideas when I did. The world is full of folk remedies and techniques for keeping healthy. However, I believe that a brown rice diet differs completely from these because it embodies a lifestyle that could well be regarded as the source and foundation of the Japanese way of life. Quite truthfully, I cannot help but be profoundly grateful at my great good fortune at having been led directly to macrobiotics as taught by Ohsawa. His approach was perfectly suited to the physical constitutions of my daughter and I.

Brown rice diets may all appear to be identical, but the effects that ensue from these diets differ considerably, depending on the school of thought. For example, if a brown rice diet that exerts a powerful cooling effect on the body is practiced in individuals who are scrofulous (have a weak physical constitution) and overly sensitive to the cold, the desired effects are not easily obtained. On the other hand, if people with this sort of physical constitution practice a brown rice diet which has a strong warming effect on the body, the diet will have a rapid and perceptible effect, producing a daily improvement in the condition of the body.

I always had too unbalanced a diet, tending to foods and drinks that have a strong cooling action on the body. As a child, I craved candies, cakes, and sweet drinks, and I also had my parent's predilection for sweet potatoes and beans; later, as an adolescent and young man, I took too many medications, imbibed too much alcohol, and ate too much fruit. This made my body scrofulous and highly susceptible to the cold. In the winter, I would always get painful frostbite on my hands, legs, and ears. When going to sleep, I would have to throw several heavy quilts over my legs to warm myself; even in the summer, I was unable to sleep without a heavy quilt over me. Given the nature of my physical constitution, I was very fortunate to have come across Ohsawa's nutritional therapy, which has a strong warming effect on the body.

Although I just noted that Ohsawa's approach to a brown rice diet has a strong warming effect on the body, that is not to say that it is inappropriate for people of other physical constitutions. The Ohsawa approach encompasses a theory and principle that can be applied to all individuals, through nutritional therapy, health-sustaining techniques, and everyday life, so as to keep our state of health from deteriorating. George Ohsawa called this the Unifying Principle, and describes the theory behind it as "the order of the universe." I studied this Universal Principle while following a brown rice diet. I came to learn in time that anyone can master the knowledge and techniques of eating brown rice in accordance with one's own physical constitution, and practice a brown rice diet appropriate for oneself. Those who wish to study and learn about this theory and principle can avail themselves of the writings of Ohsawa and his many students, as well as attend the numerous workshops, seminars, camps, and other events and organizations established for that purpose.

When I began eating brown rice, there were not as many books on the subject as we have today. Moreover, since Western dietetics was still at its zenith, only a very small number of people quietly practiced a brown rice diet, so there must have been very little demand for such books. I would get the book that I wanted by inquiring at the Nippon C.I. (publisher of Ohsawa's books in Japan), which had a habit of moving often. Things are different today. Anyone can join the Nippon C.I., and getting the books that one wants is easy. In addition, there are now many ways of studying macrobiotics, so it has become possible to study and learn more rapidly.

I read one after another of Ohsawa's books, but I found them mostly incomprehensible. The Unifying Principle in particular, which is the practical dialectic of the principle of Yin and Yang, appeared at first easy to understand, but it took quite some time before I was able to truly grasp it and apply it. In addition to reading books on macrobiotics, I attended as many workshops and other events as I could. I even participated in the health seminars held in summer and winter and often visited teachers and other more experienced adherents of macrobiotics.

The first health seminar I attended was held in the winter at Manza Hot Spring. This was after I had begun eating brown rice and the condition of my body had started improving, so I took some time off work and attended in high spirits. The seminar was great fun. The meals consisted only of brown rice and simple side dishes in very small amounts, but we spent the day skiing as much as we wanted, while at night, and at other times for that matter, there were study sessions, reports of personal experiences, music, and entertainment. The owner of the inn at which we stayed was himself a brown rice advocate, so we were able to eat macrobiotically.

On the last evening of the seminar, an unexpected feast was laid out before us. This included freshly gathered local eggs and milk. I was still in a "training" phase, having begun a brown rice diet just recently. In *A New Theory of Nutrition*, Ohsawa warns those just starting out to abstain from all animal-based foods. As I was pondering what to do, one of the leaders of the group, Dr. Moriyasu Ushio, proclaimed, "Eating freshly gathered natural food can't hurt the body. And after all, if we aren't able to eat anything freely, then we cannot become free people." This certainly made sense to me, so I sampled the food. No one was affected at the meal. The next day, the seminar came to a close and all of us returned home. On the second day after my return, I started feeling a familiar tingling sensation about my mouth and the edge of my nose. Before I knew it, those awful sores I had experienced so often broke.out over the entire lower half of my face. The pain was almost unbearable. I felt as if hot coals had been placed on my face. I tried a macrobiotic treatment, but this had no immediate effect. For several days, all I could do was moan and complain; I wasn't even able to sleep. A month passed before those sores hardened into scabs and the scabs peeled off entirely.

From this experience I realized all too well that because I had not fallen ill even once during the several months since I had begun a brown rice diet and was able to function normally without being laid up in bed, I had gained a false sense of well-being. I would prefer not to draw the simple conclusion that those horrible eruptions were the direct consequence of my having partaken of animal-based foods that were strictly forbidden me. However, after the physical training I received by skiing at Manza Hot Spring, after bringing my metabolism up to a peak by bathing in the potent hot springs, and after encouraging my body to rid itself of its toxins, the fact that I had then taken in food and drink which was stronger than necessary must have acted as a trigger for the eruptions. From this experience, I realized that my body still contained far more toxins than I had suspected.

Every time there was a reaction, I would feel wretched and depressed, thinking of how weak a person I was and what a frail body I had. Even so, I stubbornly continued my brown rice diet. In time, the reactions vanished and I became healthy. My subjective symptoms also receded and I came to feel much better than I had before. I once again acquired a cheerful frame of mind. At this point, I was telling myself that the illness and the reactions had a purifying effect; they were making my body healthy and their appearance should therefore be very welcome.

But my parents, my co-workers at the firm, and my friends all saw things differently. My colleagues scorned what I told them and warned me, "You're getting those sores because you're on a brown rice diet. Ask a doctor and he'll tell you that those sores are due to vitamin C deficiency and malnutrition. You ought to get off that diet. Nobody today has awful sores like that."

"A brown rice diet is all right I suppose, but there's no need for you to get so serious about it," my mother said. "Why don't you eat something nutritious? You were already thin enough as it is, but now you've gotten so skinny that it's hard to even look at you. Try eating more different kinds of food."

Her pleas were understandable. After starting a brown rice diet, my weight fell rapidly, and I looked like a deflated balloon. People with strong, muscular bodies do not lose weight that easily, but when you start out with a puffed-up body like I had, you invariably lose weight at first on a brown rice diet. I'm 5 feet 6 inches high. I weighed 136 pounds when I started, but within three months I had fallen over twenty pounds to 110–115 pounds. My mother's laments were endless. Imagining only the worst, she was afraid that, caught up as I was in all this brown-rice nonsense, I was getting thinner and thinner and would eventually lose all my physical strength, become sick and, unable to resist infection, would end up succumbing to an early death. For his part, when we ate together my father would scold me, saying, "You'd better eat some meat or fish and drink a little liquor to give you some strength." I don't know how many times I heard my father utter the word 'strength'.

"A man's got to have the strength to rise to the occasion," he would say looking sternly at me. "But, skinny as you are, it looks like you'd get blown away by the first stiff wind."

Since I had just started eating brown rice and yet already was so invigorated that I felt like a new man, I was unable to bear my parent's annoying objections. "What do you think it was that saved our baby's life and enabled her to begin growing healthily?" I responded. "And you always talk of nutrition, but why do you think it was that, even though I ate all that rich, nutritious food all the time, I was always falling sick? As for strength, it takes more than just the appearance of strength to get the job done."

My colleagues at work and my friends were the same as my parents. Watching me grow thinner and thinner, they asked if something was wrong and constantly urged me to go see the doctor. They all rejected my explanations about nutritional therapy and the benefits of a brown rice diet, saying, "You ought to get off this brown rice diet. If that's all it takes to get healthy, then modern medicine never would have developed as it has." At such times, I felt a strong desire to prove the merits of a brown rice diet.

But the advantages of a brown rice diet are not that easy to demonstrate. Not only are they difficult to demonstrate, in trying one often ends up showing only how inconvenient a brown rice diet can be. For instance, because I worked in sales at my company, I often entertained customers or was entertained myself. It was impossible to avoid this as well as all the other socializing connected with my job, such as parties at industry trips and meetings. Food and drink during such events consists entirely of things forbidden in a brown rice diet. As a matter of fact, once one is able to see food and drink for what they really are, it becomes clear that no foods or beverages produced for profit can be consumed with a sense of security. At the time, however, I had not yet acquired the wisdom, knowledge, or experience to realize this. I was at a stage where I pursued a brown rice diet blindly, so I would bump into this or that, most of my collisions being due to my new diet. When you're treating a guest to a meal somewhere, you can't tell him, "I'm on a brown rice diet so I can't eat together with you now, but please go ahead and order what you want." It'd be better not to invite him out in the first place. Nor is it possible for me to refuse a meal prepared in my honor by explaining that I follow a different diet. Those who are unconcerned over their success in society or business can afford to be reckless and announce that they are on a brown rice diet, but in general it's not possible to be so cut and dry in one's social interactions. Such problems proved to be quite perplexing when I was just starting out with macrobiotics. The improvement in my physical condition, which had begun as a result of my new diet, underwent temporary lapses and on occasion would even regress quite a bit. After countless failures, I arrived at my own approach to the above dilemma. This approach, which I outline below, is admittedly passive in nature.

First, I refrained absolutely from excessive drinking or eating. Second, I did not drink liquor on an empty stomach. Third, when I did eat animal-based food, I would fast for the next one or two meals. If I were able to have my way, I would ask for country-style cooking prepared without the use of chemical seasonings, but this was one wish that was very difficult to realize.

Here is a more deliberate approach. First, let everyone that you associate with socially know as soon as possible that you are on a brown rice diet. Once they have decided that you are difficult to associate with, eccentric, strange, or whatever, then the rest is easy. I was able to avoid exacerbating or hurting the feelings of others by telling them that I'm a little strange and eat brown rice, and that I prefer not to eat foods packed with too much nutrition. Second, find ways to treat others or to have yourself treated to macrobiotic cooking. Third, I found that I could resist the social pressures to eat and drink with others by talking about proper food and drink, often to receptive ears. Take the microwave oven, for example. Lately, most hotels, inns, and restaurants use a microwave oven to warm saké. These ovens are used also to cook a vast assortment of other dishes, including hot puddings, cheese gratin dishes, and so forth. Food and drink prepared with microwave ovens acquire a molecular structure that, upon entering the body, tends to induce a cancer-prone physical constitution. The incidence of cancer is greater in homes using microwave ovens. Those beautiful-looking rounds of beef or ham are treated with all sorts of food additives, edible adhesives, and coloring agents. Commercial seasonings contain many chemical substances and additives harmful to the body. Even the shrimp and fish the Japanese are so used to eating are frozen products caught in foreign waters and not at all suited to the physical constitution of the Japanese. Most domestic fish are raised rather than caught wild, and are grown using chemical feeds and the like. It is these foods containing, either directly or indirectly, chemical seasonings, chemical additives, chemical feeds and drugs and subjected to special treatment involving freezing or the application of heat or irradiation, that people today refer to as delicious food. When such food enters the body, the many foreign substances present in minute amounts act in concert to cause mysterious and inexplicable ailments. I have found that by discussing topics such as these with my dinner partners, although most do not go so far as to take up macrobiotics, they do make a point thereafter of going to restaurants or inns that serve genuine cooking and beverages.

I now clearly realize that it would have been better had I stuck strictly to the basics during the first three months after starting my brown rice diet, even had it meant sacrificing other things. Apparently, it was because I often strayed from this narrow course that I was unable to regain true health in a short time. Even so, my body improved steadily, and so I came to fully appreciate the value of brown rice. When you start feeling healthy and fit, you become complacent and certain cravings raise their ugly heads. The next thing you know, you are reaching out for forbidden foods and once again you've compromised your health. I repeated this cycle over and over. Even though I temporarily regained a sense of health and well-being, it is not as easy to completely cure an illness. It takes ten years of dietary penance to cure ten years of chronic disease. In this world, one must make retribution in proportion to the crime one has committed. Even a single small ulcer is caused by the cumulative errors of living over the period of five or even ten years that it takes to appear. Stomach cancer, intestinal cancer, liver cancer, spleen cancer, lung cancer, and esophageal cancer do not develop overnight. Judging from all the fuss and commotion that ensues when such tumors are discovered during a checkup at the hospital, it would seem as if these arose suddenly out of nowhere, but the fact is that they are the products of years and years of bad habits that could not be shed. It took years for the physical conditions permitting the emergence of such pathology to develop; after the malignant soil is slowly prepared, a malignant seed takes root, germinates, flowers, and bears fruit, becoming a tumor, a cancer, or what have you. I came to realize that those eruptions I was always plagued with were one mild example of this very same phenomenon.

As I mentioned already in the introduction, Ohsawa would sum this up as follows: "Disease is a sin. Unhappiness is a decoration bestowed upon scoundrels and evildoers." Whatever the type of decoration, identifying something as a "decoration" indicates that it is not easy to attain. If we liken cancer, tumors, and other degenerative or intractable diseases to decorations, it makes things interesting to think of these decorations as being awarded in accordance to the degree of effort devoted to previous offenses?

I received more cold sores and skin eruptions than I cared to, and these are surely insignificant decorations compared to cancer. I have no desire for any more. Still, I continued to be "decorated" on countless occasions even after I had adopted a brown rice diet. But after I began eating brown rice, these eruptions healed differently than they had before. I felt better somehow, and as these disappeared, I could sense my internal condition improving. I was fully convinced that my physical condition had improved. By the third month, I no longer had any doubts that brown rice has a very powerful cleansing and purifying effect on the body.

## Raising Children on Brown Rice

We have five children. My wife worried more than I did about whether the children would really grow properly on a brown rice diet. She is by nature healthy, so she did not sense as strongly as I did the beneficial effects of eating brown rice. Being strong and healthy regardless of what she ate, she felt that raising the children on a normal diet should do them no harm.

As for me, I believe that a brown rice diet is always good. My wife fully understands the merits of eating brown rice, but believes that this can become just another type of unbalanced diet if one gets too carried away with it. Her biggest concern is this: if I'm convinced that it's the best possible diet, then there's no dissuading me and it's unavoidable if I become slightly undernourished and skinny. However, if growing children are not fed adequately and fail to grow up strong and healthy, the damage may be irreparable. She believes a brown rice diet to be lacking in protein and calcium.

We had frequent arguments about this. I argued that because the human body is equipped with all the capabilities needed to produce nutrition essential for living, there is no special need to take protein and calcium; instead of worrying about that, I felt that we ought to concern ourselves with how to properly adapt a brown rice diet to our family situation. On this point, I didn't yield an inch. Because my wife had been brought up on Western-style cooking and was very healthy, she relied on meat, eggs, milk, and other foods rich in protein and calcium. She worried also about whether our diet contained calcium and those amino acids not produced by the human body. Although she understood my reasoning and the explanations given in the books on macrobiotics that I had, her own body and emotions craved the nutrients present in meat, eggs, and milk.

But our children were already born, and it was impossible to have them wait until we had finished improving the physical condition of our bodies for us to decide which diet was best. The fact of the matter was that it was my wife who had to feed the children, change their diapers, and put them to sleep, so although I might complain I had to compromise to a certain extent. Although we would follow a brown rice diet, the special care my wife took as the woman of the house and as a mother was also reflected in our meals. I don't recall how often I threw away some of her cooking, calling it unfit to be eaten. The very fact that I made such complaints indicated that sickness continued to reside in me.

Wondering how the children in the homes of others who had practiced macrobiotics for many years had fared, I tried running a survey of my own on the connection between a brown rice diet and the raising of children. The practice of eating brown rice dates from before the Edo Period (1600–1868), and its history as a distinctive practice continues beyond the Meiji Period (1868–1912). By all rights, there should be quite a few families who brought up their children on brown rice. Where there are families, there are, of course, children. With this in mind, I visited the homes of several teachers and more experienced individuals in my circle of macrobiotic acquaintances. Unfortunately, I found that in each home I visited, the members of the family followed only a nominal brown rice diet; in no case was the entire family consistently eating a brown rice diet. No matter how many homes I visited, the children ate according to the nutritional theories then in vogue; my visits thus served little purpose. On the contrary, they gave me a keen sense of the difficulty of practicing a diet at odds with the prevailing nutritional views of the day. Most of the homes practiced a brown rice diet for therapeutic purposes or to maintain a certain state of health; other members of the same family not suffering from pressing health problems did not share the same diet. Of course, there is no rule that says that everyone in a family must eat the same things and follow the same diet. It is perfectly okay for a family to adopt a diet or a lifestyle free of obstacles and I have no right to criticize other families for living as they see fit, but I did find it disappointing not to come upon any more instructive examples.

Ohsawa's macrobiotics is not intended merely to cure illness or maintain health. The macrobiotics and correct way of life taught by George Ohsawa have a different and more exalted aim. Even I, though still a novice, was fully persuaded by Ohsawa's thinking and philosophy as to why macrobiotics is good and why people should practice a correct lifestyle. Yet, although I had arrived at a good understanding of this thinking and philosophy, I found that putting it into practice was quite difficult. Because I was unable to come across any useful examples to follow, I realized that I would have to try to achieve this in my own way. Just at this time, I learned that Hideo Omori, a leader in Japan's macrobiotic community today, was tackling the problem of raising children on a brown rice diet with the same hopes and aspirations as I. Although I had been unable to find a good example from the past, after learning of Omori's family nearby, I have since profited tremendously from his advice and suggestions. This proved to be a source of great encouragement to me.

We have five children. Our first-born was a boy, followed by a girl, boy, girl, boy. We ventured upon macrobiotics after the birth of our oldest daughter, so our first son began eating brown rice at the age of two and the other children grew up in the course of our twists and turns in establishing a brown rice diet. The trial-and error story of our family's association with brown rice and macrobiotics is recorded in the bodies of each of our children.

Our oldest son and daughter were born while our lifestyle and diet were still in the modern mold. The birth and development of our first son was normal in every respect. My own physical condition, however, was by no means good. The back of my throat was always red and swollen; I often ran a high fever, and my body had a heavy weighed-down feeling as if a sheet of lead were strapped to my back. I would be laid up in bed for days on end. It was very early in our marriage and my wife took pains to cook nourishing food that she thought would help make me stronger and healthier. Meanwhile, I visited the doctor where I would get injections and be given medication to take at home. "It seems like the reason I married you was to nurse you," my wife would often complain. Before our marriage, I was living away from my parents so they had no idea just how weak I had gotten. I imagine also that when my wife realized how sickly I was, she must have regretted marrying me. A newly wed couple is full of dreams and hopes, but here I was always sick in bed, drenched in sweat so that my wife had to wash the bedding and the countless change of clothes. And even when I was able to stay on my feet, I was always in a bad mood and difficult to deal with—a real pain in the neck. The fact that our oldest son was born healthy and normal two years after our marriage in spite of all this can only be attributed to the greatest of good fortune. It must have been entirely the result of my wife's good health.

Had my wife been similarly feeble and also required large amounts of medication, then I have strong doubts as to whether we could have given birth to healthy children. This let me to appreciate just how vital is the health of women. But with the birth of our daughter two years later, things did not go as well as they had when our son was born. Although my wife was still basically healthy, subtle changes had arisen in unseen places.

Thanks to my daughter, our family began a brown rice diet. We tried at first to practice this by the book, but it was very difficult to do so. Even though I believed that I was strictly following the regimen in my own way, my wife felt it unnecessary to rigidly adhere to a macrobiotic diet and would soon wish to add some of the nutritious food that she had been accustomed to preparing to our meals as this had no particularly bad effects. That's why it was impossible to immediately stop eating meat, eggs, milk, and fruit. Although the amount and frequency in which we ate these fell to one-half or one-third the former levels, for one reason or another those standard notions of nutrition kept popping out. Even when our food staple was brown rice. I imagine my wife must have worried if she failed to see abundant nutrition in the secondary foods we ate with our rice. I would point my finger at such cooking and carp continuously at her, claiming that this was not true macrobiotic cooking. However, now that I think of it, for those who are not seriously ill, it does seem to be a valid approach to switch over to a brown rice diet while satisfying to a certain extent the cravings of our cells for similar cells. This may be the path of least resistance for healthy individuals who wish to take up a brown rice diet. But one must be constantly aware that with such an approach, the benefits appear later and the will to convert to brown rice or macrobiotics is more easily eroded.

Two years after the birth of our first daughter, our second son was born. Although by then we had almost completely stopped eating meat, eggs, and milk, believing whole small fish to be nourishing, my wife was including quite a bit of this in our diet at the time of his birth. He was an extremely healthy infant. The entire birth, from the labor pains to the delivery, was so light that it passed by in a flash. Unlike with our first daughter, plenty of mother's milk flowed; the baby nursed well and grew steadily without any abnormalities. Although we weren't following a strict macrobiotic diet, the fact that brown rice served as our food staple and that we were living a simple, physically active life clearly had had a beneficial effect.

Nutritional therapy gave us a correct and basic understanding applicable to all foods. People with no interest in macrobiotics or in eating brown rice may see this as excessive fastidiousness over food, but we were not being fastidious at all; rather, I thought of this as a natural concern essential for fully grasping the properties of each type of food. Without an intimate and detailed knowledge of specific foods, following a proper brown rice diet would have been impossible. We also realized that regardless of whether one eats brown rice or not, learning about nutritional therapy is extremely important.

To some, nutritional therapy may seem old-fashioned and unsophisticated, but it is Eastern dietetics. Although Western nutritional science is certainly important, the Eastern science of nutritional therapy is also very important. In Japan, we have come to realize that Western ways are valuable when adopted strictly as a point of reference, and that basically speaking, the lifestyle and diet traditional to Japan are best for the Japanese. Brown rice nutritional therapy teaches us coherent knowledge as a living and dynamic flow. It also teaches us that the phenomena of life and vitality are a part of the cosmic flow of life. This broader aspect is missing in Western dietetics.

We discovered how interesting it is to learn of the special properties of different foods. Because our oldest son was born at a time when we consumed lots of meat, eggs, and milk, he eats and enjoys vegetables such as onions, Chinese cabbage, and *shiitake* mushrooms. Our second son was born at a time when we were eating small fish together with our brown rice, and so he loves daikon, either cooked or grated. Children are often said to dislike vegetables, but having observed the foods that our children were born and raised on, we are able to give them vegetables that correspond to their physical constitutions. Onions and Chinese cabbage are compatible with meat, *shiitake* mushroom with eggs, and daikon with fish; these foods complement and neutralize each other, making it possible to break down toxins. The food preferences of children change as they grow because changes in their physical makeup create new instinctive cravings.

There is a reason why regardless of how much children are encouraged to eat vegetables not desired by their body they refuse to eat them. When vegetables are fed to children merely because they are known to contain certain vitamins and other nutrients, they are not likely to do much good unless they are desired by the body. Vegetables forced on children against their will can even result in an unbalanced diet. We found that a correct understanding of the compatibility of foods, and in particular the specific compatibilities of vegetables with animal-based foods, results in less waste in the meal and has beneficial effects on the body. Nutritional therapy based on a brown rice diet taught us what these specific compatibilities are.

Two years after the birth of our second son, our second daughter was born. By this time, our brown rice diet had become stable and well-established. Everyone in the family was now convinced of the benefits of a brown rice diet. The children were all healthy and growing normally. Only our eldest daughter, perhaps on account of her illness at birth, tended to be slightly below the norm in her physical development. While all of our children caught colds every so often, these were always light and we very rarely had any cause to go to the doctor. Even when one of the kids would get a fever and end up in bed, he or she would soon recover with proper food and rest. Our second daughter had perfect attendance at her three-year kindergarten and the other children generally averaged only one day of absence every school year.

Our third son, who was our last child, was born four years after our second daughter. Our brown rice diet had become even better established by then. Both the birth and development of our last son were perfectly satisfactory. We noticed that his skeleton and musculature were far more sturdy than those of the other children. Also, in the morning he got up out of bed the moment he awoke, while at night he fell into a sound sleep right away.

Our five children were all born at different times in our dietary odyssey. The changes our diet underwent during our period of wanderings and trial and error in passing from a diet based on principles of modern nutrition to a true brown rice diet are recorded in the bodies and minds of each of our five children. In *Physiologie du Goût*, the gastronome Anthelme Brillat-Savarin gives expression to the notion of the relationship between man and what he eats. Our experiences show this to be true.

A macrobiotic friend of mine, who has been eating brown rice five years longer than me, lives in my neighborhood. He himself was familiar with brown rice before marrying, and married a women who was a zealous adherent of brown rice. So his family has been eating brown rice from the day he and his wife set up house. The conditions in their home were different from those in ours. Both husband and wife are brown rice eaters and the children, starting from the very first, were all brought up on brown rice. Like us, they too have five children. All have grown wonderfully. They are all healthy, athletic, and bright. All are far above average, each having some outstanding ability.

Having raised five children of my own and observed children being raised on macrobiotic brown rice diets in other families, I have come to realize that there is no need for concern about whether children can be raised healthy and strong on brown rice. I now know that the more correctly such a diet is practiced, the better the children will benefit in terms of their general physical constitution, and the more superior they will be in intelligence and physical coordination. Whether or not children can be raised on a brown rice diet is no longer in doubt. Indeed, we now know that a brown rice diet is a basic and ideal diet for giving birth to and raising healthy, bright, and active children.

# 2

## Health Comes
## from the Blood

# Chlorophyll, Sodium, and Potassium

When I started a brown rice diet, I made countless blunders. Everything I saw, heard, did, and learned went counter to what I had regarded as normal common sense up until then. The first thing that I tripped up on was the macrobiotic proscriptions against eating various foods. Of course, this was only natural since I had no idea of the reasons why each of these foods were off limits to me.

People trying to establish mental and physical health are forbidden, during periods of ascetic practice, from partaking of meat, fish, eggs, milk and other dairy products, fruit, potatoes of different types, sweets, and alcoholic or carbonated beverages. Having for so long believed the consumption of many of these very foods to be the epitome of good nutrition, I had eaten them religiously and had as a result been unable to overcome my weak physical state. So now I agreed that it just might be necessary to abstain from such foods altogether.

Yet I failed to understand what was instrinsically wrong with these foods. All around us, specialists and others advise us to partake liberally of meat, fish, dairy products, fruit, and so forth. To make things worse, wherever one goes, these are usually the only nutritional foods to be found. If foods such as these are entirely banned from one's diet, then on journeys of more than a couple of days one soon runs into a dilemma over meals.

I tried asking my macrobiotic mentors about how to overcome this problem. One person's response was very tough and uncompromising: "If such a small problem prevents you from getting around in the world, then you might as well forget about macrobiotics." There certainly is some truth to that. Another person gave a more level-headed response: "For whose sake are you following this diet anyway? For the sake of society? For the macrobiotics association, or for yourself? You ought to think this over carefully and come up with your own way of dealing with the problem." This too is unquestionably true. Yet another person explained that he takes with him brown-rice balls when he leaves the house for some reason. On longer excursions, he told me that he takes roasted brown rice. In addition to this, he is careful to eat and drink in such a way as not to run counter to the nutritional approach that he has adopted.

I began by trying the latter method. On my outings I took with me brown-rice balls, roasted brown rice, or both, as the occasion called for. But this alone did not resolve all the situations that arose when eating out. While traveling and dining with a group, it was not always possible to turn down meals with others and eat alone. In such cases, I tried sticking as closely as possible to my dietary regimen by having *miso* soup with my rice, and eating innocuous foods such as pickled dishes, vegetarian cuisine, beans, and seaweed. However, I was often at a loss as to what to do in the case of Western-style cuisine. My physical condition remained unstable, and I had not yet acquired the wisdom and knowledge that enables one to successfully apply macrobiotic principles to diet. So either I would choose toast, soup, and a vegetable salad, or I would eat nothing whatsoever and later, when I was by myself, eat some roasted brown rice.

It was at about this time that Hideo Omori, in a study group he was running on the Unifying Principle of Yin and Yang, asked the participants this question: "Do any of you have any idea where the human blood comes from?" None of the twenty students ventured a response. Not knowing what the blood is made of, there was no way we could have answered Omori's question. But this was the sort of thing we ought to have learned in high school. Omori scanned our faces for a while, waiting for a response, but no one said a word. Dismayed by the lack of a response, Omori gave us the answer he was seeking: "Human and animal blood arise through transmutation from chlorophyll." Having told us this, he proceeded to write the molecular formulas for hemin, the deep-red pigment in hemoglobin responsible for the color of blood, and chlorophyll on the blackboard. Aside from the magnesium, which gives chlorophyll its green color, and the iron, which gives hemoglobin its red color, the molecular formulas were almost identical.

"Wow!" I exclaimed. This made a deep impression on me. The thought that the chlorophyll in plants is transformed into human blood had never occurred to me. The only knowledge I had of blood was what I could recollect from high school biology. I knew that blood is produced in the bone marrow, but I did not remember ever having learned anything about the raw materials in blood. Moreover, although I knew of the carbon dioxide assimilating action of chlorophyll, I had never heard before that this is transformed into blood. I did not know whether this was true or not, but just hearing this explanation made a deep and indelible impression on me. It seemed to me as if I had been struck on the head. Although I had no idea as to the scientific merit of Omori's statement, I somehow felt this to be a great truth. Many other meaningful topics were brought up at that study meeting, but the only thing I heard that day was that "blood comes from chlorophyll." This alone swept away the various doubts and suspicions I had harbored since beginning a macrobiotic diet.

**Fig. 2.1  Molecular structure of chlorophyll and hemin.**

1. Chlorophyll

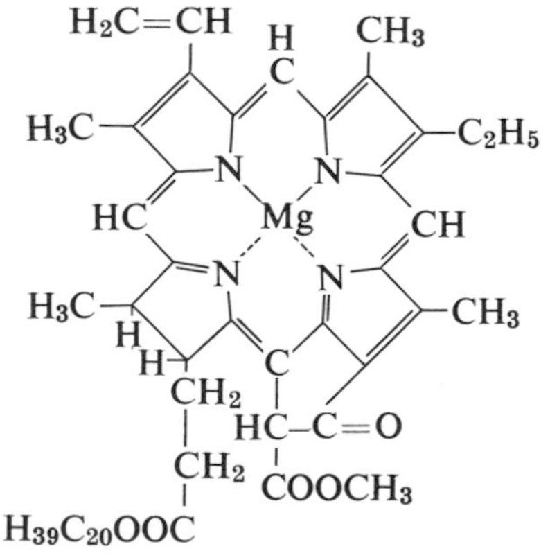

2. Hemin

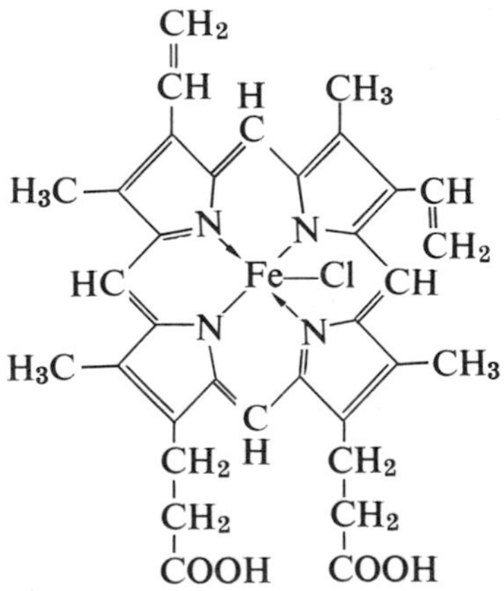

Up until then I had continued to hold childish doubts. For example, why is it that herbivores develop red blood and strong bones even though they don't eat meat? Why do carnivores begin by feeding on the viscera of their kill? Why do herbivores generally have quieter temperaments and live longer than carnivores? Is it better for man to eat meat or plants? Why does macrobiotics forbid the consumption of all animal-based food? Is it more natural for man to eat meat or plants? Why is it that a brown rice diet suits me so well? Why does the greenness of vegetation have a gentle, calming effect on people? Why is it that we enjoy lying down in a green meadow or on a lawn so much? Can people really live without eating any meat or other foods derived from animals? Is it possible to live only on chlorophyll? My questions were endless.

I felt as if most of my questions could be resolved through this one hint given by Omori. Of course, I am a layman when it comes to scientific matters, but I believed that these could be solved through a layman's sixth sense, through inspiration.

If chlorophyll is transformed into blood, then herbivorous animals must have the ability to convert the chlorophyll in the grasses and leaves they eat into blood. The same applies to human beings. Assuming this to be true, then it becomes clear which is the more advanced as a hemopoietic function—blood production from vegetable-based foods or blood production from animal-based foods. Man eats both plants and animals. I came to realize which of the two—eating vegetables and grains and creating blood from this or eating the flesh of animals and creating blood from this—is more natural and which represents a more advanced and higher order of hemopoietic function. The production of blood from plants seems to be different somehow from the production of blood from animals. Meat-eating appears to be the lazy man's approach to life because this is an attempt to obtain blood without making full use of one's own hemopoietic machinery. Doesn't the continued practice of eating meat result in the degeneration of man's ability to produce blood from plant matter, leading to the loss of an inherent capability and hence physiological degeneration? In contrast, because a vegetable diet requires that full use be made of the hemopoietic function imparted to both man and animals, isn't it fair to conclude that doing so represents physiological progress in the sense that the organism is utilizing this physiological machinery as it was intended to be used? Which is better, I wondered: that man use all of the physiological functions with which he was endowed, or that he not make full use of these functions and allow them to atrophy? Which of these alternatives, I asked myself, is in the best interest of man and most natural? In this way, I came to realize that my zealous and wholehearted efforts to take in as much high-grade nutrition as I could in the form of nutriments, medications, meat, fish, eggs, milk, butter, cheese, and so forth had in fact had a devitalizing and atrophying effect on my physiological functions; these were in a sense suicidal acts which could have led eventually to functional paralysis. I understood why my physical condition had continued to deteriorate as I consumed more nutrition and swallowed more medications. And I became fully convinced of the reasons why I continued to feel better and why my physical condition continued to improve the longer I remained on a macrobiotic brown rice diet.

I then started thinking about the food that herbivorous animals eat. They are able to thrive by eating grass because that grass is transformed into blood, meat, and bones. The real meaning of this notion of chlorophyll becoming blood may well be that animals feed on plants and are fully capable of producing blood. If not, then the question arises as to whether it wouldn't be possible to extract just the chlorophyll from plants and live entirely on pills made of this chlorophyll. Somehow I doubt that animals could live merely on chlorophyll pills. I can't be certain about this as I've never seen or heard of an experiment of this sort, but I would imagine that more is needed to live on than just chlorophyll. In other words, the idea of blood being produced from chlorophyll may only be a symbolic notion. But the fact that blood can be produced by eating plants is clearly demonstrated by herbivorous animals. The question that then occurred to me was whether any plant would do. Apparently, the answer is no. Different herbivores eat different plants. The horse, cow, rabbit, goat, sheep, giraffe, and elephant all subsist on plants, but each of these species feed on different types of vegetation. When I looked at why this should be so, it occurred to me that different species of animals eat different foods and that this difference in the foods they eat perhaps accounts for the differences between these species. I thought that the high suitability of grains as a human food might have some deep connection with the human past, or that it might reflect physiological traits inherent to man. The human body appears to be built such that man can eat both plants and animals, but it seemed to me that the production of blood from plant food utilizes a basic physiological process within us.

I am ashamed to say that until I learned of brown rice through my daughter's illness, I knew nothing of this food. During and after World War Two, a "black" rice was rationed to the Japanese population. I was just a young grade school pupil then, but I remember how we would place this rice in the large, 1.8-liter bottles used for soy sauce and pound the rice until it turned white. As a child, I thought that rice couldn't be eaten until it was pounded white in this way. Later on, after discovering brown rice and macrobiotics, I grew so found of eating brown rice that it became almost unbearably delicious. In Japan, one often hears people remark that brown rice is indeed good for the body but is a chore to eat because it is so unpalatable. In general, people who say this either have never really tasted brown rice or have not been earnest enough in their efforts to properly cook, prepare, and eat brown rice. Once we begin to appreciate how building the blood, muscles, and bones in our body from whole grains—the "meat" of plants—rather than animal flesh enables our physiological functions to work normally, prevents aging and degeneration, and is above all natural, this dispels our prejudice against eating brown rice and enhances our ability to savor this excellent food.

Since I had lived for such a long time on white rice, meat, fish, nutriments, and medications, even after adopting a macrobiotic brown rice diet, I continued to have doubts and anxieties about whether a diet consisting of just brown rice and a little bit of vegetables and seaweed was really adequate. I believe that such anxieties persisted in me until those physiological functions which had been lulled into a dormant state by my nutrient-rich diet awoke suddenly to the fact that all those vitamins and medications upon which I had depended were no longer coming in. Once my body became accustomed to a brown rice diet and those long-dormant physiological functions within me realized that from now on they would have to produce the proteins and other nutrients I needed from vegetable matter, I gradually lost my cravings for meat, eggs, milk, and other high-nutrient foods. As my body prepared itself to provide the necessary nutrients from this new food (brown rice), not only did the many highly nutritious foods that I had constantly eaten until then become superfluous, they actually became impurities.

Next, what really shocked and surprised me was the question of what type of blood is best. My astonishment and joy upon learning what healthy, natural blood is produced just as deep an impression upon me as when I had heard that chlorophyll is transformed into blood.

"The ratio of sodium to potassium in normal, healthy blood is 1: 5. One food having this ratio is brown rice."

The first to notice and study the connection between the sodium-potassium ratio in the blood and disease was Sagen Ishizuka, a pioneer of nutritional therapy in Japan. This helped to explain why brown rice is good for the body. The sodium-potassium ratio in properly cultivated brown rice of the past was 1: 5, which is the same as that in healthy blood. Of course, the sodium-potassium ratio of the blood is not the only determinant of health or sickness, but it is one important factor. Since this ratio is inherent to properly grown brown rice, brown rice is far more natural, effective, and beneficial than other foods in the course of consumption to assimilation in the blood. By replacing brown rice with white rice, we disrupt this ratio and also eliminate minerals and other nutrients. No matter how well we try to compensate for this loss with meat, fish, eggs, milk, fruit, and other foods, we cannot hope to match a composition so judiciously assembled by nature. What this means is that eating white rice invites an irrational and uneconomical way of life.

When I heard about the normal values of sodium and potassium in blood, I at once got some food composition charts, and checked for myself the compositions of various foods. It is indeed true that the sodium-potassium ratio varies from food to food. I found that brown rice and buckwheat have the closest sodium-potassium ratios to that of blood. Eggs also have a good balance of ingredients, but because this is an animal-based food, I excluded this from consideration. Upon closer examination, I found that the sodium-potassium ratio in brown rice deviates more widely as one approaches the present, changing to 1: 8, 1: 16, and 1: 20. Although properly cultivated rice used to have the same sodium-potassium ratio as that of healthy blood, the ratio for rice grown more recently has become increasing deviant. The reason for this has to do with changes in rice cultivation practices and in the nature of the soil. With the use of chemical fertilizers and pesticides, the chemical makeup of most rice grown today is no longer the same as it used to be. This is not a problem limited only to rice. Unnatural farming methods have led to unnatural and unhealthy crops, and since we eat those crops, there can be little doubt that the chemical makeup of humans has also become unnatural and unhealthy. Although brown rice and people with a sodium-potassium ratio of 1: 5 existed during the Edo Period, today both the food is sick and so are the people; I have come to understand that this is as it should be. Also, from this it became clear to me that if one truly wishes to become healthy one must eat healthy food; that to obtain healthy crops, one must build healthy soil; and that building healthy soil is itself the very foundation of health.

Crops grown by natural farming or organic gardening, whether they be rice, vegetables, or fruit, are truly more delicious. Recovery from illness with such food is also entirely different. Beginning with this single notion of blood being produced from chlorophyll, I was able to learn about healthy blood, healthy food, and a way of self-development, merely through the practice of a macrobiotic brown rice diet.

## The Seven Conditions of Health

There are times when one's muscles ache for days on end after vigorous exercise or work. When I skied or did some physical labor that I was unaccustomed to, my muscles and joints would ache for days and I would also end up catching a cold. A half year to a year after starting out on a macrobiotic brown rice diet, however, I stopped experiencing pain or fatigue even after doing more vigorous exercise or work than I had before. I became laid up in bed much less often than before. For me, this was an enormous step forward.

George Ohsawa lays out what he calls the seven conditions of health:
1. Absolute freedom from fatigue
2. Good appetite
3. Sound sleep
4. Perfect memory
5. Excellent mood
6. Precision in thought and action
7. Total honesty

When I first read this in one of his books, I thought that such conditions for health were impossible to achieve. I was certain, for example, that no living person could be absolutely free from fatigue. Whenever we work or exercise, waste products form in the body and since these waste products are the cause of fatigue and pain, I refused to believe that there could be a person anywhere who never got tired. I thought of this as just so much claptrap. I could see how having a good appetite and sleeping soundly might be conditions for health, but how in the world was it possible for someone to have a perfect memory? And no one could forever remain in an excellent mood. As for precision in thought and action, I doubted that anyone could always be precise in everything they did or thought. With regard to the last condition of total honesty, as much as I wished to be perfectly honest, this was certainly not something I could be fully confident of.

So at first I regarded these "seven conditions of health" as nonsense. But the longer I remained on a brown rice diet, the more these appeared to make good sense instead. Even though it still is impossible for me to be absolutely free of fatigue, I am largely free of fatigue; and when I do feel tired, the fatigue vanishes after a good night of sleep. I now do believe, therefore, in the possibility of becoming absolutely free of fatigue. As for the other conditions, each of these appear to me today to be very convincing. In fact, I even use these seven conditions of health as a diagnostic chart of my own health and as a guide to good health.

When I was a child, my family frequently relied on the services of our doctor and on medications. Both my father and mother had chronic ailments, while my sisters and I all had weak stomachs and bowels. Our entire family was constantly afflicted with gastrointestinal disorders and colds. Nor was this everything. I had three older brothers, but they died at the ages of 8, 4, and 1. I was born after their deaths, so I never knew them, but I learned that they had all died from ekiri, a type of dysentery endemic to children in Japan. It was common at the time for families to lose one or two children to this disease. Since my brothers died at ages that were multiples of four, even as a young child I remember being worried that I too would die at some multiple of four. I often wondered also why it was that some families such as ours had lost three boys to ekiri, while in other families the children grew up healthy and strong, easily resisting bouts with the illness. Why was it that some families were able to hold up so well during the worst epidemics? How were they different, I wondered. Being sickly as I was, I seem to have developed at an early age a strong interest in becoming healthy. It was not until I had adopted a macrobiotic diet that I came to understand the errors of my family's eating habits while I was growing up. Our daily diet gave us a physical constitution that made us an easy target for pathogens. In a sense, there was little order to our diet since we were not constrained by any dietary principles. We ate pretty much what we pleased and as circumstances permitted. The food situation during my childhood did not allow for luxuries. Under such circumstances, the lack of proper dietary practices soon results in an unbalanced diet, which leads to unforeseen results. For example, we often ate sweet potatoes or white potatoes in place of rice. These were favorite foods of my father. We were not aware of the effects of eating potatoes and sweet potatoes on the body. We also used liberal quantities of sweeteners such as sugar, saccharin, and Dulcin. Not only were we ignorant of the harm these do to our body, we positively delighted in the delicious flavor this gave our food. Social circumstances today and the modern living environment are vastly different from what existed in my youth, and so both the approach and thinking with regard to diet have also changed. Yet, while it is understandable that life styles change with the times, the desire to be healthy and to live a healthy life is the same in all ages. This being the case, it clearly would seem wise to acquire for ourselves knowledge and techniques that enable us to live healthily regardless of how the times and social circumstances change. It is with this in mind that I resolved to somehow build up, in our life with our children, a household that is healthy and happy. I believe that this was the desire also of my own parents. By becoming healthy myself and making my own family healthy and happy, I felt that I would at last be able in some small way to repay my debt of gratitude to my parents.

Seeing as our eldest daughter had been saved by brown rice and the frequency with which I caught colds and was laid up in bed had dropped dramatically, my wife had no objection to continuing a macrobiotic brown rice diet. However, an unforeseen problem arose in getting the entire family on a brown rice diet. Even though we were able to buy brown rice and had no difficulty getting hold of a pressure cooker, naturally fermented miso and soy sauce of macrobiotic quality, and other essential products such as sea salt, sesame oil, and seaweeds through distributors of macrobiotic products, we ran headlong into the problem at home of personal food preferences. We live together with my parents. Although they eat separately from us, my wife does the cooking for everyone. My parents flatly rejected a macrobiotic brown rice diet. They were adamant, saying that to begin eating brown rice at their age would mean robbing them of one of the great pleasures left in life; even if it meant dying younger, they insisted that they would prefer to continue eating white rice, meat, fish, eggs, milk, and fruit just as they had up until then. Had my parents really been healthy, I wouldn't have minded, but both had chronic illnesses so I very badly wanted them to take up a brown rice diet. I did everything I could to encourage them to try eating brown rice, even to the point of serving it to them in spite of their objections, but they ate only the side dishes and would refuse to touch the brown rice. My parents did not believe that my daughter and I had regained our health on account of our brown rice diet. In addition to their reluctance to believe that brown rice can be so effective, they had a preconception of brown rice as bad-tasting. No matter how good a food is, it can hardly be beneficial to the body if it is eaten unwillingly by someone who can't stand it, so we stopped trying to force my parents to eat brown rice and prepared for them the same sort of meals as before. This doubled my wife's work at mealtime. Unfortunately, the problem did not end here. When food suited to different tastes was prepared under one roof, this soon began to affect the attitude of our children toward our way of life. Children are fond of things that look and taste delicious. They would eat their meal with us, then go over to their grandparents and eat something else with them. Or just the reverse might happen; they'd be unable to eat their meals with us because they had already eaten with their grandparents. We had a hard time dealing with this at the beginning. There is no denying that brown rice cooking appears to be crude and backward while a Western-style nutritious meal looks hearty and attractive. It is difficult to tear children away from what attracts them so strongly. Before giving any thought as to how best to remove the temptations of these foods, I would often yell at the children. Knowing how much to scold children, if at all, is never easy. However, in matters concerning diet and food, I did quite a bit of scolding. Even now, I keep a sharp eye out for self-indulgent eating and drinking and continue to scold when I have to. My parents and sisters told me on countless occasions that my harsh disciplining over matters of such little import as food would have a negative influence on the children. I would reply that I was being strict precisely because this concerned food. Because I felt, as the saying goes, that "food is life," regardless of how I handled other matters, I had no intention of relaxing my discipline in matters concerning food.

When someone is on a brown rice diet, any surplus nutrition taken above and beyond a brown rice diet immediately manifests itself in that person's physical and mental state; thus, by keeping a watchful eye on the children I was able to detect at once any changes that arose in them. I was even able to tell when they were lying to me.

The "seven conditions of health" served as a very useful barometer of health. By observing the daily life of our children and applying this barometer, I learned how to read with great accuracy their physical condition each day. Children, however, forget quickly; even after getting scolded by me, they would continue to eat unwholesome food, upsetting their system. In time, these experiences taught them how food and the condition of the body are interrelated. As their bodies became accustomed to a macrobiotic diet, they gradually ceased to crave unwholesome foods. We learned that when one eats a brown rice meal in silence, one's life comes into line with the seven conditions, and that when one eats strange foods and develops strange cravings, this inevitably triggers colds and indisposition.

It took time, but through persistent efforts on my part to have them try eating just a mouthful when they were of a mind to, even my parents, who had refused to have anything to do with brown rice, came to realize that it tasted better than they had thought, in addition to which they noticed that it quickly improved their bowel movements. Eventually, they came around to the view that eating brown rice was good for the bowels. When the bowels improve, then of course the stomach feels better; and when the stomach starts feeling better, the condition of the entire body improves. In order to be easy for older people to eat, brown rice should be cooked on the soft side. The secret to maintaining peace and harmony in the home is to strive to have older members of the family eat brown rice of their own free will.

## Why Eat Brown Rice?

"Why is eating brown rice good," I wondered. "Or is it that brown rice is especially good for me alone?"

It even crossed my mind that because it was good for my body, perhaps I was forcing it upon my family in order to see whether it worked for everyone else as well. That it was good for my daughter was undeniable, and there was no doubt that it had worked wonders for me as well. But that isn't to say that it was necessarily beneficial for anyone and everyone. Many other people have gained health or been saved from chronic illness by brown rice. Yet there are also countless individuals who are healthy even though they don't eat brown rice. It dawned upon me that the suitability of a particular food is strongly connected with one's basic physical condition. I also came to realize that one's condition improves or deteriorates, becomes healthy or ill, in accordance with one's daily diet and way of life.

In eating brown rice, I realized for the first time that to eat is to receive life. This act of receiving the life of the various foods we eat allows us to make such life our own. This is what is meant by the expression "food is life." In order that this may be so, one must receive fresh food that has a life-force or vitality, but what sort of food has vitality? Such questions further deepened my interest in food.

My view of food up until that time had been totally one-sided. I had seen food as consisting of protein, fats, carbohydrates, vitamins, calcium, calories, and other components; I had considered it in terms of measured values and units. Needless to say, grounds do exist for this view of food, but I came to believe that an appreciation for the life within food is also extremely important.

Macrobiotics holds as an ideal the consumption of a food in its entirety. Instead of eating just select portions of a food, the entire food is eaten. By eating the entire food, one is able to more naturally receive and assimilate the full vitality of that food. Individual plants and animals, when considered as whole organisms, each have within them a balance of nutrients and exhibit a vitality or life-force. Eating only one portion of these individual organisms readily leads to an unbalanced diet. If one is eating meat, then ideally one should eat the entire pig or cow. By consuming a bird or fish in its entirety, one can eat without upsetting the overall nutritional balance. However, when only a portion of the animal is eaten, the invariable result is an incomplete diet. Eating an organism in its entirety results in the generation of little toxicity once this food enters the body. However, in the case of partial consumption, the ensuing imbalance in nutrient distribution renders the body unable to fully neutralize any toxins that form.

In countries where meat is the food staple, there remain even today forms of cuisine and customs whereby the animal—whether it is a cow, pig, sheep, or fowl—is prepared and eaten in its entirety. Of course, it is impossible for one person to eat an entire cow or pig. So one ends up by eating just a portion, and compensating with other foods for the nutrition not received from other parts of the animal. This must be how dietetics developed in the West. The fact is that foods can be eaten in their entirety much more easily when the diet consists mainly of grains and vegetables than when it is based on animal flesh.

If man has the ability to turn plant matter (such as grains, vegetables, or seaweed) into blood and sinew, then isn't it his true physiological nature to make full use of that ability? One's own body should create the nutrition necessary for one to live. I believe that this is the basis of self-support. Although eating meat, consuming nutrition-packed food, and swallowing vitamins and food supplements that give some of our physiological functions a rest is indeed efficient and convenient, this is much like doing business on borrowed funds. The household, the company, or even the public treasury may get by very well on loans, but the moment that all hope is lost of paying back those debts and repayment becomes impossible, then the only possible outcome is bankruptcy, running out on the creditors, or suicide. In this sense, the body can be compared to running a business, where it is best to get by without taking out any loans, regardless of the hardships this may entail. Once money (or nutrition) has been borrowed, then the result that must inevitably follow is a decline or degeneration proportional to the size of the "loan" in the inherent capabilities, be they fiscal or physiological.

Applying this metaphor to my physical self, my body was riddled with "debt." The more "debts" I accumulated in the form of nutritious, vitamin-enriched foods and nutriments, the more each of the parts of my body came to rely on deficit operations and the more it lost the desire to work for itself. It only stands to reason that over the long term, my body lost the ability to revive itself and collapsed of its own accord. I was awakened to the realization that I was not making full use of my physiological functions. Debts should not be paid off with more debts. Hard as it may seem, one must work those debts off with one's own efforts and pay off those debts oneself, even if this takes a long time.

I recall an episode about my mother and debts from my childhood. My father had been in business for himself, but a major client of his folded and, faced with large debts, my father borrowed from the bank to pay those debts off. But business never recovered; to make matters worse, my father fell seriously ill and was forced to stop working. All that remained of his business were those debts from the bank. I was only in grade school then. Given the state of affairs at home, it was impossible for us to pay off those large debts. My mother had someone from the bank come over, and explained the real situation to him. Since it was absolutely impossible for us to return the money all at once, she promised to repay the debt in small monthly installments. The next day, she began taking in some manual piecework at home. At the time, it wasn't easy to come by even such work as this, yet my mother managed to find and bring home work from various places; she stayed up late every night doing that work. My older sisters and I also worked on this along with her. We did many different things, but the work paid very little considering all the labor that went into it. Even so, we never looked at this as a hardship, pursuing it rather as a sort of game in which we made so much today and wondered how much we would make the next day. My mother would take the money we earned from this work and use it to make payments on our debt at the bank. I have no idea how large the debt was, but I do remember someone coming from the bank at the end of each month to collect. It took quite a few years, but at long last we paid off the entire amount. When we had made the last payment, the director of the local branch came over to see us and I recall how proud I was when he told us, "Your mother is a remarkable woman. This is the first time anyone has ever fulfilled their obligation to pay back a debt to our bank without once going against their promises over such a long period of time." The fellow who had collected the monthly payments from us was also very kind, and had evidently reported to the branch chief how my mother was taking in manual work at home to pay off the debt. Later on, even after he had been transferred elsewhere, this person occasionally stopped by when he was in the neighborhood, and would never fail to compliment us on the wonderful mother we had.

Of course, this episode has nothing to do directly with the body itself, but when I realized that my own body was being sustained on "loans"—namely, high-nutrition food and nutriments, I recalled how my mother had paid off our debts. She had not taken the short-term stopgap approach of borrowing new funds from somewhere else to pay off the debts. Pushing aside concerns over appearance and outward respectability, she turned to manual piecework at home, with all the hardships this entailed, cut back on our living expenses, and somehow we scraped through. The experience made life later on for us much easier. I realized that, in the same manner, I would have to adopt a radical approach in order to regain physical health. A macrobiotic brown rice diet based on the notion of eating whole foods was not regeneration through debt. It was a self-reliant means of regeneration.

In the case of a cow or pig, it is absurd to think of eating an entire organism; only a very small portion can be eaten in one meal. But brown rice is a different matter; in a single meal one is able to consume thousands of grains, each endowed with a vitality enabling it to germinate and develop into a full plant. I came to understand that, from the standpoint of receiving life, brown rice is the best food that exists.

Just at about the time that I began eating brown rice and my physical condition improved, pesticide pollution started becoming a serious problem. Another major problem that arose was pollution by industrial wastes. Word spread that eating brown rice was dangerous because this meant directly taking pollutants into the body. I too became very concerned. Clearly, rice grown on unpolluted soil without the use of large amounts of pesticide was preferable, but I had no idea where the rice that I ate was produced. At the same time, I had my doubts as to whether this concern would vanish merely by polishing the rice.

After adopting a macrobiotic brown rice diet, my bowel movements improved tremendously: I stopped feeling tired all the time; and even when I thought I had caught a cold, instead of getting laid up in bed for days, I would wake up refreshed and recovered after a single good night of sleep. All of this thoroughly persuaded me that brown rice does indeed enhance the body's metabolism. The excellent effects of brown rice have also been demonstrated through experimental research. For example, in one experiment on the effects of eating rice on mercury pesticide residues in the body, it was found that the amount of mercury eliminated in the stools of brown rice eaters is greater than that eliminated in the stools of white rice eaters. True, some voiced the opinion that this is because brown rice contains more pesticide residues, but such is not the case. The level of impurities detected in the stools of brown rice eaters is higher not only because brown rice has a greater ability to eliminate impurities present in the rice itself, but also because it has the ability to excrete impurities and toxins that have been ingested and retained within the body. The reason that bowel movements improve, that one's ability to recover from fatigue improves, that skin eruptions as well as nasal and mucous discharges become very active for a while is that brown rice contains substances which bring the body's metabolism to a peak of activity. I have not heard of any cases in which people fell ill from pollution-related diseases due to the consumption of brown rice. On the contrary, cases have been reported of individuals among the victims of the atomic bombings at Hiroshima and Nagasaki who were saved from radiation sickness by their strict adherence to a brown rice diet.[1] Brown rice contains within it the strength to enhance the natural powers of healing.

For a while, both my wife and I were even concerned that a macrobiotic brown rice diet might lead to malnutrition. We were so used to thinking of food in terms of the stereotypic Western notions of nutrition according to which meat, fish, eggs, and milk serve as the sources of protein, fats are obtained from butter and cheese, calcium comes from milk and fish, and vitamins are obtained from fruits and vegetables. The presumption here, of course, is that the staple of one's diet is white rice, white bread, or meat. But even when one adopts a brown rice diet, this standard view of nutrition keeps popping up from time to time, upsetting the vision of food in macrobiotics as the consumption of life.

I thus set out to study the nutritional composition of brown rice. I approached with great interest the question of how white rice and brown rice differ nutritionally by trying to determine whether it is better to eat white rice and compensate for the nutrients stripped from this rice during polishing with a combination of other foods or whether it is preferable instead to ingest the nutrients as they exist in brown rice and minimally compensate for what is thought to be lacking.

Table 2.1 compares the nutrients in white rice and brown rice. From this, it is apparent that white rice is higher in carbohydrates and calories, but brown rice is higher in all other nutrients. I also discovered that the protein in rice is of excellent quality compared to that in other foods. But is it enough for a food to have an abundance of high-quality nutrients? If all that is needed in a food is an ample quantity of high-grade nutrients, then the production of food meeting these conditions with advanced processing technology ought to suffice. The status of production today by the food processing industry is founded on the view that what is essential is that there be an abundance of high-grade nutrition. But has this resulted in a decline in disease and in the number of sick people? The answer to this,

---

[1]   Tatsuichiro Akizuki. *Nagasaki genbaku ki* [An Account of the Atomic Bombing of Nagasaki].

unfortunately, is "no." So it does not appear as if simply providing nutritious, high-quality foods is the solution. It then occurred to me that the problem had something to do with the vitality and the life-giving properties of the food itself; the fact that brown rice is good for us not only on account of its high quality and the good balance of its components, but because it has latent within it the power to germinate and bring forth new life, a property lacking in white rice. This I felt to be the most crucial aspect of brown rice. Even if the components present in brown rice were gathered together in exactly the same proportions, and the quality and amount of the nutrients as well as all other conditions of this mixture made to precisely duplicate those in brown rice, it would be impossible to bring forth new life from this aggregate of ingredients. I cannot help thinking that this life-force enters the human body and manifests itself as differences in the effects and influence of eating brown rice. In addition, as I have already noted, the sodium-potassium ratio in brown rice is close to that in healthy blood.

Blood donation campaigns have been very active recently in Japan. According to the director of the Red Cross Blood Center here, the proportion of blood donated that is unhealthy and cannot be used has become very high. Blood collected after the New Year's holiday season is often of especially poor quality. This apparently is due to all the feasting that goes on during New Year's; the blood components become contaminated with nutrients from all the food and drink consumed in the course of the festivities. How unfortunate both for the donor and the recipient that blood which has been donated cannot be used because it is of such poor quality. One can see from this that the blood is very sensitive to what we eat and drink. I acquired a correct understanding of the blood only after adopting a macrobiotic brown rice diet. Up until then, I had had absolutely no interest in the connection between one's health and one's blood. I had thought all along that I had a fair understanding of such matters, only to discover that my understanding was superficial and largely incorrect. The same was true of blood; I thought I understood this, but as it turned out I knew not a single thing of importance about the blood. Had I not been on a brown rice diet, I might have continued all my life to be tormented by my poor health and sickness without ever learning why the blood is so important; my entire life would probably have been wretched and cheerless. One major gain I made by adopting a brown rice diet was the chance to deepen my understanding of the blood.

Before I turned to macrobiotics and brown rice, if my head hurt for some reason, I would take headache medication; if I had a stomach ache, I would take a digestive and some cold medication; for a fever, I would take an antipyretic. Likewise, there is insulin for people with diabetes; antihypertensives for people with hypertension; tranquilizers for people suffering from irritation; carcinostatic agents for cancer; tonics for fatigue; and high-nutrition diets for maintaining health. That is the basic pattern. By living in accordance with this approach, it is possible to keep one's respect as a person of common sense. But this view fails to take into account the blood; nor does it show any concern for the process of rendering the blood healthy.

It was only when I began eating brown rice that I realized that food becomes blood, that blood in turn becomes cells, and that it is these cells which make up our tissue, organs, muscle, bones, and nerves. At the same time, I saw for the first time that illness, recovery from illness, health, and happiness are all connected with the condition of the blood. When I realized that this blood is created from our daily food, I saw how wrong I had been in my former view of food and my former way of life.

I also gave some thought to the drawbacks of a macrobiotic brown rice diet. The first and greatest disadvantage is that our society is not organized in such a way as to facilitate a brown rice diet. Second, a brown rice diet appears coarse and unsophisticated. Third, one cannot become lax in following such a diet. One must be attentive when eating and when preparing meals; one must chew well; and one must allow one's internal organs and bodily functions to carry out the work they were made to perform. This is not really a disadvantage at all, but it may appear to be so to those who wish to take the easy way out or to "profit" in some way. However, none of the above are true disadvantages.

I was unable to find a real disadvantage to eating brown rice. I recall a period when rumors against rice-eating were common. Eating rice, it was claimed, would turn one into an idiot, give one diabetes, etc. When seen as criticisms of a white rice diet, these rumors were not entirely off the mark, but there is no denying that such views greatly undermined people's understanding of rice as a food. It is also a fact that such prejudices led to the widespread belief and adoption of the basic tenets of Western dietetics, particularly the reliance on animal-based foods and meat-eating. The consequence of this has been the gradual abandonment of the rice-based diet traditional to Japan. Those who ate white rice were unable to distinguish between what was true and what was false.

When I took up a macrobiotic brown rice diet, not only did I at last become healthy, I gained, through a very smooth and orderly process, an understanding of the essence of things and of life itself.

**Table 2.1    Just look at all the nutrition in brown rice!**

Results of rice analyses (amounts given are per 100 grams of rice)

|  | white rice (commercial) | three-quarter-milled rice | half-milled rice | one-quarter-milled rice | brown rice |
|---|---|---|---|---|---|
| protein | 5.6% | 6.3% | 6.5% | 6.7% | 6.7% |
| lipid | 0.4% | 1.3% | 1.9% | 2.3% | 2.4% |
| ash | 0.4% | 0.8% | 0.8% | 1.2% | 1.2% |
| fiber | 0.2% | 0.4% | 0.5% | 0.7% | 0.7% |
| carbohydrates | 80.7% | 78.2% | 77.5% | 76.4% | 76.2% |
| calories | 362 cal | 361 cal | 359 cal | 349 cal | 349 cal |
| iron | 0.32 mg | 0.70 mg | 0.95 mg | 1.30 mg | 1.26 mg |
| calcium | 4.29 mg | 6.11 mg | 7.16 mg | 7.86 mg | 8.37 mg |
| vitamin $B_1$ | 0.07 mg | 0.24 mg | 0.35 mg | 0.38 mg | 0.44 mg |
| vitamin $B_2$ | 0.02 mg | 0.04 mg | 0.04 mg | 0.05 mg | 0.05 mg |
| vitamin $B_6$ | 0.082 mg | 0.206 mg | 0.287 mg | 0.330 mg | 0.494 mg |
| pantothenic acid | 0.48 mg | 0.78 mg | 0.86 mg | 0.99 mg | 1.33 mg |
| niacin | 0.76 mg | 2.26 mg | 2.90 mg | 3.32 mg | 5.74 mg |
| vitamin E | n.d.* | 0.7 mg | 0.8 mg | 1.0 mg | 1.1 mg |
| folic acid | 0.002 mg | 0.003 mg | 0.003 mg | 0.005 mg | 0.005 mg |

*Limit of detection by gas chromatography for vitamin E is 0.5 mg.

(Analysis performed by Japan Food Analysis Center; Data No.: OS 22090266–22110020)

## Table 2.2   Nutrients in rice.

| | energy (kcal) | protein (g) | lipids (g) | sugars & starch (g) | fiber (g) | calcium (mg) | phosphorus (mg) | iron (mg) | potassium (mg) | $B_1$ (mg) | $B_2$ (mg) | niacin (mg) |
|---|---|---|---|---|---|---|---|---|---|---|---|---|
| | | | | **carbohydrates** | | | | | | **vitamins** | | |
| brown rice | 351 | 7.4 | 3.0 | 71.8 | 1.0 | 10 | 300 | 1.1 | 250 | 0.54 | 0.06 | 4.5 |
| half-milled rice | 353 | 7.1 | 2.0 | 73.9 | 0.6 | 8 | 220 | 0.8 | 170 | 0.39 | 0.05 | 3.5 |
| milled rice with attached germs | 354 | 7.0 | 2.0 | 74.4 | 0.4 | 7 | 160 | 0.5 | 140 | 0.30 | 0.05 | 2.2 |
| white rice | 356 | 6.8 | 1.3 | 75.5 | 0.3 | 6 | 140 | 0.5 | 110 | 0.12 | 0.03 | 1.4 |

From *Nihon Shokuhin Hyojun Seibunhyo* [Reference Table of Components in Japanese Foods], 4th ed.

## Fig. 2.2   What are the nutrients in brown rice?

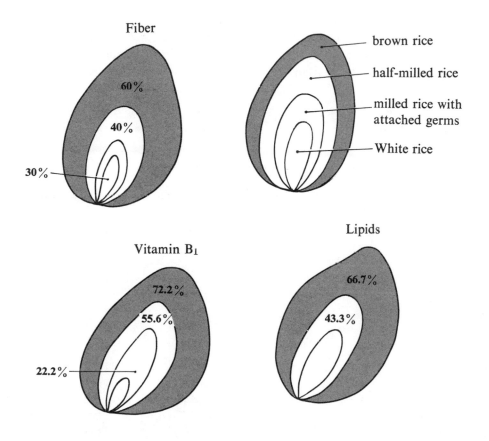

Fig. 2.2 compares the levels of fiber, vitamin $B_1$, and lipids in brown rice, half-milled rice, milled rice with attached germs, and white rice. The percent of each is shown, based on a value of 100 for brown rice. These all decline as the degree to which the rice is milled increases.

**Fig. 2.3   Nutritional value of white rice, based on value of 100 for brown rice.**

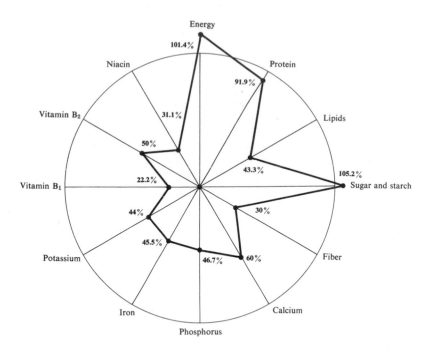

Fig. 2.3 compares the nutrition in brown rice and white rice. It is clear from this just how little nutrition there is in white rice compared with brown rice.

**Fig. 2.4   From brown rice to white rice.**

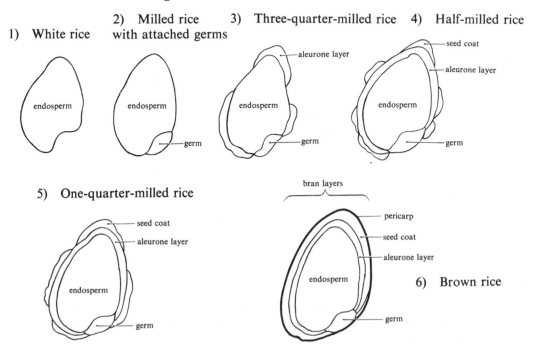

# The Digestion and Absorption of Brown Rice

A great many people are convinced that brown rice is a food that is difficult to digest. When they notice the epicarps or outer seed coats, which retain the original shape of the brown rice kernels, in their stools, this surprises them and they start raising a fuss about how the brown rice wasn't digested properly. However, if they bothered to take a close look, they would notice that everything on the inside of the kernel of rice has been digested and that only the outer integument has been eliminated from the body. Children, no matter how much one keeps after them, never chew enough. That's why so many seed coats shaped like grains of rice are found in their stools. However the interior of the rice grain is digested and absorbed by the body, leaving only an empty case. There is no cause for concern on this account. The epicarps discharged in the shape of brown rice are ideal fiber capsules that help to regulate bowel movements.

**Fig. 2.5   Longisection through a grain of brown rice.**

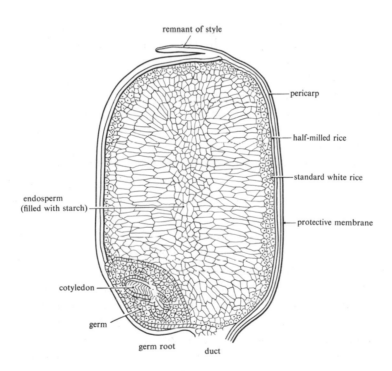

Thus, many prejudices exist against the consumption of brown rice. People tend to think of brown rice as difficult to digest, hard, and unpalatable, but this is hardly a problem limited just to brown rice. Any food that is cooked and eaten improperly can be hard to digest and assimilate. On the other hand, when cooked and eaten properly, any wholesome food can be enjoyed in its own way and be fully digested and absorbed by the body.

66

**Fig. 2.6    The structure of rice (160×).**

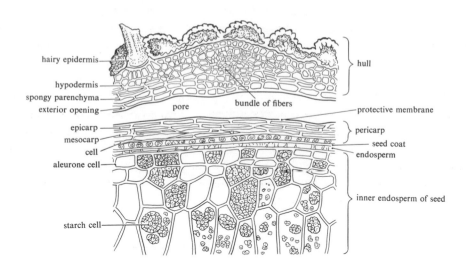

hairy epidermis

hypodermis
spongy parenchyma
exterior opening

pore

bundle of fibers

hull

protective membrane

epicarp
mesocarp
cell
aleurone cell

pericarp
seed coat
endosperm

inner endosperm of seed

starch cell

I believe that no food is as easy to digest and assimilate as brown rice, and certainly no other food is as good for the body as this. Of course, at first I too wondered exactly what brown rice is and whether it can really be eaten, so I can understand why so many people who have never eaten this food question its value.

But if, as is generally thought, brown rice were indeed hard for the body to digest, then I would probably have long since ruined my health. I may never have survived the experience. After all, my stomach and intestines had grown very weak. Not only had I been frail from birth, as a young boy I had continuously feasted on the foods I loved, such as sugar and cakes, hard candies, caramels, chocolates, sweetened azuki beans, condensed milk, and so forth. Unaware of just how bad such foods were for me, I was so fond of these that I would even eat them on the sly. As a result, I constantly had gastrointestinal complaints, my stomach always sloshed around as if it were full of water, and I suffered from heartburn, indigestion, and endless belching. In x-ray images, my stomach hung low in my abdomen; I had a classic case of gastroptosis and gastroatonia. This condition persisted from the time I was in grade school until I was about thirty years old. Until I found out about macrobiotics and brown rice, I was plagued with chronic ailments such as these, so if brown rice were really as difficult to digest and absorb as so many people claim, then I could not possibly have continued surviving on a brown rice diet up until now. The truth is, however, that the condition of my gastrointestinal system improved steadily as a consequence of my new diet, so brown rice is not only capable of being digested, it has strong healing powers. The fact of the matter is that brown rice has a most incredible and extraordinary power to heal what doctors and drugs cannot cure, a power far greater than the best medicines devised by man. In this section I will describe the digestion and assimilation of brown rice by the body to illustrate the amazing properties of this food.

I can state here with total conviction that no food is as easy for the body to digest and absorb as brown rice. In fact, the gastrointestinal system positively welcomes the arrival of brown rice. "When you eat brown rice, your stomach and intestines are all smiles"—that's the way I think of it. There are some people who say that brown rice doesn't agree with them, that their condition deteriorates when they eat it. These people have a gastrointestinal system unable to accept brown rice. I plan to discuss this problem more closely in a later chapter, but it is a fact that cases do exist in which the nutrients in brown rice appear to be incompatible with the components within a person's body. The cause of this may well be that eating habits which do not agree with brown rice have become too deeply ingrained in that person's physical constitution.

Principles for pleasing the gastrointestinal system do exist, but unless these principles are correctly learned and applied, one develops a negative attitude toward brown rice. I don't think that this is limited only to brown rice. Any food which is said to be nutritious and is claimed to be easily digested and absorbed by the body will hardly be welcome by the gastrointestinal system unless eaten and used correctly.

One must eat the right foods in the right combinations, and these must be prepared and eaten properly; that is the basis of the meal. If these principles are adhered to each day, the stomach and bowels are pleased; and if, on top of this, one's staple food is brown rice (or another unpolished grain), the result is gastrointestinal ecstasy. There is ample reason physiologically why this should be so.

Because I am no scholar, I cannot furnish proof of this myself. Perhaps it is because my proof rests on personal experience that these are subject to prejudices and arbitrary judgments by others. But I will leave it up to the scientists and researchers to provide incontrovertible proof for what I say, and will get on instead with my views.

As I noted above, "When one eats brown rice, the stomach and bowels smile." But there is a precondition here. It is very simple: How far are you able to educate yourself? Let me give some examples. Your ability to make one of the following your daily creed will have a very large influence on the effectiveness of your brown rice diet.

"I will be reborn through this brown rice diet."
"This brown rice diet will make me healthy."
"This brown rice diet will cure my illness."
"Brown rice will revitalize me."
"A proper brown rice diet will improve my body and mind."
"Brown rice is the best food for man."

Believing that the only way to save my daughter and I was through brown rice, I embraced this diet by throwing my entire faith into the vitality or life-force of brown rice. At first, I had neither theory nor reason with which to justify this. All I did was cling to brown rice with my entire heart and soul. If the life-force in brown rice would not save me, then I had to resign myself to fate. I had no choice but to leave the fate of my daughter and myself up to the life-force of brown rice. I resolved to place everything in the hands of God (the cosmic life-force) and not call the results into question; with this determination, I threw myself wholeheartedly into a brown rice diet. The new way of life that came about from such self-abandonment turned out better than I could have anticipated. The life in the proper food that we ate started to become a life-force for my daughter and I.

Had I instead begun a macrobiotic brown rice diet with the following sort of attitude, I can well imagine how it would have turned out:

> "I wonder if a brown rice diet really heals illness?"
> "Will I really become healthy by eating brown rice?"
> "Will a brown rice diet be nutritious enough?"
> "I feel silly eating brown rice."
> "Just the idea of a brown rice diet sounds awful."
> "A brown rice diet sounds crude and backward."
> "I'd rather die than have to eat brown rice."

It's better not to eat brown rice if doing so is unpleasant and distasteful. Clearly, the effects and benefits of brown rice differ enormously depending on one's attitude and approach. As the expression "mind over matter" suggests, most illnesses can be overcome depending on our mental attitude.

Macrobiotics is a powerful method for returning the body's life-forces or *ki* to normality.

Seen in this light, I, who appeared sickly and miserable, was in fact blessed with truly good fortune and happiness. George Ohsawa teaches us that "those who know hardship have the capacity to be grateful" and "the way is steepest for those who are greedy." When I chanced upon a brown rice diet, I had reached a state where retreat was no longer possible, so I undertook this diet with a sense of total devotion. This decision turned out to be truly fortuitous.

Let us look more closely now at the digestion and absorption of brown rice.

*The Correct Way to Eat Brown Rice (How to Chew):* If your true desire is to cure an illness now, then my advice to you is to take small mouthfuls of brown rice approximately the size of your thumb (80–100 grains) and chew each mouthful at least 100 times.

Although it may seem so single-minded as to be ridiculous, I continue even now to follow this practice. I take a mouthful of another dish with each three to five mouthfuls of brown rice, and find that the results are best when the amount of secondary foods eaten is kept to a minimum. I am often asked whether eating so little of the accompanying foods in a meal doesn't result in malnutrition by preventing the intake of adequate nutrients. At first, I too had strong doubts about this, but when I went ahead and tried it anyway, I learned that keeping the amount of secondary or side dishes consumed to a minimum is most effective in curing illness. The reason for this is as follows.

Illness and a poor physical condition are caused by imbalances in the body and mind. The primary cause of an imbalance in the body is an erroneous diet which encompasses the food itself, how this food is cooked, and the manner in which it is eaten. An erroneous diet means a diet without order, a diet that is inconsistent with the universal order. Without one being aware of what is happening, a diet controlled by one's impulsive preferences and self-centered cravings ultimately upsets the physiological mechanisms within the body. When this confusion becomes habitual, one becomes accustomed to an unbalanced diet. Habituation to an unbalanced diet results in an imbalance in the body's physiological functions, tissues, and overall physical constitution.

An imbalanced diet refers to a condition in which one has lost a sense of the proper dietary order. An imbalance in the physiological functions, tissues, and physical condition of the body represents a loss in the proper order of the body. This is why recovering the proper dietary order is so critical.

Disorders of the human body are more often a result of excess nutrition than of malnutrition. Although continuous and extended malnutrition makes the body more susceptible to illness, the diseases associated with modern civilization are almost all caused by supernutrition, and so I shall discuss below a means for dealing with such disorders.

When someone eats a large amount of secondary foods (nonstaple foods), adjustment of the excess nutrients within the body becomes difficult. People in which all nutrients are present in excess throughout the entire body should fast, whether they are ill or not. However, because gluttonous people who are overweight due to an imbalanced modern diet suffer from both supernutrition and malnutrition, their bodies are not suited for fasting. Such people have extremely self-indulgent, cumbersome bodies. Excess nutrients must be gradually eliminated from their diet and they must be supplied with a very minimum level of nutrition. Brown rice contains the minimum level of nutrition required by the human body in a good balance. When the amount of secondary foods taken in is reduced, this accelerates the digestion and consumption of components that are stored in excess within the body. Such an approach produces tremendous results.

The dietary approach of taking in the bulk of one's nutrition through secondary foods is not very effective in reestablishing a normal physical condition, normal physiological functions, and a normal balance of components in the body. In fact, such an approach requires more effort and is less advantageous.

My own view is that, up until the stage of digestion and assimilation, the nutrients in properly chewed brown rice more than satisfy the minimum nutritional requirements of the body. Brown rice by itself has enough basic, balanced nutrition. Moreover, during mastication, digestion, and assimilation, the body produces the necessary nutrients by a mysterious process that is beyond the comprehension of the human mind. Initially, when someone starts out on a macrobiotic brown rice diet, certain rhythms and aspects of the diet incapable of fully carrying out the physiological activities of the body arise, but as one learns how to properly cook and eat brown rice, the nutrients in the rice regulate the various physiological activities and restore them to order. The first indication of this is that the bowel movements improve; once the bowel movements improve, this means that the passage of food and liquids through the body becomes more regular, thereby fulfilling the first basic condition for invigorating the metabolism.

So, by chewing mouthfuls of about 80 grains of rice at least 100 times and making sure to thoroughly chew secondary foods as well, the bowel movements gradually improve, eliminating both constipation and diarrhea. Let us take a look at why it is that eating brown rice improves the passage of stool by examining what happens starting at the mouth and teeth.

What is this thing that we call the "mouth"? And what in fact are the "teeth"? Anyone can see that the mouth is an opening or intake for admitting food and drink while the teeth are tools for chewing the food that has been admitted into the mouth. Now, I'm not very fond of the notion of the mouth as an "intake" and the teeth as "tools," but there is no denying that the purpose of these body parts is to admit food and chew it. Nor can there be any doubt that the first business of the mouth and teeth is to chew. An infant that hasn't teethed yet drinks mother's milk by suckling at the breast. It moves its jaws as if to chew, but does not in fact chew with teeth. From this we can see that chewing is performed through the joint action of the mouth and the teeth.

Well then, why is it that we chew in the first place? One typical response to this would be "to aid in the digestion of the food we eat." Another explanation one would expect to hear is that the act of chewing serves as a "pretreatment" for sending the food smoothly onward to the esophagus, stomach, and intestines. An understanding based on such an explanation is generally adequate, but this taken by itself can hardly serve as a macrobiotic explanation or interpretation. I would thus like to discuss what I believe to be the macrobiotic view of the mouth and the teeth and what it means to chew.

I see the mouth and the teeth as existing in the relationship of a macrocosm (nature) with a microcosm (the body). The mouth and teeth serve as the gateway for the transformation of a macrocosm into a microcosm. The natural food brought forth by the sun, earth, and air is an embodiment of the macrocosmic life-forces. The distinctively individual character of food arises from differences in the manner in which this process of embodiment takes place, which in turn depends on how the macrocosmic life-forces are concentrated. As discrete individual entities, each and every thing has a universe of its own—its body; this applies to viruses, amoebae, plants, insects, fish, birds, beasts, and people. If we refer to these as individual microcosms, then in man the point of tangency and the locus of transformation between the macrocosm and the microcosm is the mouth and the teeth. Man is unable to introduce and assimilate nature in its original form within his body. He receives nature in the form of food, and the actual process of transformation is begun with the mouth and teeth. The function of the mouth and teeth is then to start the process of selection and assimilation by which man takes in macrocosmic life-forces.

The mouth and teeth act in unison to chew. This is reflected in the Chinese character for chewing (嚼), which is a combination of the characters for mouth (口) and for teeth (齒).

Next, I'd like to discuss what it means to chew.

When I started eating brown rice, I had no idea of the importance of chewing. I had been told to chew each mouthful of brown rice at least 100 times so I blindly obeyed. Before adopting a brown rice diet, I had never chewed anything 100 times, nor had I even paid any attention to the act of chewing itself. So when I began chewing each mouthful of brown rice at least 100 times, my temple and the joints and muscles in my jaw started aching. Everyone who starts a brown rice diet has the same experience. Chewing can be very tiresome. I thought of what a great relief it would be if there were some way to eliminate this irksome task. I even tried thinking of ways to eat brown rice without having to chew. For example I thought of cooking the rice until it was soft and mushy—like a cream or thick gruel, making a juice out of it with a blender, or grinding it to flour and preparing it in the form of a bread, dumplings, or even as a milky liquid. I seriously considered all of these as reasonable ways to prepare and eat brown rice. I wanted to simplify the job of chewing.

But I realized that the reason we have a mouth and teeth in the first place is to chew; if we were meant to eat by swallowing only, then *Homo sapiens* wouldn't have been given teeth to chew with. We would have been created as animals with just a mouth, an esophagus, and a stomach, like infants. But the fact is that human beings have teeth. This is because we were meant to chew. If this were not so, we would have no teeth.

At this point, I then asked myself again why it is necessary that we chew. There are in fact many reasons why we chew, but let us examine this from a macrobiotic point of view.

Naturally, the primary object and mission of chewing is to break down food that enters one's mouth in order to make it easier to digest. And what is meant by making a food easy to digest and absorb is to enable that food to be effectively assimilated and integrated into one's life; this may be regarded as the first step in the transformation of the outer macrocosm (nature) into the inner microcosm (the body).

The act of chewing itself comprises the selection and assimilation of food that has been placed in the mouth, but it does not necessarily follow that all food from the natural world is appropriate for all people. There are times when food containing harmful ingredients is placed in the mouth. Among other things, the process of chewing also functions to reduce or eliminate such harmful agents. Chewing results in the secretion of saliva, and the more one chews the greater the amount of saliva produced. This saliva has mysterious powers that boggle the imagination. For instance, not only does it function in digestion, it also serves to disinfect, render harmless what is harmful, cure injury, and invigorate the life-forces in the food. This deserves renewed appreciation as an extremely important fluid of life.

According to a recent report on experimental research conducted by Professor Hajime Nishioka at Doshisha University, the saliva is able to render certain carcinogenic substances present in food innocuous. One can see from this the importance of eating and chewing properly.

As the critical role played by mastication continues to be clarified from various perspectives—philosophical, biological, physiological, biochemical, physical, and cultural—this process assumes ever increasing importance. Taking all of this together, macrobiotics makes it a practice, based on empirical knowledge, to chew at least 100 times. A book entitled *Children with Poor Teeth Have Poor Minds*[2] was recently published in Japan. Children with poor teeth not only are not as bright as they could be, they also have weak bodies. The only way to prevent this is to encourage them to chew. Whether they have teeth or not, and whether those teeth are strong or not, they should be made to chew. By building a culture in which he need not chew, modern man is working toward his self-destruction.

---

[2]  Kunio Matsuhira. *Ha no yowai ko wa atama mo yowai.*

Here then, in summary form, is my macrobiotic view on chewing:

1. In Japanese, the word for chewing (*kamu*) is an abbreviation for God (*ka*mi) and to greet (*mu*kaeru).
2. "Kamu" means to take sin (*ka*) and eliminate it (*mu*).
3. The Japanese "kamu" sounds like "come" in English, which signifies the coming of God (the macrocosmic life-force).
4. The Chinese character for chew (嚼) is composed of the characters for mouth (口) and teeth (齒).
5. The more one chews, the more saliva is secreted. Saliva contains a large amount of hormones, digestive enzymes, and life-activating elements with disinfective and detoxifying actions.
6. The more one chews, the smarter one becomes; chewing stimulates the nerves and cells of the brain.
7. Chewing strengthens the teeth, jaw, and temples, and improves one's physique and facial features.
8. The more one chews, the more obesity-preventing hormones are produced (it is possible in this way to become slimmer without eating less and without doing sports or special weight-reducing exercises).
9. Chewing improves your vision.
10. Chewing reduces the amount you eat.
11. Chewing will result in food savings, lessening the burden on both household finances and the national treasury.
12. Chewing strengthens the stomach and intestines. This in turn will strengthen the other internal organs, eliminating disease, reducing worries, enabling one to become healthy, and increasing one's zest for life.
13. Last of all, there is the song written and composed by George Ohsawa:
    Make sure to chew your food very well.
    As you chew and chew and chew and chew,
    Your body will grow stronger.
    (chorus refrain)

I have discussed above the digestion and absorption of brown rice, and I have mentioned that brown rice is very easily digested and absorbed and that the stomach and intestines smile when brown rice is eaten. When brown rice is properly cooked and eaten, all this is true. But yet some people claim that brown rice is not easy to digest and absorb. Modern nutritional scientists have put out the following data on the digestion and absorption of different foods.

The data in sources A, B, and C were obtained from three different researchers.

In this table, the analytic results presented by each researcher show brown rice as having the worst ratio of digestion and absorption. Based on these figures, most people would (and do) conclude that brown rice is not easily digested and absorbed by the body.

In spite of these results, I firmly maintain that brown rice is more easily digested and absorbed than any of the other rices in the table, and I continue to insist that eating brown rice pleases the stomach and intestines.

**Table 2.3  The digestion and absorption of various types of rice.**

| | Name of food | Protein (%) | Starch (%) | Lipids (%) | Mineral (%) | Calories (%) |
|---|---|---|---|---|---|---|
| A | White rice | 85.8 | 99.7 | 86.8 | 90.9 | 97.0 |
| | Three-quarter-milled rice | 83.8 | 99.6 | 80.5 | 87.3 | 95.9 |
| | Half-milled rice | 82.0 | 99.3 | 74.4 | 84.4 | 94.5 |
| | Brown rice | 74.9 | 98.6 | 58.3 | 78.0 | 89.6 |
| B | White rice | 85.5 | 99.6 | 81.7 | 86.8 | 96.1 |
| | Three-quarter-milled rice | 83.0 | 99.4 | 74.5 | 81.9 | 94.6 |
| | Brown rice | 76.1 | 99.0 | 61.7 | 73.4 | 91.2 |
| C | Brown rice | 87.3 | 97.8 | 21.0 | — | 91.4 |
| | 1% milled | 89.6 | 98.3 | 28.6 | — | 93.2 |
| | 2% milled | 91.4 | 98.5 | 43.1 | — | 94.9 |
| | 3% milled | 92.3 | 98.7 | 48.6 | — | 96.0 |
| | 4% milled | 93.3 | 98.9 | 54.7 | — | 97.2 |
| | White rice | 94.7 | 99.1 | 58.6 | — | 98.0 |

From the *Handbook of Dietetics* [Eiyogaku Handbook].

The nutrients contained in food are digested and absorbed in relation to the body. It is not possible to determine the true quality of a food based only on the percentage of digestion and absorption of the protein, starches, lipids, minerals, and other components within that food.

For example, foods high in fiber have a low percentage of digestion and absorption, but scientists and others have begun to recognize that this fiber has a beneficial effect on the gastrointestinal system and that it also helps prevent one from becoming prone to cancer. What is most important about a food is the overall effect it has on the human body, the nature of its beneficial properties, and the extent to which the vitality of the body is enhanced by that food. True, narrow evaluations and judgments based on isolated numerical values are also of importance, but at the same time it is essential that we make more accurate evaluations and judgments for life and the body as a whole. White rice has a higher ratio of digestion and absorption than does brown rice, but once inside the body, brown rice has a better effect on metabolism than white rice. White rice tends to cause an imbalance in the distribution of nutrients within the body, whereas brown rice has the opposite effect of improving that balance. Although white rice does not have a beneficial effect on the intestines, brown rice promotes the healthy functioning of the gastrointestinal system. Macrobiotics takes a comprehensive look at all of life's activities, and from this vantage point is able to unequivocally claim that brown rice is better for the body than white rice.

# 3

## A Renewal of Life

# Proper Food Is the Best Medicine

With what is the word "medicine" associated in your mind? I used to think of medicine as something that cures sickness, something that makes one healthy. Indeed, the purpose of drugs and medications is to cure illness and restore health. That is why when we become ill or fall out of sorts, many of us soon reach for medications of one kind or another. Without having the slightest idea of what real medicine is or the different kinds of medicine that exist, I was a drug junkie, a blind believer in pharmaceutical fixes. Because I firmly believed that the synthetic drugs created by modern science are the best medicines known to man, I paid no attention to other medicines. I thought that I was correct in my judgment; after all, most of the drugs dispensed and used by hospitals, physicians, and pharmacies in the most advanced therapies are chemical pharmaceuticals. So I continued for many years to make habitual use of various chemical preparations. But my physical condition improved not one iota as a result. Instead of improving, in fact, I felt certain that my condition was deteriorating year after year. How could this possibly be when I always carefully followed the advice of my physician and made certain to use the latest medications and eat the most nutritious foods? Many people must surely have the same doubts and suspicions that I had.

Later on, when I turned to a macrobiotic brown rice diet, this resolved all my doubts and suspicions by steadily curing every one of my chronic ailments.

When I began eating brown rice, I stopped using pharmaceuticals altogether because I had begun to feel a strong distrust for chemical preparations and I realized also that it would be impossible to accurately gauge the true effectiveness of a macrobiotic brown rice diet if I were to continue at the same time to swallow medications and take shots. More importantly, I knew that taking chemical medications while on a brown rice diet would hamper the effectiveness of the brown rice. This, of course, is not true only of a brown rice diet. I did not have a proper understanding or knowledge of either food or medicine.

Most people think that drugs and medications are the answer to disease. At one time, medical associations and the Ministry of Health and Welfare in Japan urged people to "see a doctor at once when you get ill." One intention may have been to place the Japanese health care system on a firm footing. "Treatment at home by medical non-professionals is dangerous, so make haste to visit your doctor or hospital when you notice anything abnormal about your state of health." In this way, the idea that someone who is ill or not feeling well should visit the doctor or hospital became widely accepted. But physicians and hospitals found it difficult to properly handle the extra caseload brought on by the sudden surge in the number of patients. They became unable to thoroughly diagnose and treat patients, which led to an excessive reliance on medications. Clearly, the notion that one should combat illness with drugs has become accepted and ingrained within us. Let us consider here the wisdom of fighting disease with medications.

I personally have no quibble with this notion as expressed above. There is no question that medicines of some sort are needed to treat illness. The problem has to do rather with our use of medicines and our attitude toward them.

Our family had a long and close association with one physician that began with my own parents. This doctor was of course very familiar with the state of our family's health and the physical constitution of each member of our family. Whenever he examined me, he would always cock his head to one side with a quizzical look on his face. I was fifteen or sixteen years old back then.

"Your stomach almost looks like someone stuck a washboard underneath the skin."

When I was about twenty he again commented, with the same puzzled expression, on how hard my stomach was: "Why it feels almost as if you've got a steel plate in there." He said the same thing about the back of my neck, and repeatedly expressed amazement at the abnormal hardening of my muscles. My stomach and neck muscles were totally inflexible. But since I had no idea what healthy muscles were like, I didn't worry very much about whether these muscles were normal or not. Convinced that nutrition should be my uppermost concern in maintaining daily health, I was very careful to eat nutritious food and take gastrointestinal medications and nutriments. In addition to the medications prescribed by the doctor for illness, I bought medicine at the druggist's and used this constantly as I saw fit. The amount I used was probably more than I would dare imagine now. Not knowing that I was taking a lot of over-the-counter drugs, the doctor was unable to give me correct advice or guidance. I clearly remember our family physician and other doctors warning me: "At this rate, your body isn't going to hold out past the age of thirty." When I was told things like this, I would turn all the more to nutrition and medications I thought were good for the body. I was entirely convinced that only medicine could make my body strong and healthy. Had I not come across macrobiotics and brown rice and continued instead my life of dependence on medications and nutritious food, it's quite likely that I would never have lived past the age of thirty-five or so. The reason I'm convinced of this is that the doctors I saw were unanimous in giving me up to about the age of thirty to live; a fortune-teller I went to see at the time also told me, "You're only going to live to be about thirty-five."

However, as soon as I began eating brown rice and stopped taking medications, the condition of my body rapidly improved. How strange that my physical condition should improve when I quit taking medicine. Why in the world should this be?

As I have already related, with my adoption of macrobiotics I experienced many different physical reactions, the first of which was skin eruptions. Time after time, these appeared around my mouth and lips, under my nose, on the back of my hands, on my arms, and in my mouth and nostrils. At times, my whole body broke out in hives and eczema. Before long, my fingers and toes turned a dark color and countless large purple spots the size of quarters appeared on the joints in my hands and feet and on my elbows and knees. This was the same color as black ink. Cloudy yellow snivel, eye mucus, greenish-yellow phlegm—large discharges of all of these arose. I also suffered diarrhea, in addition to which I had sore throats, headaches, chest pains, fevers, stomach aches and, to top it all off, the most annoying and persistent case of flatulence.

Every time reactions such as these occurred, I started to worry that discontinuing all my medications and eating brown rice may have made my condition worse; I thought those reactions might be the symptoms of a general degradation of my internal organs. I asked others who were more experienced with macrobiotics about my fears and reread books on nutritional therapy. Now that I look back on it, I can see just how foolish I was.

These reactions were in fact signs of a general cleansing of the body. The vitality and metabolic forces of brown rice had begun to promote the purging and detoxification of the many contaminants, poisons, and other materials that had accumulated within me over all those years.

Furthermore, every time such reactions occurred, both my physical condition and my subjective symptoms would improve, giving me a deep sense that this brown rice diet was indeed cleansing my body, repairing my debilitated organs and tissue, and revitalizing my metabolism. The discomfort and malaise that I had exerienced while relying on drugs and a high-nutrition diet had disappeared; in place of this I now felt a sense of joy surge up within me every time I carefully chewed and ate my brown rice. Brown rice must certainly have an amazing power, a life-energizing force that is beyond compare with pharmaceuticals or a modern diet based on Western principles of nutrition. Even so, why is it that brown rice and synthetic drugs produced such vastly different results in my body?

To address this question, I must turn now to the Unifying Principle.

## The Difference in Vitality between Brown Rice and Synthetic Drugs

The body consists of a balance between Yin and Yang (for the moment, we shall understand Yin and Yang to be two opposing and complementary forces). When the balance between Yin and Yang is upset or destroyed, the body always gives out a signal. The nature of the signal—whether it is large or small, urgent or restrained, strong or weak—depends on the degree of imbalance in Yin and Yang.

My body was constantly sounding signals of Yin-Yang imbalance and abnormality: "The Yin-Yang balance has been disrupted! The Yin-Yang balance is awry! Bring Yin and Yang into harmony! Harmonize Yin and Yang!"

But I knew absolutely nothing about Yin and Yang. The moment I sensed that my body was out of sorts, I would rush right over to my doctor or the hospital. Physicians and hospitals in Japan today do not take a Yin-Yang view of the world. Modern medicine insists on treating illness with drugs. The primary mode of treatment is the administration of synthetic drugs. My body became permeated with drugs. Because of my constant intake of medications, my stomach and neck muscles became as hard as iron and my muscle tissue was in a senescent stage.

Drugs are produced from specific ingredients that are extracted by special processes. This extraction is in fact a great villain. We forcibly collect only those active ingredients which are helpful, beneficial, and convenient for man—I call this "the ideology of extraction." Drugs are typical products of this way of thinking. It is clear that when only certain components are extracted from something having a harmony of its own, both that which remains after such extraction and that which is created have lost the original harmony. The aim of pharmaceutical drugs is to induce the characteristics of this disharmony to act upon those parts of the human body lacking harmony such as to aid in the restoration of harmony to the human body. This explains why it is necessary to use drugs with such extraordinary precision and accuracy. For this to be possible, a very close and reliable diagnosis of the ailment must be made and exactly the correct amount of medication prescribed. But such perfection is not within the realm of what is humanly possible. This is why the body's natural powers of healing are said to be supreme. However, I did not believe this; I believed that the more medicine and nutrition one takes the better.

I'd like to take a very brief look at the process of extraction. Extraction may be regarded as the selective removal or withdrawal of certain substances contained in a given object or material. What then is the opposite of extraction? I suppose that this could be called "introduction."

An understanding of the above can be arrived at through a fundamental study of the Unifying Principle of Yin and Yang. Let us thus take a look here at the yin and yang of "extraction" and "introduction." The very process of extraction can be regarded as yin. In contrast with the source entity, which existed in a state of harmony, the extracted ingredient is a substance that has emerged through the disruption of harmony. This substance is of a nature, then, that seeks to extricate itself from its unstable state by finding a mate suited to itself and immediately establishing together with this mate a new harmony. This property is applied in the treatment of disease.

Since I had no knowledge of the true nature of medication, I thought that the more I took the better this would be for me. In fact, I was even more grateful for the medication I took than for the food I ate. Chemical components taken in too great an excess to be entirely discharged from the body search out complementary substances and seek stability by finding a home within cellular tissue. The cellular tissue in my body, unable to completely fight off the invasion of synthetic drugs, became sites for the deposition and accumulation of chemical substances, resulting in the progressive hardening and aging of not only my stomach and neck muscles, but my entire body.

Drugs come from various sources. Technical advances have brought many skilled and ingenious methods for the extraction and synthesis of active ingredients. These ingredients include substances that have been extracted from animals, substances extracted from plants, substances extracted from mineral matter, and substances created or synthesized from combinations of these. While the technology was still primitive, the ingredients necessary for drug manufacture were obtained from readily accessible sources by crude techniques. The history of civilization shows evidence of a change in the sources of these raw materials from animal to vege-table to mineral.

This shift in drug manufacture from the use of animal-based raw materials to plant-derived materials, from plant-derived materials to mineral substances, and from mineral substances to gases, heat rays, and electromagnetic waves represents a change from the use of yang materials to the use of yin materials. Hence, one could say that with the advance of civilization, medications have become increasingly yin. Generally speaking (and there may, of course, be exceptions), medicines prepared from raw materials of mineral origin are more strongly yin than those extracted from plant- or animal-based materials. Drugs that are more strongly yin work more quickly in humans because we are warm-blooded. The human body is far more yang than plants or mineral matter, so the more yin a drug, the more rapid an effect it has. This explains why mineral-based synthetic drugs are so welcome and why the drug industry has prospered so greatly in our materialistic civilization.

But has the health of the human body seen an improvement proportional with the development and supply of synthetic drugs? From my own personal experience, I feel very strongly that such drugs do far more harm than good to man. The drug industry is now beginning to move in the opposite direction in terms of where it obtains its raw materials; the trend is now moving from mineral to plant, from plant to animal, and from animal to human. This has come about because of a growing desire for safety and more rapid efficacy. For example, human insulin causes fewer side effects and has greater affinity to the human body than does insulin taken from the cow or pig. The use of donated human organs is superior to that of artificial organs. In the name of genetic engineering, man has already begun to treat the human body as a resource for the production of pharmaceutical products. There is no denying that organs and other materials obtained from the human body have greater affinity for, and are thus better suited for use in, the human body. Both the vision of science and technology as enabling human waste products as well as tissue and organs extracted from the human body and even cadavers to be utilized as resources and the understanding of the human body and human life as things or substances are achieving general acceptance and legitimacy. The world view that informs modern scientific civilization is analogous to the "ideology of extraction"; it is an ideology founded in the notion of elitism—the living over the dead, the strong over the weak, the affluent over the poor, the superior over the inferior—that leads to discrimination and the division of humanity into those who shall consume and those who shall be consumed.

One thing I am certain of with regard to synthetic drugs is that, when administered in the wrong way, in the wrong dosage, or with the wrong timetable, these invariably have an adverse affect on the internal body environment. The habitual use of synthetic drugs, like illicit drugs, renders one a physiological invalid.

Next, I would like to discuss what brown rice is and why it was good for my body. Figs. 3.1 and 3.2 are diagrams adapted or taken from Michio Kushi's *The Book of Macrobiotics*.[1]

The chapter entitled "Food and the Human Constitution" describes in very clear, easy-to-understand terms why grains are such an excellent food for man. I heartily recommend that those who are interested read what he has written. Below, I add my own perspective on this subject.

The mass of atoms we know as the earth arose from the ethereal world of elementary particles. It was not until after the earth and its atmosphere—the environment serving as the stage for the emergence of organisms—was in readiness that individual bodies having life (monocellular organisms) at last appeared on the face of the earth. These monocellular organisms emerged as viruses and bacteria, adopting at first a plant-like way of life. After repeated division in response to the demands placed upon them by changes in the environment, these monocellular organisms became primitive algae. The establishment of a stable existence by certain types of primitive algae probably led to the emergence of primitive animals capable of living by feeding primarily upon these algae. Billions of years of coexistence and interdependence by primitive algae and invertebrates in the sea must have brought about some change in the living environment that eventually resulted in

---

[1]  M. Kushi with A. Jack, p. 45, revised and enlarged edition, Japan Publications (1987).

**Fig. 3.1 The complementarity and evolution of plants and animals.**

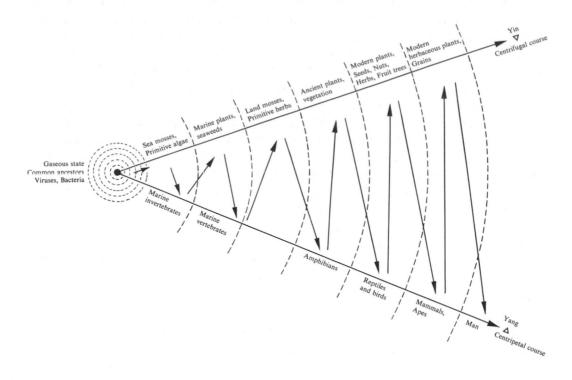

**Fig. 3.2 The principle of food according to biological evolution.**
(Diagram borrowed from *The Book of Macrobiotics*)

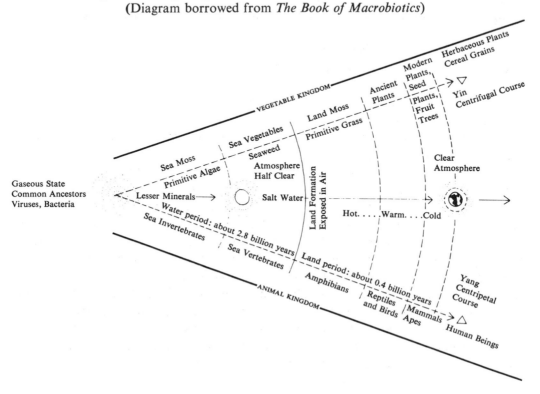

a change in vegetation. The seeds of new plants replaced the seeds of vanishing plants. Animals that fed on the vanishing plants had to adapt in order to go on surviving. Those species able to develop a mode of life or morphology adapted to the new environment became the dominant force in the animal kingdom of this new age and prospered. While complementing each other in this way, plants and animals went on changing and adapting to the environment, yet continued to retain their respective biological identities. Plants could not have lived, changed, and evolved independently of animals, and vice versa. In this way, plants changed habitat, moving from the water to the land, and animals followed suit, moving from the water to the land, and from the land to the air. The most recent arrivals among plants in this long evolutionary chain are the herbaceous plants, and it is the cereal grains that are the fruit of these plants which serve as the foods that have enabled man to become what he is. Animals are nurtured by plants. The existence of animals became possible through the lives of plants. This is a principle of life that cannot be overturned; it is the order of the phenomenon we call life.

This is what I understand from the above diagrams. Why don't you try looking at these diagrams from different perspectives and bringing away interpretations of your own?

If such development in organisms is regarded as evolution, then one cumulative effect of past changes in plants and animals has been the evolution of gramineous plants through the natural environment, bringing forth cereal grains, which are the seeds of these plants. When man began to eat cereal grains, the development of his intelligence speeded up. Of the cereal grains, rice in particular is rich in ingredients suited to the formation, growth, and development of brain cells. Latent within the rice seed is a vitality that develops and brings out the powers of human judgment to their highest degree. Following their emergence on the earth, animals lived in water for about 3.2 billion years, then another approximately 400 million years on land. This gives a ratio of the length of life in water to that on land of 8: 1. This ratio has been inherited by man in the ratio of water in his body to all other components; namely, 7–8: 1. The life of the rice plant capped by the fruition of new seeds reflects the course of biological history on earth. Other cereal grains include wheat, barley, and millet, but it seems to me that the yin-yang ratio of the ingredients in rice make this the most suitable of the cereal grains for the mental and physical growth of man.

I used to have a blind and absolute faith in human science. But this science we take such pride in is not even 1,000 years old. How silly I was to have thought that I could control my body, which after all is the product of 3.6–4 billion years of biological history, with the knowledge gleaned from less than 1,000 years of medical and nutritional science. Doesn't this alone explain perfectly well why, after having ruined my body by years of immoderately ingesting drugs and high-nutrition food, my physical condition began immediately to improve when I stopped taking these and switched to a brown rice diet? If the scientific method were used to examine this experience of mine from a different perspective, I am certain it would demonstrate that a traditional life in general conformity with the biological history of organisms constitutes a truly scientific approach to living.

After such contemplation, I realized that this boiled down to the question of whether one should live one's life dependent upon synthetic drugs or dependent upon brown rice. Reliance upon synthetic drugs involves the application of human judgment to the use of man-made products produced by extraction and synthesis; this is clearly a human- and self-centered way of life. On the other hand, brown rice represents a way of living dependent upon God, in which the decision as to what pharmacological ingredients to extract from the brown rice is left to the divine nature within one's body (by which I mean the body's natural powers of healing).

Before I learned of macrobiotics and brown rice, I thought that my life was unique and unlike any other in this world. Convinced that I had to do what I could for the sake of my own existence—that I had to see the doctor, go to the hospital, get shots, take medication, and eat plenty of nutritious food—I was completely caught up in my ridiculous cleverness and contrivances, all of which had the reverse effect of destroying my physiological well-being. This happened because I ignored the divine nature within my body and chose instead to live a life that relied on brainpower, a life that was centered on the self and on man.

The only duty to myself I have now is to correctly eat brown rice. That is absolutely all. I have no idea how the brown rice that I eat is used or acts within my body. I leave this work and its results up to the divine nature of the body; all I do is to make full use of the life-force and vitality I receive. This alone has blessed me with such improvement in my physical condition and general health as I was never able to achieve while I depended upon doctors, synthetic drugs, and nutritious foods. That is why I cannot refrain from urging you to change your life too—if you haven't already done so—through macrobiotics.

The very first thing one should know is that "proper food is the best medicine." At the same time, it is vital that one grasps the difference between the power of brown rice and the power of drugs.

## A Macrobiotic Brown Rice Diet for Curing Illness

I stated above that "macrobiotics develops the divine spirit within the body." I believe that by exploiting the divine spirit within me to the extent I am able, I can make full use of the life in this body given me by my parents and thereby justify my existence. You too were born with and bear your own divine spirit. If each of us were to fully exploit our divine spirits, then we would be able to lead happy lives.

It is necessary first to free the divine spirit within the body. This divine spirit must not be oppressed, shackled, or hindered in any way.

Based on my shallow, superficial knowledge of drugs and nutrition, I chose only actions that disregarded the divine spirit within the body. Clever, egoistic "knowledge" is incompatible with this divine spirit, something which I first came to realize when I turned to a macrobiotic brown rice diet. Even when one practices the same macrobiotic diet, however, the effects manifest themselves in different ways depending on the approach one takes. There is a large difference between eating brown rice based on reasoned knowledge and justification, and completely surrendering oneself to the divine spirit inside by obediently following the fundamental path of macrobiotics and gratefully receiving life from brown rice.

*Curing Disease with a Macrobiotic Brown Rice Diet:*  The first thing I did was to make a difficult resolution: "If my daughter is not saved by the power of brown rice, then that will be the end for her." Once we had so decided, then it became a matter of faith to my wife and I that brown rice would surely save our child.

I made just as drastic a resolution for myself when I started eating brown rice: I threw away all the drugs and medications I had. This was a frightening action that filled me with anxiety. But I had resolved that if throwing away my medications and eating brown rice aggravated my ailments and brought me to death's door, then I would resign myself at that time to death. I clung to brown rice with the desperate conviction that if it would not cure me then nothing I ate could.

I clung to the god of life we know as brown rice. I was desperate at the time and understood nothing. Looking back on it now, I had turned to a truly welcome guardian spirit of life. A fool who knew nothing of the essence of "food" was clinging to the lord of food—the guiding principle that "food is life."

Fortunately for my daughter and I, we still had enough recuperative strength to be saved by brown rice. People often ask me what should be done in the case of someone who is already dying—a terminally ill patient at the last stage of disease or someone who has been gravely injured—if that individual is too far gone to eat brown rice.

My answer to this is: "Death itself is the ultimate cure." If life and resuscitation are the supreme cure, then I believe that the same can be said also of death. I discuss this later on in the book; when one carefully examines my Life Cycle Diagram (Fig. 5.1) and judges life and death with the Unifying Principle of Yin and Yang that represents the cosmic order, then life and death can be seen as merely a pair of exactly equal phenomena. If man is intent on making judgments egoistically from a standpoint favorable to himself and laden with self-justification, then some kind of value-based distinction does arise between life and death. But judged from the standpoint of God and from the cosmic macrobiotic perspective, life and death are opposite sides of one reality.

The fact is, however, that man is trying to gain control over life and death. Advances and developments made in science and technology have given him the illusion that he can influence and even control life and death. This is a source of great misfortune, for life and death are the work of God alone. Yet modern man thinks and believes this to be the work of science and technology. The majority of scientists and scholars are striving to push forward scientific and technological development that reinforces such thinking in people. Modern man has become terribly arrogant and blasphemous.

One proof of this is the following experience I had recently. I met with the director of a well-known Japanese hospital. He had read a book of mine (*Seikatsu kakumei＝Genmai seishokuho* [Life Revolution＝Macrobiotics]) in which I wrote that my association with macrobiotics and brown rice came about because my daughter's physician had frankly admitted the limits of medicine and left the matter of her life or death in the hands of God.

This director told me that the judgment and action taken at the time by my daughter's physician were today inconceivable. When I asked him in what way these were inconceivable, he said that physicians are bound by ethical codes and regulations from abandoning or discharging patients from the hospital on the grounds that no method of treatment exists or a condition is incurable. Although his attitude of doing everything that is medically possible to treat a patient is admirable for its devotion to the physician's sense of mission, if modern medicine—which represents only a fraction of the vast range of treatment modes known to man—is regarded as "everything," this actually reflects a very arrogant, self-serving attitude. It is highly unfortunate and regrettable that such a tendency is so strong in the modern medical profession.

What I desire most of modern medicine in regard to the treatment of patients like this is that, if physicians are truly devoted to the mission of healing, they leave open the final option of allowing the physician, the patient, and the patient's family to select together an appropriate mode of treatment from the many that exist, including not only Western medicine, but Chinese herbal medicine, Arabian medicine, Ayurvedic medicine, and other folk therapies indigenous to various parts of the world, as well as natural medicine, of course.

Macrobiotics maintains that "food is life." Hence, it follows that "food is the best medicine," which is, in fact, what macrobiotics asserts. Moreover, adherents of macrobiotics practice a way of life which maintains that macrobiotic medicine is the best medicine. It is no exaggeration to say that macrobiotic medicine is divine therapy. The only way for someone to master this mode of treatment and successfully administer it is if the person under treatment is himself a strict adherent of macrobiotics and understands and embodies the Unifying Principle of Yin and Yang, which is the fundamental principle of life activity. My own teacher, Hideo Omori, who is the leading practitioner of macrobiotic medicine in Japan, once told me, "Unless one eats properly, no therapy or technique for maintaining good health will be of any use." That's a frightening statement, isn't it?

What does macrobiotic medicine do in the case of someone in the final stage of a terminal illness or someone who has suffered a life-threatening injury? The answer is that it administers warm, attentive nursing and care far beyond anything imaginable in modern medicine. Although I did write above that "death is the ultimate cure," this is not to say that one should stand by with folded arms waiting for death. In macrobiotic medicine, those treatments selected from the food about us that appear as if they will work best on this particular critically ill person at this particular time are tried one after another, these being administered to the best of one's ability with the fullest devotion and love. If death ensues in spite of this care, then I think it fair to say that "death is the ultimate cure." Whether to entrust the final treatment to the hands of God, to the hands of modern science, or to some other method or means is a problem to be decided by you, your family, and those around you who have influence over you.

The decisive factor in curing illness through macrobiotics is whether or not the afflicted person and his or her family devote themselves wholeheartedly to macrobiotic medicine. This is the first and most important condition. Through macrobiotics, some people recover rapidly from illness while others are much slower to show improvement. Proper desire, will power, and vigor are indispensable for curing disease. An intractable disease cannot be overcome in the absence of a strong internal desire and force of will by the patient to recover. The same is true of the family and others around one.

Because macrobiotic medicine draws from cosmic life and life-forces to treat man, one must clearly understand that the foundation for treatment through macrobiotics is a way of life that faithfully observes God and the Order of the Universe.

## Modern Medicine and the Body's Natural Powers of Healing

The forces which protect, maintain, and regulate the body, which repair cellular tissue and functions that have been damaged or disrupted, and which restore the body to health are collectively called the natural powers of healing. My brown rice diet was more effective in restoring these natural healing powers in my body than were the medications, tonics, and high-nutrient foods to which I had been accustomed.

Before taking a look at these natural powers of healing, I would like to consider first the question of what treatment is. I believe that true treatment consists of restoring the body's natural powers of healing and its natural ability to heal itself. Therapy must begin by aiding and returning to normal the healing powers of the body and the vitality that is lacking.

What about modern medicine then? It seems to me that this disregards the natural healing powers of the body. It appears to rely totally on the intervention of artificial or man-made forces to conquer and subdue the illness or the afflicted part of the body through the power of drugs and other treatment modes. I myself was totally reliant on doctors, drugs, and nutritious food for so long because I believed these forces to be stronger and more reliable than the natural powers of healing. I thought that I was always prone to illness because my body was weak; after all, I soon fell ill over nothing at all. I was certain that the only way to win out over my inherent frailty was to borrow strength from outside of myself. Unaware that I myself am blessed with wonderful powers, the only thought that arose in my mind was that I had to compensate for my weakness by drawing strength from without.

I am totally convinced that modern medicine makes the same mistake as I made. It seems to me that the basic thinking in medicine today can be summarized as follows: "Medicine acts in place of the natural powers of healing," or "Modern medicine takes over for the natural powers of healing because these are impaired."

"I can't be concerned about the natural powers of healing." "We have no time to wait for recovery of the natural healing powers." "If we waited around for the natural powers of healing to take effect, the patient would be dead." "Relying on the natural powers of healing would be bad for business." "We practice physical therapy because you can't depend on the natural powers of healing"—it seems to be attitudes such as these which have propelled modern medicine to its present stature. Such thinking manifests a fundamental distrust in the natural powers of healing. Rather than "distrust," this might more accurately be called neglect or disregard.

Physicians and others engaged in the practice of medicine reply that I am wrong in my views. They say that careful screening and tests are conducted on patients and an overall diagnosis arrived at to assess the degree of vitality in the patient.

But modern medical procedures, which rely so heavily on diagnostic testing, drugs, and surgery, are forcing upon patients increasingly artificial and invasive treatment. Clearly, it is the physician who is doing the treating here. I think it fair to characterize such treatment as "excessive" and "arrogant."

What I used to do was select certain doctors, hospitals, drugs, foods, and so forth based on what I knew, advice and suggestions from others, and other information. I sought in this way to cure not only myself, but also my daughter and the ailments of the rest of my family. The doctor or hospital would, with the resources they had available, set out to handle the patient and treat the disorder. But, when viewed in overall terms, the so-called miracles of modern medicine have not brought us a decline in either the frequency of disease or the number of those who are ill. With scientific treatment as advanced as it has become, one would expect a drop in disease and illness proportional to the much-heralded advances of science and medicine. Yet, contrary to all expectations, it has not been possible to resolve or reduce even very common disorders such as the common cold, headaches, urticaria, rheumatism, diabetes, gastroptosis, and insomnia.

However, when I changed my diet and started eating brown rice, I gradually stopped catching colds, one after another of my chronic ailments vanished, and I no longer felt constantly fatigued as I had; this was clearly a result of the increased healing powers of my body. A condition that modern medicine was unable to do anything about was resolved completely merely through a change in diet. How could this be? Is this not an indication of the limits to human technology and abilities? Modern medicine and health care throw their full energies and resources at the problem and administer scientific treatment. As more and more therapy is administered, the natural powers of healing weaken and degenerate to the point where the body's inherent powers of resistance and vitality decline. This is why medical care that relies upon drugs, equipment, and facilities becomes necessary. In view of this, I do not find it at all surprising when our modern health care system turns seriously ill or injured people into "vegetables" and merely keeps them alive.

I feel that true health care must at all times strengthen and enhance the natural healing powers of the body, but it must not go further than this. How I wish that the medical establishment would wake up to the fact that excessive medical care can never be in the best interests of the patient. Because it is difficult to determine the appropriate limits of care, I would like here to suggest a simple guide to these limits: the presence or absence of a desire by the patient to eat with his own mouth, of a will to live, and of alimentary functions. These must be diagnosed with great care and precision.

This would represent a great departure from the basic thinking of modern health care. Let me return for a moment to the conversation I had with the hospital director of a large hospital. In my book, I had written that because a doctor had been forthright enough to admit to me that my daughter could not be saved by modern medicine, we were able to save her through nutritional therapy. The director refused to believe this, saying repeatedly, "That's just impossible."

"What do you mean it's impossible?" I asked.

"A respectable university hospital would never abandon a patient like that."

"Why not?"

"Because the work of doctors and hospitals today is to watch over that patient by whatever means possible until he or she is cured. It is inconceivable that a physician would tell a patient that no mode of treatment exists for his or her condition."

"In other words, a patient beyond hope of recovery is unable to leave the care of the physician or the hospital, right?" I couldn't avoid pressing this point home.

To this, the director replied with conviction: "Those in particular who are gravely ill or injured should not be taken out of our care. That is the work of the physician."

As I listened to him speak, I pictured my infant daughter at the time; she was not even six months old. Had the doctor in charge of her been less candid with us and kept her in that hospital, she would surely have died in their care. Had that doctor held the same views on health care as the director before me, he would probably have treated her with various drugs and equipment, but would not have succeeded in saving her. I couldn't help thinking that it would all have ended with an "I'm awfully sorry." The reason is simple: while modern health care does have somewhat of a positive effect in patients with good physical strength, it has the opposite effect in weaker patients of robbing them of their remaining vitality.

The hospital director's thesis is really very clear: modern-day physicians and hospitals can treat patients until they kill them, and must not relinquish such medical care even if it kills the patient. The idea here, of course, is that the fate of the patient is entirely in the hands of the physician or hospital, who claim to do everything that is humanly possible for the patient.

But isn't there something wrong here? I have serious doubts about whether health care that extends the life of an unconscious patient while keeping him barely alive with round-the-clock infusions, oxygen tents, and artificial organs, that filters the blood with sophisticated machinery, supplies alimentation, removes body wastes, and in general permeates the body with a contant barrage of drugs and injections is true health care.

One time-honored way for the layman to gauge the vitality of an invalid is very simple: "If he can't eat, then it's all over." I believe that this unsophisticated method of making a judgment is very valuable.

Aside from those cases in which an individual is already dying from illness or injury, most diseases in general—including degenerative diseases, acute and chronic ailments, intractable and exotic illnesses—can be cured by a change in diet. Although this may appear to be an extreme statement, if someone cannot be saved through a new and proper diet, then it would be wise for that person to resign himself to death. I believe that gaining general acceptance for this life view is the true work of medicine. Modern health care is very technologically advanced. However, it has forgotten the origin of life as expounded in such tenets as "Food is life" and "Without food, there is no life." I wish with all my heart that modern medicine would establish a correct view of diet as the key to health care, a view that would seek answers to such questions as "What sort of a diet is necessary for eliminating disease and curing invalids?" "What kind of a diet strengthens and invigorates the natural healing powers of the body?" and "How can diet be used to reduce disease and the number of those afflicted with disease?" Medical technology today is advancing from physicochemical therapy to biological and natural therapy. It has become clear that there are limits to physicochemical therapy; people have come to realize that perfectly natural and acceptable biological and ecological techniques are in fact surprisingly effective. I earnestly hope that the medical establishment will undertake as a research topic of the utmost importance the question of nutritional therapy (macrobiotic medicine), which is the most sensible of these latter therapeutic techniques. I believe that only after this awareness has been raised will it be possible for the natural healing forces within each of us to be properly awakened and revived.

## Is Your Body Your Own?

This question of the body's natural healing powers made me stop and reflect on whether my body was indeed my own. I had never given the matter any serious thought, but the answer seemed to me perfectly simple and obvious. Descartes' famous dictum, "I think, therefore I am," and other conventional wisdom led me to decide by association that one's body belongs to oneself. It was on these same grounds that I had come to believe that one's body must be treated according to one's way of thinking. In the case of a family, and especially with children, I felt that it was up to the master of the house or the children's parents to make the decision.

"I am my own master"—such an understanding may be necessary to a certain extent. But if this feeling is too strong, it leads to a self-centered, self-serving "me-first" attitude and to a human-centered way of thinking that always places man first and foremost. I suspect that all people today share to some extent such attitudes and notions.

Believing that my body belonged to me, whenever it was out of sorts, I would run immediately to the doctor's or the hospital. For their part, the doctor or hospital would, as they are wont, administer medications, nutrients, and surgery. Thinking that I was the master of my own body, I selected the doctor or hospital; likewise, when it comes to therapy, the doctor thinks of himself as the patient's master and accordingly selects what he feels to be the appropriate drugs, nutrients, or surgery. This I, this doctor, and this hospital all share the same view of man as master of the body.

When I started eating brown rice, my thinking changed completely. I strove only to eat brown rice silently and correctly. I no longer needed to worry, as I had before, about whether I should go see the doctor, whether I should have a checkup at the clinic and get some shots, and whether I should continue to take my medication. All I did was quietly and correctly chew my brown rice and leave things up to the rice. That was the extent of my thoughts. Yet at some point, I had adopted a way of life that relied on brown rice. I had placed myself in the hands of brown rice, in the hands of providence, in the hands of God.

This series of changes may appear at first to be nothing special, perhaps even quite ordinary. However, looking at the matter calmly, the change that I underwent was to me a great revolution.

Before I was fully aware of what was happening, my life style, which had been largely self-centered, changed completely into one that left things up to providence and to God. What a strange and marvelous transformation! I had heard of the amazing powers of brown rice, and everything I learned turned out to be true.

None of this was forced upon me. Rather, I underwent first a change in my awareness and attitudes. This change came over me unknowingly. As I continued eating brown rice, I, who had thought all along of the body as being one's own possession, came to believe instead that one's body belongs to God.

In fact, the truth of the statement that the body is man's and yet belongs to God rather than man is starting to be demonstrated even in the world of science. In this regard, I describe below several items of information that I've picked up from the news recently.

Up until now, the heart has generally been regarded as a pump for sending blood throughout the body. The following description is typical: "The heart is a pump: a muscular organ that contracts in rhythm, impelling the blood first to the lungs for oxygenation and then out into the vascular system to supply oxygen and nutrients to every cell in the body. That has been known since the publication in 1628 of William Harvey's *Essay on the Motion of the Heart and the Blood in Animals.*"[2]

It was from this perspective that development of an artificial heart began. "Because the heart is a pump, a prosthesis for the heart need function only as a pump." This is how the idea came about of using an artificial heart in place of a real human heart that has been diagnosed as damaged, dysfunctional, defective. The egocentric thinking and over-optimistic expectations of both the medical practitioners, who maintain that treatment is possible by replacement of the damaged organ, and the patient and his family, who hope that replacing the heart will free the patient of heart disease, completely disregard the as yet unknown and mysterious workings of the heart—what I like to think of as the special solicitude of God. Yet another aspect of the unfathomable ways of God has been brought to light recently by the hand of man. The same article continues with this passage:

> Within the past few years it has been discovered that the heart is something more than a pump. It is also an endocrine gland. It secretes a powerful peptide hormone called atrial natriuretic factor (ANF). The hormone has an important role in the regulation of blood pressure and blood volume and in the excretion of water, sodium and potassium. It exerts its effects widely: on the blood vessels themselves, on the kidneys and the adrenal glands and on a large number of regulatory regions in the brain.

As a medical layman, this new information raises the following doubt in my mind: "Can an artificial heart also be capable of functioning as an endocrine gland?"

The heart we were all born with no doubt possesses other unknown yet critical functions. Scientists may investigate and elucidate each of these in turn, adding such discoveries to the greater glory of man's technological prowess as advances in medicine and health care. But there is more to the body than just the heart. Regardless of how much science is practiced in different disciplines, the more research man does, the larger becomes the world of the unknown. Achieving perfection that

---

[2]   Marc Cantin and Jacques Genest, "The Heart as an Endocrine Gland," *Scientific American* 254, No. 2, 62–67 (1986).

permits application to the human body as a whole might take thousands and even tens of thousands of years; and even if man does spend all that time, he is not likely to obtain fully satisfactory results.

Can the way of life and thinking of modern man, who nonetheless applauds the replacement of a defective human heart with an artificial one as the triumph of scientific medical care, be right? I think not. This carries the blasphemy of God too far. It certainly serves as a prime example of the great conceit and arrogance of man.

Let us take the kidneys as a second example here. The medical profession applies the same thinking and methods to the kidneys as to the heart. It is a view of the kidney as merely an organ for filtering out waste products and impurities from the blood that has brought about the development of hemodialytic technology and equipment. As a result, the world of health care has seen the creation of a new type of patient who is tied to and controlled by equipment. Everyone now is aware that the kidney is more than merely a blood filtering device. We know that it has a wide range of baffling endocrinal functions. Yet, in spite of this, kidney extractions, transplants, and the use of artificial kidneys have grown almost commonplace. These actions by physicians and hospitals are supported, except in the case of blatant failures, by a system of health care that justifies therapeutic intervention, even when a hundred physiological functions are sacrificed in the bargain. Although a procedure may destroy God-given bodily functions, as long as the treatment produces the desired effect, no one is called to account even if the patient should die as a result. On the other hand, if someone dies without receiving treatment within the modern health care system, the members of the surviving family are subjected to social sanctions for their contempt of modern medicine and their cruelty and heartlessness. This view that regards as wicked the entrusting of matters of life and depth to the hands of God and as virtue the entrusting of life and death to the hands of man—or, more precisely, modern health care—is a very queer and anthropocentric ideology.

A third example has to do with the liver. Liver cancer is so intractable a disease that it has been called incurable. Yet a ray of hope has begun to emerge now with the development of what is called "fresh plasma therapy."

In his recent book *Realizing New Ideas* (Hasso no genba), the Japanese author Kunio Yanagida states that one large factor in achieving success in liver cancer surgery is the growing success of "fresh plasma therapy" in preventing postoperative liver dysfunction. I quote here from his book:

> Yanagida: Doctor Hasegawa, I understand that two key conditions for successful liver cancer surgery are the improvement of surgical technique within Japan and the use of large-volume fresh plasma therapy for preventing postoperative liver dysfunction. As I understand it, the basis for this large-volume fresh plasma therapy is the presence of *something special* in fresh blood . . .?
> Hasegawa (Director of Hepatic Surgery and Pediatric Surgery at National Cancer Institute): When children are given transfusions of their mother's blood, they become incredibly lively and energetic. We found that the effect is far more immediate than when the salt level, pH, and so forth are controlled. We therefore concluded that *there must be something special in fresh blood.*

However, when too much whole blood is used, the blood becomes viscous, so what we do is transfuse just the supernatant after operating on the liver.

Both Yanagida and Hasegawa talk of *something special* in the blood. Research proceeded from the observation that the mother's fresh plasma appears to be very effective in preventing hepatic dysfunction following liver cancer surgery. From this emerged "fresh plasma therapy." Even a rank amateur such as I could have guessed that blood or blood plasma from a child's own mother would be more effective than synthetic drugs or artificial blood.

One would never expect the presence of that "something special" in artificial man-made products. Yet, we live in a world where, in the absence of proof to the contrary supplied through research by medical specialists such as these, we end up believing that man-made products are more reliable and proper. It does appear as if we place more confidence in the artificial: artificial hearts, artificial kidneys, artificial lungs, artificial livers, artificial bones, artificial blood vessels, artificial blood, artificial insemination, artificial organisms, and so forth and so on.

For many years, my wife and I have been active supporters of the "mother's milk movement" which encourages mothers to nurse their babies with their own milk. Mother's milk, which is essentially mother's blood that has been transformed into milk as food for the infant, surely is the best possible food for infants. The divine spirit within the mother's body converts blood into an ideal food for the baby. Incredible as it may seem now, there was a time when the medical community, nutrition experts, and the formula milk industry joined hands to promote the use of formula milk. Claims were made that children raised on this would be smart because of the excellent ingredients in the formula, spurring the production and sales of formula milk. Even some mothers who lactated readily were persuaded by these claims to raise their children on formula milk.

I would like to introduce one last and very recent example along these same lines. The following excerpt is from an article entitled "Substance that Increases Number of Cells Confirmed in Amniotic Fluid" which appeared in the March 27, 1986 issue of the *Mainichi Shimbun*.

A research group led by Professors Masahiko Mizuno and Yuji Takeya of the Department of Gynecology at the Tokyo University Faculty of Medicine has ascertained for the first time that a strong cell-propagating factor is contained in the amniotic fluid which protects the human fetus. Although this substance has not yet been definitively identified, the investigators believe that it may be a peptide consisting of a chain of amino acids and having a molecular weight of about 1,000. This substance is thought to be closely associated with the growth of the skin, lungs, and gastrointestinal system of the fetus. It may help to elucidate the riddle of the growth mechanism in infants, and also open up a new avenue toward the treatment of growth-impaired infants. . . . For reasons having in part to do with the difficulty of obtaining amniotic fluid, relatively little research has been done on this fluid *and so it has been thought to provide merely physical protection of the fetus.* However, because a small amount of amniotic fluid in the womb (normally this is about 500 cc at term) is associated with incomplete development of the infant's lungs, the group undertook their studies believing the amniotic fluid to contain a substance that stimulates cell growth."

As can be seen from the blunt statements in the above article, even the medical community regarded the amniotic fluid as nothing more than a material providing physical protection. The starting point of this research—the suspicion that a substance which promotes cell growth might be present in amniotic fluid—was vital in the discovery that amniotic fluid is more than just a physical buffer. However, it is clear that the amniotic fluid does even more than what is described here. That which is disclosed to us is only a tiny fraction of a fraction of the whole.

As I have repeatedly pointed out, we are egocentric and anthropocentric in all that we do. Every single part of the human body—not just the heart, the kidneys, the liver, or fresh blood—contains a mysterious *something* beyond which any effort of the human imagination or technology pales into insignificance. God has carefully seen to the perfection of each detail. What this means is that our bodies may seem as if they belong to us, but they do not. I believe that the day has come when we must humbly admit that no matter how perfect and complete human artifice and invention may appear, it is always hopelessly flawed. And having admitted this, we must set out once again on our journey by changing our diet.

# 4

## Nurturing a Body
## that Does Not
## Catch Colds

# What Is the Common Cold?—The Cold Is a Signal of Death

The common cold is often called the root of all illness. Many people have heard this, but few give it much thought. This once was true for me too.

After starting to eat brown rice and study the Unifying Principle, I came to appreciate the meaning of the above words. I even realized that not only is the cold the root of all illness, it is also the root of death.

I used to naively believe that a cold was something that was cured with drugs and the doctor's ministrations. "Why am I so prone to catching colds?" I wondered to myself countless times. Yet I had not once considered the meaning of the common cold. I had never given any thought to what colds are and indeed believed them to be of no particular significance. I thought that colds were caused by bacteria and viruses, and that these could only be cured by injecting or swallowing medication that killed the pathogens. I felt that colds were caused by extraneous factors such as microbes, stress or fatigue from work, and temperature changes.

But the causes of a cold all lie within oneself. One theorem of the Unifying Principle states that "nothingness (emptiness) is the source of all things." This may be reworded thus: "nothingness (emptiness) is the source of the creation of all things." The creation of all things means the birth of all things, so it is possible to recast the above as "nothingness is the birth (誕生) of all things." By abbreviating this further, we get "nothingness (emptiness) is life (生)." Ohsawa's cosmic spiral and my Life Cycle Diagram (see Fig. 5.1) graphically represent this above notion.

I have just stated that "nothingness is the source of life" in order to contrast this with the notion of the common cold as the root of death.

What sort of a world is the vast, limitless, unbounded cosmos that contains a countless number of infinitesimally tiny universes such as the solar system or the Milky Way? This is a world that cannot be expressed except with words such as "nothinginess" or "emptiness." The two elements of *ki*, Yin and Yang, emerge from this world of nothingness (emptiness). Yin and Yang are the order (law) of the universe and have brought forth all things. I understand this as being the true or proper cosmic spirit (*seiki*). True cosmic spirit can be understood as being the *ki* of creation.

In contrast, I shall call the *ki* that opposes the cosmic order the false or perverse cosmic spirit (*jaki*). Although *seiki* and *jaki* are but different sides of the same reality, if *seiki* is the *ki* of creation, then *jaki* can be called the *ki* of annihilation (destruction). Evidence of the two *ki* and their respective properties can be seen even on this earth in the natural phenomena of creation and growth on one hand and of destruction and annihilation on the other. The phenomena that occur on earth take place in exactly the same way within the human body.

The common cold is an evil *ki* of the body and mind, a wrong *ki*. When the body and mind are dominated by an evil or wrong *ki*, this results in symptoms of illness. The cause of a cold is just this and nothing more.

But what is a right *ki* and what is a wrong *ki*? And how does one distinguish between the two? Let me describe my own personal experiences in this regard.

Through macrobiotics, the *seiki* of the universe began flowing into my body. Proper natural food is an embodiment of *seiki*. The *seiki* of the universe created and grew plants as food. Plants made the existence of animals possible. Part of *seiki* and the life-force of the universe is embodied in the cereal grains, and it is with one of these grains, brown rice, that I cast my lot. Because food is obtained through the condensation of all terrestrial elements—sunlight, air, land, and water—the presence of right or wrong *ki* in the food that one eats can have an enormous effect on the amount and type of *ki* that controls the body. By examining the *seiki* and *jaki* of the universe, it is possible to understand why eating proper natural food is important and why artificial and unnatural foods are bad for the body.

The notion of the human body as a universe is familiar. The body is an infinitesimally small universe within a large universe. It is the child of a large universe. When *seiki* is in control, vigorous growth and activity occur; but when *jaki* is in control, the result is annihilation and destruction.

It is extremely important that one carefully distinguish between food that has been created by cosmic *seiki* and fraudulent, deceptive foods produced through the *jaki* of monetary gain. One yardstick for distinguishing between proper foods and improper foods is to ask oneself whether it is food having the *seiki* of the universe and nature or food resulting from the *jaki* of human stupidity and greed. An even more effective yardstick is the symptom of *jaki* we know as the common cold.

Catching a cold means that one is under the influence of *jaki*. My body was formerly a constant haunt of *jaki*. Because I was controlled by *jaki*, I relied on whatever drugs, doctors, nutrition, and other available means of "healing" I could avail myself of. Since these are not products of *seiki*, I was unable to eradicate the *jaki* within me. This is why the common cold is the root of death, and thus "a signal of death."

Those who catch colds are people who violate the proper order of life.

## How Not to Catch Colds

Few people must catch colds as easily as I did. During my youth, I was always going from one cold to the next: I would get laid up sick in bed with every change of season; I would catch colds from fatigue whenever I overtaxed myself a little at work or sports; regulation of my body temperature would get out of kilter in the winter and summer whenever I entered and left well-heated or air-conditioned rooms; and all I had to do was to hear about a flu epidemic to catch it. I was always among the first to catch a cold in any epidemic.

I had a constant fear of colds. All I had to do was think that I might catch a cold, and without fail I would. First my throat would start to swell and get feverish. Before long, it would be all red and swollen and I would no longer be able to stay on my feet. I'd get into bed and pile on one quilt after another. If I didn't warm my body, swallow some medication, have my doctor give me some shots, and try sweating off the bug, I was unable to rid myself of these symptoms. Whenever I got laid up like this with a cold, I would have to take at least a week off from work. After repeated copious sweating, my fever would at last come down and I would start feeling better. Once I had arrived at this stage, cold sores would break out around my nose or mouth and on my lips. My cold would never pass without the appearance first of these sores, which had an unpleasant tingling sensation and later became red swellings that would begin to positively ache. The blisters eventually broke open and dried. Once these had turned into scabs, this signaled that the cold was at an end. It took ten to fourteen days for the scabs to fully heal. Therefore, all told, it took three weeks to a month for me to recover completely from a cold. Since I would take a week to ten days off from work with each cold, when I returned to the office I would have to work hard to catch up on the backlog. But if my exertions led to overwork as a result, I would catch a new cold that would again land me sick in bed. I spent my youth and early adulthood constantly battling one cold after another in this way.

I desperately wanted to make my body healthier and more robust. Whenever I wasn't feeling too bad, I would try joining in some sports or hiking with my friends. But after a little athletic activity or walking, the muscles in my arms, legs, back, abdomen, and elsewhere would ache and feel feverish. If I were exposed to stress while in this state, my throat would soon start swelling red, I would become unable to stay on my feet, and the same cycle that I have described above would be repeated once again.

I always found it strange and incomprehensible why I was so prone to catching colds and why I was unable to stay on my feet when I had them. I knew nothing of the order of the universe at the time. I depended on doctors, medications, nutritional food, profuse sweating, and rest, and still the same thing happened over and over again. Neither I nor the doctors could understand why I caught colds so easily.

After taking up a macrobiotic brown rice diet, however, I stopped catching colds. Even when I did catch a cold, it became possible for me to recover without staying in bed. As my body became accustomed to macrobiotics, I fell ill less and less often. Today, I have changed so much that now it seems strange when other people catch colds.

A cold is generally associated with such symptoms as a sore throat, nasal discharge, aching of the throat and chest, coughing, and fever; it is thought that, if one is not careful, tissue of the respiratory system, primarily the bronchi and lungs, will be invaded by viruses, resulting in infection. In other words, colds are thought to be caused by cold viruses and bacteria. But why does a cold "bug" invade the body? Is it the fault of the microbe or the body?

I used to think that it was the fault of the cold germs. I believed that in order to recover from a cold, it was necessary either to kill these germs or drive them from the body. That's why I was a big fan of drugs and injections; I thought that these killed the cold germs. Through a medical examination, the doctor attempts to detect the causative organisms in the patient's body and determine what drugs to administer in order to kill those organisms. Such an approach is by no means limited to colds; even today, modern medicine is working hard to discover new viruses and bacteria. The treatment mode is decided on the basis of the test results. For some time now, the notion of microorganisms as the cause and the malefactor in disease has predominated in medical circles.

After having adopted a macrobiotic diet, I came to realize that it is not the bacteria which are at fault; it is the fault of the body that is invaded by bacteria. Bacteria are in the air, water, and earth; they are in our food and even in our body; they are everywhere. Now why would bacteria which are ubiquitous pick and choose between people, making some ill and leaving others healthy?

Cold germs have an affinity for some people and a dislike for others. People with the sweet blood and body fluids that bacteria are fond of and with the type of cell tissue that these microbes find ideal habitats may dislike the germs, but there is no way of keeping the germs from what they like. If people with physical constitutions for which these germs have an affinity are out of sorts or fatigued, then the germs soon take up residence in the nose, throat, and bronchial tissue. This is the process of infection. Infection is not immediately followed by the outbreak of illness. For a certain period, the body resists the microbial invader. If at this time the stomach and bowels are healthy and in good condition and if pure blood is working in the body's internal metabolism, the infection is kept in check and vanquished without the body becoming ill. However, if poor eating and drinking habits and an immoderate life style cause enteric toxins to contaminate the blood, then the body is unable to completely fight off the microbial invasion. The proliferation of microbes gives rise to new toxins; when these toxins begin to circulate throughout the body, chills and fever arise. This is the mechanism behind the onset of a cold.

I myself was to blame for catching colds. In my eagerness to build up resistance to this ailment, I continued to take a high-nutrition diet. I followed the advice of doctors and nutritional experts by including in my diet meat, eggs, fish, dairy products such as milk, cheese, and butter, fruit, and supplements. The predominance of animal-based foods in my diet was a heavy burden on my weak gastrointestinal system. But even more serious, these became toxins in my bowels; since my body was unable to completely neutralize such toxins, I had chronic autotoxemia. My blood was incapable of carrying out healthy metabolism. So cold germs constantly parasitized me, making me a year-round star in the theater of the common cold.

There is really only one way to avoid catching colds, and that is to maintain healthy bowels. Various other techniques seem to be at least partially effective, such as sunbathing to improve the health of the skin, bathing in the sea, or a daily rubdown with a cold, wet towel or a dry towel. However, the point of each of these is simply to make the bowels and the entire gastrointestinal system healthy, to keep the stomach and bowels in a constantly healthy state—that is all. Without fully realizing it, macrobiotics improved my body so that I no longer caught colds.

## The Cold as a Way of Renewing the Cells

Let us now apply the Unifying Principle to an examination of the common cold, limiting ourselves here to the relationship between food and the body.

I used to catch colds even in midsummer. In Japan, they say that only fools catch colds in the summer; to be sure I was just such a fool. When it is hot and the outdoor temperature is high, the exterior of the body is yang ($\triangle$). The body adjusts itself to the outside temperature, becoming yin ($\triangledown$).

The question at this point is what type of yin the body becomes. Whether or not ones catches a cold depends on whether this is the right yin or the wrong yin.

As a boy, I was fond of foods that make the body extremely yin—foods that are sweet and cold, such as ice candy, ice cream, sherbet, soda pop, fruit juices, watermelons, cantelopes, and bananas; foods that are sour and cold such as mandarin oranges with baking soda added or vinegared gelidium jelly, a typical Japanese treat. Later on, as a young man, I added to the above such beverages as beer, whiskey, iced coffee, and coke. In addition, I took medications and ate my fill of nutritious food. My stomach and bowels were without doubt filled with exceedingly yin foods, although of course the degree of yinness depended on the particular items and the amount in which I consumed them. My stomach was far too yin (▼) for the yang of the outside temperature. It was as if I was always lugging around a refrigerator inside of me. This may be all right when the temperature during the day is high or there is a hot spell lasting for several days. However, suppose that the temperature drops suddenly (▽) and the weather stays cool for two or three days in a row. Or suppose that the temperature at night drops lower than expected. The bowels are packed with yin food. In order to respond rapidly, the yin retained in the intestines must be discharged and the yin *ki* reduced by however little. This results in diarrhea and bedwetting, due to night chills while asleep. However, both the yin components present within the cells and the yinnized cells themselves are not that easily replaced. The nerves take the emergency measure known as goose bumps to prevent the loss of body heat from the skin. Simultaneous shivering and chills forces the cells to generate heat. The bowels and cells are made more yang until the environment within the body corresponds to the decline in the outside temperature (▽). In my case, this always took seven to ten days. People in normal health are able to rid themselves of the *ki* of a cold in the two or three days that it takes for the material within the bowels to be replaced. However, with me, because the tissues and cells of my internal organs were yin, I had to suffer several times as long before these attained the proper degree of yangness. That is why the colds that I always seemed to catch at the turn of the seasons represented also a "renewal" of my cells. The cellular renewal that takes place quite naturally and inconspicuously in people with a normal metabolism would, in my case, put me through a period of forced metabolism that had me laid up sick in bed and sweating profusely.

When the seasons change from winter to spring, the opposite happens. The yang components within the bowels and cells are metabolized to a degree that corresponds with the outside temperature. In me, the means for carrying out this process was again the common cold. Seen in this light, colds served as "rescue squads" that labored hard to keep me alive. Yet I hated, feared, and felt threatened by them.

If the cells are formed in such a way that they maintain a healthy moderation, then metabolism takes place smoothly. When the formation of cells leans too far toward yin or yang, the metabolism becomes excessive in exactly the same degree as the extent of this imbalance. The properties and nature of the cells are determined by the blood. The blood in turn is determined by the daily food and drink consumed (one's diet). As long as there is a good yin-yang balance in one's diet or one lives in accordance with one's environs, as long as proper food is properly eaten and sent on to the stomach and bowels, the body is able to respond without difficulty to both cold and hot temperatures, sudden changes in climate, and dramatic changes in the environment.

# The Root of Human Life Is the Stomach and Bowels

It was not until I began eating brown rice that I heard of the maxim that the root of human life is the stomach and bowels. People who correctly observe plants and live a humble life together with nature know that the life activities and energies of a plant rely completely on the roots of that plant. If the roots are cut off or otherwise rendered incapable of activity, then the plant dies. The same is true of animals.

I did not have the eyes to learn directly from nature. Instead of learning from nature, I resorted to my wits; I relied on the knowledge and learning of man. In addition to having no interest in nature, I did not know how to learn from nature. Macrobiotics and the Unifying Principle taught me how to see and how to think of nature and the universal order.

In the preceding section, I stated that the secret to not catching colds is the stomach and bowels. I learned from my own experiences that as long as these organs are truly healthy, one will not catch colds. When I took up a brown rice diet and the condition of my gastrointestinal system improved, I stopped catching colds. This to me was a startling discovery. The experience taught me that the stomach and bowels hold the key to our health and the secret to life.

People often ask me: "Why are you macrobiotic?" At first, I was only able to give a vague answer or explanation of my reasons. Now, however, I can answer with conviction: "Because this pleases my bowels." The way I see it, the stomach and bowels are far happier with a brown rice diet than a nutritious diet of white rice, meat, fish, eggs, milk, and fruit. Even allowing for individual differences between people, there can be no doubt that in almost all people a brown rice diet prepared and eaten correctly is pleasing to the bowels.

Figs. 4.1(a) through 4.1(d) show, for the sake of visual comparison, diagrams of normal, healthy intestines and unhealthy intestines.

**Fig. 4.1 Schematic diagrams of normal and unhealthy large intestines.** [1]

**(a) Sites of disease in the intestines.**      **(b) Large intestine of people with gastropathy**

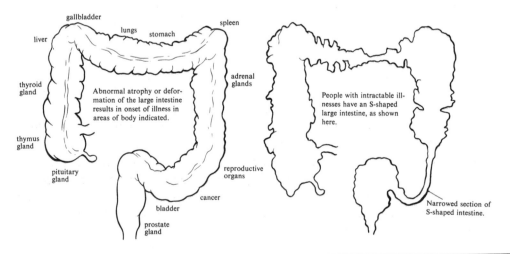

---

[1] From *Teate ryoho* [Palm healing] by Jiro Asuke.

**(c)  Large intestine of people with poor adrenal glands**

**(d)  Diagram of diarrhetic large colon**

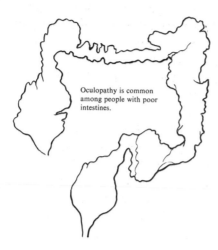

Oculopathy is common among people with poor intestines.

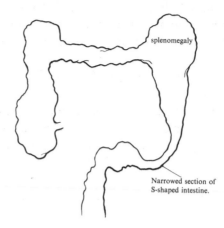

splenomegaly

Narrowed section of S-shaped intestine.

I have no doubt that my intestines were far worse even than the abnormal intestines depicted in Fig. 4.1. People who are chronically afflicted with some ailment or are critically ill have abnormal intestines such as these.

Only the external appearance of the intestines has been shown in these drawings. If this is what they look like from the outside, then imagine just how awful the internal condition and functioning of the intestines must be. A mere glance is enough to tell me that someone with a large intestine like this must not only have poor bowel movements, but must also have old, impacted fecal matter lodged against the walls and folds of their intestines. The ill effects of coprostasia (impacted feces), as this is called, on the entire body are immeasurable. Clearly an intestine such as this is incapable of functioning properly.

When I was about fifteen years old, I was told that I had gastroptosis. In an X-ray checkup taken at the age of eighteen, my stomach had descended to my pelvis. This drooping stomach of mine was always sloshing around as if it were full of water; I felt heavy throughout my chest and my abdomen, I constantly had heartburn, and acidic belches would well up all the time. So I always took gastrointestinal medications, digestives, and nutriments. My alimentary tract was certainly in rickety shape.

The first thing that a macrobiotic brown rice diet did was to clean out my intestines. The proof of this is that in place of my burps, I had an endless discharge of intestinal gases. While keeping strictly to a macrobiotic diet, I also applied ginger compresses and taro plasters to my abdomen and lower back. When a taro plaster is applied, gases within the intestines begin moving and a blackish-purple color rises to the surface of the skin. Intestinal gases are easily expelled and bowel movements also improve. Occasionally you may become constipated or diarrhetic. As these and other changes repeat themselves, you are able to feel the condition of the gastrointestinal tract gradually improving. During evacuation, long, thick, earthen-colored stools push right out, leaving one with a pleasant feeling as if a draft of cool air were blowing over the entire body. The discharge eventually becomes so clean that one has no need for paper or water to clean up afterward. When things got to this point, not only were my bowels clearly delighted, I experienced a pleasurable sensation as if I had been reborn. Involuntarily, I joined my hands as if in prayer and intoned a word of gratitude.

The seed coats of the brown rice contain many elements that are ideally suited for cleansing the intestinal walls. This fibrous matter is a material having many valuable functions. It plays a mysterious role that is partly, but not entirely, physical, chemical, physiological, and ecological.

Let us consider, for example, the intestinal bacteria. Fecal matter consists essentially of a mass of bacteria. I started paying attention to the intestinal flora when I noticed major changes taking place in my stools shortly after I began eating brown rice. Up until then, bowel movements had always been an extremely unpleasant experience for me. Following the start of my brown rice diet, however, an enormous change occurred in the color, odor, shape, and amount of the discharge. This in a sense provided an experimental demonstration of the great influence that my diet and eating habits had on the types of bacteria in my bowels, and on their activities and energy. The stools serve as sort of a report card on the activity of the intestinal bacteria. If food that makes healthy coliform bacteria happy and comfortable is sent to the intestines, the bacteria will work full out to make the life of their host easier, enabling one to be healthy and active. Those bacteria are what keep us alive.

Once things get to the point where intestinal gases are being properly expelled and bowel movements become pleasant and regular, this shows you that your intestines are being cleaned and are probably assuming a normal shape. Impacted feces is also eliminated. The intestinal wall is reborn again and again until it eventually becomes new. With a renewal of the intestinal wall the metabolism of the body becomes vigorous. To the human being, life means metabolism, so a more vigorous metabolism results in a greater vitality.

This is how I regained full health and my physical condition improved.

Improvement in the gastrointestinal tract can be achieved from within, but there are also many methods and techniques for improving the intestines from without. In addition to aiding the intestines, many such methods serve also to correct physical deformation and reestablish order within the body. Athletics or various types of exercises may be practiced in accordance with one's physical nature and condition; there is also a great variety of traditional or nonstandard healing and health-sustaining arts, such as shiatsu, acupuncture and moxibustion, and chiropractics. It is possible to develop and assiduously apply a suitable combination of these that is suitable to one's own condition and goals.

Deformation of the intestines prevents complete elimination of feces; imcomplete elimination results in impaction; impacted feces keeps the intestinal walls from functioning properly; and improper intestinal wall activity lowers the intake of necessary nutrients and hemopoietic activity. Impacted feces hampers elimination, which results in further impaction; as the number of areas of impacted feces increases, the intestines become increasingly deformed, which in turn facilitates further impaction. This negative cycle leads ultimately to death. The root of the problem is a mistaken diet in which proper food is not cooked and eaten properly.

# Making the Stomach and Bowels Healthy

Sickness begins with fatigue of the gastrointestinal system. That, at least, is the way I see it. In his book, *The Workings of the Internal Organs and the Hearts of Children*,[2] Nario Miki, a professor of physiology in Japan, even goes so far as to say that, "Internal organ discomfort leads to evil passions."

I passed the first half of my life in constant gastrointestinal distress and discomfort. The doctors diagnosed this as chronic gastroenteropathy and treated me accordingly. Unfortunately, however, none of the treatments they gave me were fundamental. I know this because I never once felt cheerful and lively; I rarely experienced pleasure. When I started a macrobiotic diet, however, my mood became pleasant and cheerful, so brown rice must surely have an amazing and mystical force. I mentioned in the preceding section that a macrobiotic diet creates an ideal environment for coliform bacteria. Now I would like to add to that some observations on the intestines themselves.

I was diagnosed at the age of fifteen as having gastroptosis, but I had no idea what state my intestines were in. People generally pay attention to their stomachs, yet tend to have little interest in their intestines. That's because if the stomach is okay, then the intestines do not cause that much trouble. However, in people like me who have had gastroptosis for many years, the intestines are most likely in a correspondingly poor state of health. It was only after I began a macrobiotic diet that I learned that the intestines are at least as important as the stomach, if not more so. Not until I started eating brown rice and began passing a great deal of intestinal gases did I become intensely curious as to what state my intestines were in at the moment and what exactly they were doing.

Gastroptosis arises due to a loosening or weakening of body tissues and cells, and the overall condition of the body. Why was I afflicted with this? The reason was very simple: because I was consuming foods and beverages that cause this weakening effect. When I was a little boy, I was crazy over sweets. I'd pick a moment when my mother wasn't looking and would literally stuff myself on candy, cake, and soda. Sweet, sugary drinks are yin. Sugar has the property of softening, expanding, and loosening body cells and tissue. Because I was crazy about yin foods, my cells and organs all ended up flabby and loose. This was true also of my intestines.

The diagrams in Fig. 4.1 should give some idea of what it means for the intestines to become weak or "slack." A weak intestine stores old fecal matter (see Fig. 4.2(a)).

As can be seen in this drawing, abnormal areas of "slackening" in the intestine wall form abnormal folds, and stercoromas (impacted feces) collect here. Clearly, the larger the number of folds, the greater the amount of impacted feces. Old impacted feces is a mass of toxins. When such masses lie deep within the intestinal wall, they cannot be easily eliminated. When a large number of these masses of toxin is present in the abdomen, it is not surprising if the condition of the body doesn't improve. With the intestines in such a state, what chance is there of one feeling refreshed and invigorated? Weak intestines such as this establish a large

---

[2]   *Naizo no hataraki to kodomo no kokoro.*

106

**Fig. 4.2  The diverticula that form in the folds of the large intestine, and the stercoroma that remains there become result in constipation.**
(From "Seimei Kagaku Dokuhon" [The Book of Biology], by Shuichiro Musha)

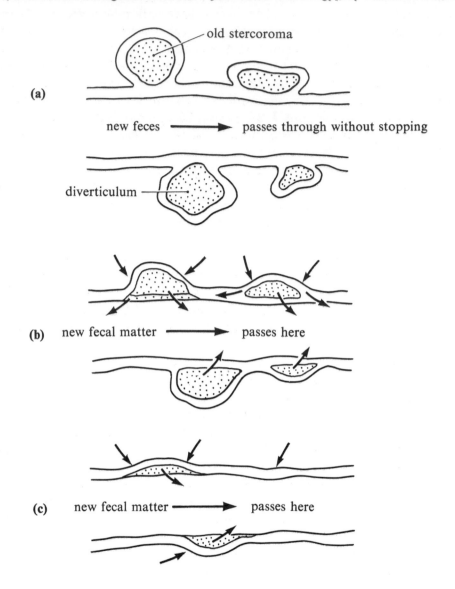

number of diverticula that allow toxins to rest, but in so doing this robs the master of the body from resting.

I had no idea that my intestines were in this sort of a state. I learned of the weakened condition of my stomach when I was diagnosed as having gastroptosis, but I knew nothing whatsoever of my intestines. Yet, although I knew nothing, macrobiotics guided me in the right direction. Macrobiotics firmed and tightened up my cells and tissue slowly but gradually. If to loosen or slacken is yin, then to firm up or tighten is yang. A macrobiotic diet may be either yin or yang depending on the method of cooking and eating, but the method which I first encountered was a yang-type brown rice diet. This suited my physical condition perfectly. Using the intestines as my example, I'd like to show what happens when loose cells and tissue "tighten up," Please refer to diagrams (b) and (c) in Fig. 4.2.

When intestinal tissue tightens up, the folds are pulled into the correct intestinal shape. The stercoromas—masses of toxin that have until now rested quietly in the diverticula—are pushed out from the walls into the main cavity. If one patiently and faithfully follows a macrobiotic diet, the abnormal folds and diverticula in the intestinal walls gradually are pulled tight so that what ultimately remains is a correctly shaped intestinal tract and nothing more. Once impacted feces has been eliminated in this way, the intestinal walls stay in constant contact with new food, bringing renewed metabolic vigor and gradual healing to other parts of the body. With the elimination of each stercoroma and the disappearance of each diverticulum, a sensation of freshness and vigor returns.

A variety of other methods exist for eliminating impacted feces. Some consist of fasting or semi-fasting where only very small quantities of food are ingested. Some involve the use of drugs. Other means frequently resorted to are shiatsu and surgery. Combinations of any of these may also be used, depending on the physical condition and constitution of the patient. However, the only reasonable way to completely and permanently resolve this condition is through food and the manner in which it is eaten—in a word, diet. Looking at it from the standpoint of the enteric environment (which consists primarily of coliform bacteria) as a whole, a macrobiotic diet based on yin-yang judgment (diagnosis) is the best possible approach to gastroenteric health. Please take a good look at diagrams (a), (b), and (c), in this order. I leave it up to you as to what diagram (d) will look like. Whether one advances to a better state or regresses is determined solely by the food one chooses to eat, the way in which one eats this food, and the sort of life style one lives. It depends on your way of living and eating.

The approach taken by modern medicine in curing the symptoms in diagram (a) would probably involve a surgical procedure in which the diverticula are excised and the old stercoroma removed. By using a sharp scalpel, the unseemly irregularities in the intestinal wall and the masses of toxins can be removed in one quick operation. The methods of modern medicine are the same for cancer and for all other organ and tissue disorders. One can surmise from the diet-based therapeutic approach I have outlined above for tightening or "firming" the intestines just how senseless, dangerous, and unnecessary such drastic methods are.

The diagrams I have used here depict only a small portion of the intestines. When the same symptoms exist throughout the entire intestines, the result is systemic disease. The only way to prevent this from happening is to learn how to properly eat the right foods and how to live properly.

# AIDS and the Unifying Principle of Yin and Yang

(1)  *A Look at AIDS in Terms of the Unifying Principle:*   Let us first study the fundamentals of yin and yang essential for examining and diagnosing AIDS.

The greatest characteristic of yin is an outwardly directed force. This may also be called centrifugal force or action. It can expressed with such verbs as to extend, expand, swell, stretch, slacken, melt, crumble, separate, open, divide, rupture, break down, explode, tear, cool; and with such adjectives as chilly, cold, large, slow, loose, slack, light (as in "lightweight"), and so forth. Many other words are characteristically yin, but I have selected only a few here that appear to have a bearing on AIDS.

Colors and shapes which are typically yin include violet, blue, white, long, thin, slender, and the inverse triangle ($\bigtriangledown$).

We use the symbol $\bigtriangledown$ to represent yin, and the symbol $\blacktriangledown$ to represent very yin.

Yang is likewise characterized by an inwardly directed or "center-seeking" force, and may be described as centripetal force or action. The reverse of the properties of yin may be regarded as characteristics of yang. Thus, for example, verbs such as to contract, close into oneself, shrivel, harden, become knotted, join with, link with, fuse together, push or press, force, create, warm; adjectives such as hot, warm, small, fast; and colors and shapes such as red, orange, yellow, round, short, thick, circle, and upright triangle ($\bigtriangleup$) are all yang characteristics.

The symbol $\bigtriangleup$ stands for yang, and $\blacktriangle$ for very yang.

The above yin characteristics are drawn in part from the yin-yang chart that appears in George Ohsawa's book, *The Unifying Principle and the I Ching*[3]. Because this table is useful not only for the diagnosis of AIDS but also for all observation and inquiry, I have included it in this section.

I list below those among the twelve theorems of the Unifying Principle which pertain to AIDS. The numbers preceding the theorems are the same as the numbers used by Ohsawa in his *The Order of the Universe.*[4]

3)  That which has a centripetal, compressed, descending nature is called yang; and that which has a centrifugal, spreading, rising nature is called yin (thus, action and heat come from yang, while quiet and coolness come from yin).

4)  Yang attracts yin and yin attracts yang.

7)  Nothing is entirely yin or entirely yang; all things are both yin and yang.

8)  Nothing is neutral; there is always an imbalance of yin and yang.

11)  An excess of yin creates yang, and an excess of yang creates yin.

12)  All things are yang at the center and yin at the surface.

(2)  *Characteristics of AIDS Patients:*   The data on AIDS that I use is primarily information that I have picked up from the Japanese media—newspapers, magazines, and TV and radio broadcasts. The more data that comes in, the more accurately a Unifying Principle (PU) diagnosis can be carried out. However, there is a limit to the information available to the general public. I would urge individuals

---

[3]  Japanese title: *Muso genri–eki.*
[4]  Japanese title: *Uchu no chitsujo.*

**Table 4.1   Yin-Yang chart of everyday world of science and chemistry.**

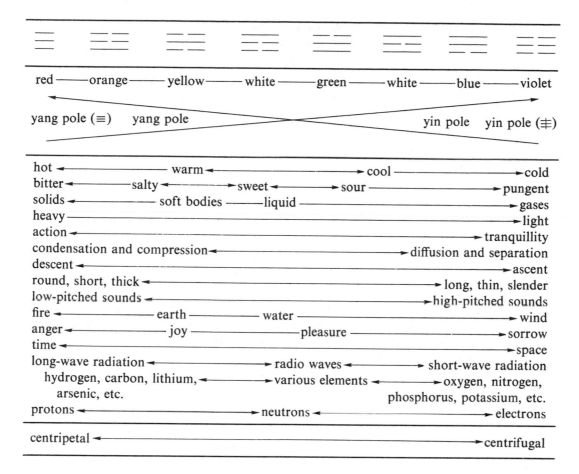

in a position to obtain more specialized data to apply PU to that data. Even my own PU diagnosis, which I arrived at based on the scant data I have been able to gather (and assuming all along that the information I do have is accurate and not misleading), is full of insights and predictions that go beyond technical diagnoses.

Let us begin then by examining the characteristics of AIDS patients. The following are for the most part the characteristics of AIDS patients in the United States.

1.  Male homosexuals;
2.  Users of narcotics;
3.  Frequent users of synthetic drugs (pharmaceuticals, tranquilizers, stimulants, tonics, etc.), excluding narcotics;
4.  People who have received blood transfusions (including hemophiliacs);
5.  People who take in a great excess of sugar (white sugar) and sugar-containing drinks on a daily basis (10 times that of normal people);
6.  People who eat several times the normal amount of fruit and milk or other dairy products;
7.  Inveterate drinkers of alcoholic beverages;
8.  60% have a history of hepatitis;

9. 40% have a history of malignant lymphoma;
10. 100% have hypoglycemia;
11. 65%–80% have drug allergies.

The above are the primary symptoms observed in AIDS patients. Of the AIDS patients in the United States, (a) about 73% are male homosexuals, (b) 17% are narcotics addicts, and 10% are others who belong to neither category (hemophiliacs or individuals who have received blood transfusions, for example).

Based on the above symptoms, I would pose the following questions.

*Question 1*: Why do homosexuals, drug abusers, hemophiliacs, and transfusion recipients contract AIDS?"

*Comments:*
1. Hemophilia is a disease whereby *the blood does not coagulate* on account of an abnormality in the coagulating factor.
2. Japan has many patients with adult T-cell leukemia, a disease dreaded as much as AIDS. This illness is also a hereditary disease in which *the blood does not coagulate*. The patient must receive constant injections of a blood coagulating factor preparation prepared from donated blood. In Japan, the vast majority of this preparation is imported from the U.S.; if the AIDS factor is contained in this preparation, the chances of infection increase. Cells infected with adult T-cell leukemia (ATL) are also highly susceptible to infection by the AIDS virus.

*Question 2:* Is the symptom of poor blood coagulation or a lack of coagulation in comments 1 and 2 above yin or yang?

(3) *The Characteristics of AIDS Viruses:*

1. Shape and Form:
   The AIDS viruses are shaped like confetti (photos in December 25, 1985 issue of *Asahi Shimbun*).

cylindrical                               hollow cylinder

A third AIDS virus having a double membrane has also been discovered (photo from June 25, 1986 issue of *Asahi Shimbun*).

2. AIDS Virus Transforms One Million Times Faster than Human Cells:

A group led by Dr. B. Hearn at the University of Alabama Medical Center has learned that the genes of the AIDS virus transform at *a speed one million times faster* than the genes of ordinary organisms. A high speed of viral transformation had been suspected, but this is the first experimental confirmation of that fact. The genes of most organisms, including man, are made up of deoxyribonucleic acid (DNA), but the genes of the AIDS viruses consist of ribonucleic acid (RNA). When these viruses infect human cells, they use reverse transcriptase to convert the genetic information contained in the RNA into DNA. This DNA "sneaks" into the DNA in human cells and immediately begins to rapidly multiply. The members of the research team isolated viruses from three AIDS patients every several months over the course of one to two years, and examined the changes in the nucleotide bases that serve as the letters of the genetic code. In one of the patients, a three-year-old child who had been infected as a fetus, a total of 2,571 bases were studied for three AIDS viruses. From this, it was learned that the first and second viruses differ by 69 bases while the first and third viruses differ by 52 bases. Given that the three viruses all split off from common ancestors 1–5 years before, this represents a speed of mutation at least one million times faster than for humans and other organisms. When the change in the viral genes is this fast, the viral coat antigen proteins also are constantly changing and elusive, making a vaccine difficult to create. (from July 24, 1986 evening issue of *Asahi Shimbun*)

*Question 3:* Is the rapid rate of mutation in this virus yin or yang?

3. AIDS Viruses also Attack the Brain:

A research group headed by Dr. D. Howe at the Massachusetts General Hospital and a group led by Dr. L. Resnick at the National Institutes of Health have reported finding evidence that the AIDS virus not only invades and destroys leukocytes as formerly thought, but also *enters and multiplies within brain tissue....* Because the brain has a "barrier" that prevents the movement of almost all drugs into the brain parenchyma, the development of drugs for treating AIDS is difficult. In addition to a decrease in immunological resistance that makes them susceptible to infection, AIDS patients often develop as complications such brain illnesses as meningitis and dementia.... This "barrier" in the brain is called the blood-brain barrier; it protects the brain by checking the ready entry of foreign matter through the blood. For the AIDS virus, the brain is a sanctuary inaccessible to therapeutic drugs. The development of an antiviral agent capable of breaking through the blood-brain barrier is extremely difficult.
(Excerpted from December 12, 1985 issue of *Asahi Shimbun*)

*Comment 1:* The AIDS virus is known to be attracted to yin. The brain is the most yin part of the body and is located in the most yin position.

**Fig. 4.3  Schematic diagram of AIDS viral (HTLV-III) particle.**
(From R.C. Gallo, *Scientific American*, Jan. 1987)

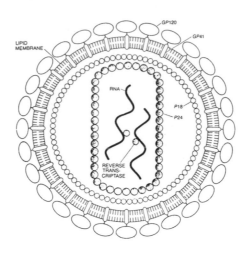

HTLV-III VIRION, or virus particle, is a sphere that is roughly 1,000 angstrom units (one ten-thousandth of a millimeter) across. The particle is covered by a membrane, made up of two layers of lipid (fatty) material, that is derived from the outer membrane of the host cell. Studding the membrane are glycoproteins (proteins with sugar chains attached). Each glycoprotein has two components: *gp*41 spans the membrane and *gp*120 extends beyond it. The membrane-and-protein envelope covers a core made up of proteins designated *p* 24 and *p* 18. The viral RNA is carried in the core, along with several copies of the enzyme reverse transcriptase, which catalyzes the assembly of the viral DNA.

*Question 4:*   Is a virus that favors yin places and environments yin or yang?

*Comment 2:*   Although the blood-brain barrier prevents the passage and movement of drugs into the brain tissue, it does not prevent the entry of AIDS viruses.

*Question 5:*   Is the blood-brain barrier, which rejects drugs but accepts AIDS viruses yin or yang?

4.   The AIDS Virus Directly Attacks the Brain:

In the United States, it is known that most AIDS patients develop brain dysfunction, which presents new difficulties. Now, a group led by Professor Richard Axle of Columbia University has come across evidence that the AIDS virus directly attacks brain cells. The research group found that when the virus infects a cell, the substance that adheres to the cell surface and secures a foothold for invasion of the cell is present not only in lymphocytes, as formerly believed, but also on the *surface of brain cells....*

AIDS viruses invade and destroy the lymphocytes called T4 cells, which play an important immunological role. At the time of infection, the viruses invade the cells by bonding with the glycoprotein "receivers" called T4 present on the cell surface. Professor Axle reports that his group has found a virus "receptor" like that of the lymphocytes in the cells of the cerebral cortex as well. In addition, the group also found new "receptors" only about one-quarter as large.... (from February 10, 1987 issue of *Asahi Shimbun*)

*Question 6:* Is the surface of brain cells more yin or yang than the surface of cells in other parts of the human body?

5. AIDS Occurs More Frequently in Areas with a Warm Climate than in Areas with a Cold Climate:

*Question 7:* Is a cold climate yin or yang? What about a warm climate?

6. The Onset of AIDS Declines in Winter and Rises in the Summer:

*Question 8:* Is winter yin or yang? What about summer?

7. Most AIDS Patients are Men; Few are Women:

*Question 9:* Are males yin or yang? What about females?

8. Substance with AIDS Promoting Effect Present in Semen:

The transfer substance research group of the Research Development Corporation of [Japan's] Hayaishi Biological Information Transmission Project has discovered the existence of a substance in human semen that promotes the onset of AIDS. They reported that when the acidic, lipid-soluble physiologically active substance prostaglandin E$_2$ (PGE$_2$) present in large amounts in human semen was periodically injected *anally into rats, a decline was observed in the immunological functions of male rats only*. In addition, they also reported that when PGE$_2$ was added to human lymphocytes cultured in a test tube, these became more susceptible to infection by the AIDS virus.
(from February 18, 1986 issue of *Asahi Shimbun*)

*Question 10:* Why is the semen readily absorbed by the large intestine in the vicinity of the anus?

*Question 11:* Why is it that a decline was seen in the immunological functions of just male rats?

*Question 12:* Is the semen and the prostaglandin E$_2$ in semen more yin or yang than other body fluids?

9. Semen Promotes Cancer:

A research group led by Professor Osamu Yoshida (urology) and the late Professor Yohei Ito (microbiology) of the Medical Faculty at Kyoto University has discovered a substance in human semen that promotes the onset of cancer. The observation that cervical cancer is almost nonexistent in women who have never had sexual relations led to the conjecture that semen might somehow be associated with the onset of cancer, which prompted the present study.

The special proteins produced by EB viruses appeared in about 50% of the semen samples collected from several thousand people, and awakened cancer viruses. Yoshida and his colleagues applied dimethylbenzanthracene, a strong carcinogenic substance, to the skin on the backs of the mice as a cancer "trigger," following which they took the substance extracted from semen, dissolved it in acetone, and applied it to the same area. In the case of substances extracted from virus-awakening semen, tumors known as papillomas began to form on the skin during week 7; by week 20, 40% of the mice had cancer. (from October 20, 1986 issue of *Asahi Shimbun*)

*Question 13:*  Is semen yin or yang?

10. UV Irradiation for Eradicating AIDS Viruses:

Namiko Yoshihara, director of the HB antigen laboratory at the National Institute of Health in Japan, and her colleagues have found through their research that *ultraviolet irradiation* is effective in the destruction of AIDS viruses.... The researchers cultured AIDS viruses in T cells (a human lymphocyte), then irradiated the viruses with ultraviolet light when the viral count reached 100,000 per cubic centimeter of culture fluid. They found that 75% of the viruses died after thirty seconds of UV irradiation, 90% died after one minute of irradiation, and more than 95% died after two minutes of irradiation. It was also found that the T cells serving as the hosts for the AIDS viruses were all destroyed after about one minute of irradiation.
(from March 23, 1987 issue of *Saitama Shimbun*)

*Question 14:*  Is ultraviolet light yin or yang?

11. Differences in Method of Contraception Used:

|      | Tubal ligation | Vasec- tomy | Birth control pill | Dia- phragm | Condom | Other modern methods |
|------|------|------|------|------|------|------|
| U.S. | 23.2% | 11.4% | 30.0% | 7.9% | 12.9% | 14.6% |
| Japan | — | — | | 11.6% | 78.4% | 9.3% |

(from March 11, 1985 issue of *Newsweek*)

*Question 15:*  Don't tubal ligations and vasectomies upset the hormonal balance and other physiological aspects of the body, rendering the internal environment abnormal?

Do the pill and other oral contraceptives make the body fluids and physical contitution yin or yang?

How does the degree to which semen is absorbed within the body differ in the U.S. and Japan, and how do the body fluids and physical constitution differ as a result?

(4) *AIDS and the Unifying Principle ( Yin=▽; Yang=△):*

- The Yin and Yang of Males and Females:
  Males are dynamic, favor outdoor work, have a muscular physical constitution, and are extroverted; thus, outwardly, they are △. Females are static, favor indoor work, have a fatty physical constitution, and are introverted; hence, they are outwardly ▽.
- The Yin and Yang of Sperm and Ova:
  The sperm has a long, slender shape. In a single ejaculation, hundreds of millions of sperm are discharged, and so these represent fragmentation. The ovum has a spherical shape. Only one ovum is discharged in each ovulation. The ovum absorbs the sperm and thus represents synthesis. Hence, the sperm is ▽, and the ovum is △.
- Males (△) produce sperm (▽) within themselves, while females (▽) produce ova (△) within themselves. The respective internal and external constitutions form yin and yang (▽△). This can be expressed in the following way:

male= △    female= ▽

- Likewise, one would expect sperm and ova to be composed such that, within their respective interiors, spermatozoa (▽) contain △ and the ova (△) contain ▽. If we describe this by saying that the spermatozoon has a spermatozoon core and the ovum has an ovum core, then these cores can be expressed as follows.

spermatozoon= ▲    ovum= ▽

- The universe is so constructed that the smaller and more minute the core of a substance, the more active and vigorous its activity. Hence, the core strengths of the spermatozoon and the ovum are quite considerable. The interior of the core is again constructed of microcosmic yin and yang. This can be expressed as follows (structural ▽△ diagrams for males and females).

male= △ < spermatozoon / body    female= ▽ < ovum / body

● The Yin and Yang of Male Homosexuals:

male+male=spermatozoon+spermatozoon= $\triangledown$ + $\triangle$ = ▼

    Thus, not only are those most at risk of contracting AIDS already very yin (▼) by nature, this yin principle is increased and enlarged even further as a result of homosexual acts.

● Narcotics are highly yin ($\triangledown$) substances which loosen ($\triangledown$) the nerves ($\triangle$) and nerve function and which divert ($\triangledown$) one from worries ($\triangledown$), anxieties ($\triangledown$) and fear ($\triangledown$), affording one a temporary escape in the realm of ecstasy.

    Tranquilizers, synthetic drugs, chemical food additives, and alcohol are all yin substances ($\triangledown$) to differing degrees. These have the effect of loosening ($\triangledown$), dissolving ($\triangledown$), and fragmenting ($\triangledown$) the body and mind.

    In other words, narcotics ($\triangledown$) and synthetic drugs ($\triangledown$) are all very yin (▼) substances which make the body fluids and the physical constitution more yin. The yin and yang of drugs and other chemicals can be determined through spectroscopy.

● Sugar causes nothing but yin effects such as cooling ($\triangledown$), melting ($\triangledown$), breaking down ($\triangledown$), loosening ($\triangledown$), and stretching ($\triangledown$).

    Thus, when a large amount of sugar and sugar-containing processed foods are used, this inevitably results in a yin ($\triangledown$) physical constitution.

    If an individual ordinarily takes in ten times as much of these as a normal person, the bodily fluids and physical constitution come to exhibit very yin (▼) symptoms. The result is a body without firmness ($\triangledown$) and incapable of tension ($\triangledown$), a temperament and life style that is licentious and immoderate ($\triangledown$), slovenly and untidy ($\triangledown$), and disorderly ($\triangledown$).

● Although fruits are more gentle than sugar, they also have strongly yin effects such as cooling ($\triangledown$), loosening ($\triangledown$), and thinning ($\triangledown$). Fruits, therefore, are yin substances and yin foods.

● The Yin and Yang of Red and White Blood Cells
Red blood cells are yang ($\triangle$), as symbolized by their red color ($\triangle$). Hence, their first and most important function is that of transporting oxygen, a yin substance.

    In contrast with red blood cells, white blood cells are yin ($\triangledown$), as symbolized by the color white ($\triangledown$). Their primary function is thus to produce antibodies and to prevent infection by microbes, which are animals and thus yang (these perform the function indicated in Theorem 4).

    In other words, the $\triangle$ of red blood cells takes in and binds the $\triangledown$ principle oxygen, while the $\triangledown$ of white blood cells absorbs and takes in microbes, a $\triangle$ principle.

        red blood cells=$\triangle$;              white blood cells=$\triangledown$

● Because AIDS is a disease that concerns white blood cells, let us examine these. The structural $\triangledown$ $\triangle$ of the white blood cell is presented below (this is done in the same manner as in the preceding paragraphs on spermatozoa and ova, and on males and females).

expansion

white blood cells ▽ ⟶ ◁▷ (below)

- **This Should Be the Structure of Theorem 12:**

The bactericidal action of white blood cells operates in the following manner: the ▽ of the outer membrane draws in and traps the microbe (△) while the △ at the core acts upon the core matter (▽) of the microbe, destroying the microbe (Theorem 4).

T4 cells, T8 cells, B cells, and other cells are present within the core matter of the leukocytes. Each of these have structures and compositions with subtly differing degrees of yin and yang. Their role is to respond to antigens. When the △ within the core matter of the leukocyte is stronger than extrinsic ▽, infection does not occur; when the reverse is true, infection occurs. The reason why the AIDS virus (HTLV-III) especially favors T4 lymphocytes as its host is that the respective yinness and yangness of the virus and the lymphocytes fit the state described in Theorem 4, indicating that their forces are in a state of equilibrium.

Dr. R.C. Gallo makes the following observation with regard to the above (from January 1987 issue of *Scientific American*).

> In the case of HTLV-III the host cell is often a *T*4 lymphocyte, a white blood cell that has a central role in regulating the immune system. Once it is inside a T4 cell, the virus may remain latent (▽) until the lymphocyte is immunologically stimulated by a secondary infection. Then the virus bursts into action (△), reproducing itself so furiously that the new virus particles escaping (▽) from the cell riddle the cellular membrane with holes (▽) and the lymphocyte dies (▽). The resulting depletion of T4 cells—the hallmark of AIDS— leaves the patient vulnerable to "opportunistic" infections by agents that would not harm a healthy person.*

- On the outside, the AIDS virus has a spherical shape (△), but the viral coat consists of a membrane punctured with glycoproteins (proteins with attached sugar chains). The fact that the coat has an uneven, confetti-like shape indicates that this is formed of ▽ △ components corresponding to the interior and exterior thereof.

Outside shape  = △　　　　According to Theorem 12, the interior is very yin (▼).

Thus, the AIDS virus can be said to have the structure △⧩

(5)  *Conclusion:*  Of the multifaceted environment of the living body (component substances of the body, physical constitution, acts, conditions, state, etc.; in short, all aspects of life), I have observed and discussed AIDS from the standpoint of food and sex. Here are my conclusions.

---

* The ▽△ symbols in the above text are mine.—the author

First, graphically representing the fact that the bioenvironment of AIDS patients is very yin (▼) in all aspects, we get:

$$\triangledown+\triangledown+\triangledown+\triangledown+\triangledown+\dots\dots\dots\dots+\triangledown=\blacktriangledown\rightarrow$$

"An excess of yin creates yang." (Theorem 11.) In other words, the symbol of this body is the same as that for the AIDS virus; although the two differ in degree, both are of the same type. However, it so happens that when the overall strength of the AIDS virus becomes greater than that of the patient's white blood cells, the viruses demonstrate the strength to destroy the patient's body. This is illustrated as follows:

Infection and incubation period      AIDS virus $\simeq$ leukocyte

Onset of symptoms to death      AIDS virus $>$ leukocyte

Healthy condition without symptoms      AIDS virus $<$ leukocyte

Thus, when the coat of the AIDS virus penetrates the outer membrane of a leukocyte T4 cell and the inner core material of the AIDS virus absorbs and swallows up the inner core material of the leukocytes (Theorem 4), this results in the onset of AIDS; if the patient is in a physical state that allows the vigor of the AIDS virus to increase unabated, the result is a progression of the patient's condition toward death.

Even if AIDS does not arise, this very yin organism continuously causes illnesses favored by very yin bodies, such as cancer, intractable or unusual diseases of the nervous system, or various milder but chronic yin ailments.

Quoting again from the above *Scientific American* article by Dr. R.C. Gallo:

It has become increasingly clear that immune deficiency is only one effect of the AIDS agent. The other main type of disease caused by HTLV-III is seen in the central nervous system. . . . In the brain and spinal cord the virus appears to have a direct pathogenic effect that is not dependent on the immune deficiency. . . . People infected with the virus have an increased risk of at least three types of human tumor: Kaposi's sarcoma, carcinomas (including skin cancers often seen in the mouth or rectum of infected homosexuals) and *B*-cell lymphomas, which are tumors originating in *B* lymphocytes.

(6) *Curing and Preventing AIDS:* The PU observations throughout sections (2) to (5) above are full of hints as to ways for treating and preventing AIDS. Since I have already pointed out the characteristics peculiar to AIDS viruses and leukocytes, what remains is how to skillfully handle the interrelationship between the two; this is the largest problem with the current treatment of AIDS. Modern medicine regards the AIDS virus as the enemy. As long as this and other pathogens are viewed with hostility and treated as if they were bitter enemies of mankind, it will surely be impossible to eradicate not only AIDS but diseases in general, The AIDS virus is ubiquitous on earth, and it would be no exaggeration to say that it already exists in the bodies of all people today. Indeed, it might even be said that all people today are AIDS patients. The fact that AIDS patients are becoming common even

in areas where homosexuals are rare (such as southern Africa) and even among people without homosexual experience indicates that it is at once a disease incidental to and divorced from civilization in which the balance between extremes of yin and yang has been upset by civilizing influences.

The methods of treatment and prevention that I indicate below are not the sort of symptomatic treatment for which modern medicine and modern society are searching so frantically today. Thus, my approach lacks somewhat in the rapidity of its effects. To those people who expect rapid effects, this may be difficult to comprehend and accept. However, if their desire is to treat the roots of AIDS and to prevent this dread disease from later reemerging on earth, only by taking the steps I indicate below can they hope to achieve this end.

1.  Immediately ban meat, eggs, milk and other dairy products (butter, cheese, cream, etc.), fish, fowl, sugar, fruit, alcohol, soda and fruit juices, sweets (ice cream, chocolate, etc.) from the diet.
2.  Strictly prohibit drugs (narcotics, stimulants, excitants). Reduce drugs currently being administered in inverse proportion to changes in the diet, and phase administration of these drugs out as soon as possible.
3.  Clearly impress upon all people that AIDS is a result of damage caused by improper diet and drugs; have people devote themselves to treatment and improvement of their life style.
4.  Diet must be entirely vegetarian and based on whole cereal grains (macrobiotics).
5.  People should spend time by the sea and go bathing in the water when appropriate; sunbathing should be kept to just short periods.

Properly and faithfully observing the above steps is the best possible method of treatment and prevention. To improve the rapidity and reliability of the above method of treatment and prevention, I would need the following data:

(1)  The climate and natural features of the place where the patient was born and grew up.
(2)  The dietary history of the patient and his or her parents. For example, what and how much of such foods as milk, eggs and egg products, other dairy products, fish, fowl, sugar, fruit, sweets, alcoholic beverages, carbonated drinks, etc. did the patient and his/her parents consume at various times in his life—as a fetus, during weaning, as a small child, as an adolescent, and so forth. In addition to the above foods, how much grains were consumed?
(3)  Patient's clinical history and history of therapeutic as well as recreational drug use (including injections). At what age and in what way did the patient use what drugs? Clearly indicate all drugs that are remembered, including specific narcotics, pharmaceuticals, non-prescription drugs, etc.
(4)  Clinical history of patient's family.
(5)  Record of examination at onset of patient's illness.
(6)  Analytic chart of patient's blood and lymph components during periodic checkups.

(7)  Detailed description of overall diet of patient following onset of illness.

(8)  Types and amounts of drugs administered to patient.

(9)  Ability of patient to express himself/herself orally and in writing.

Needless to say, a statistical study on the above data would serve as a valuable reference for the methods of treatment and prevention sought by modern medicine. However, it is always possible to cure, treat, and prevent any intractable disease even without the above data. The fundamental method is laid down in the approach I describe in steps 1 to 5 above. I shall refrain from discussing here subsequent basic methods.

In any case, the idea is to promote a yin-yang balance in the proper direction (e.g., by making $\triangledown$ more $\triangle$, and by making $\triangle$ more $\triangledown$), and in this way to master as quickly as possible a life style that advances $\triangledown$ $\triangle$ to the state of ✡ When we seek the yin-yang that forms the core of this state to infinity, what happens? Even if the core does not attain an ultimate state, it should become spherical in shape; a perfect spherical state should have biological characters that are not attacked by the pockmarked spherical shape of the AIDS virus. The only way to form cells with such characters is to follow a correct life style based on the consumption of proper food. A macrobiotic brown rice diet is one of the best of such life styles.

# 5

## A Journey to Cosmic Life

# Yin and Yang in the Order of the Universe

With the help of George Ohsawa's book, *The Order of the Universe*[1], I, who had known nothing whatsoever of "life" and "life-force," followed the flow of life and awoke to life and the source of life. From this book I learned by what process the vast, boundless life of the universe came to be my own life. I did not come to know just the roots of my own existence, but was able to learn the principles by which life exists.

"The world of the finite (this world) emerges from the world of the infinite (emptiness, nothingness, absoluteness)."

"The beginning of the finite world starts with the two extremes yin ($\nabla$) and yang ($\triangle$), from which emerge light and all things."

Lao-tzu stated it thus: "Two arise from one, three arise from two, and all things arise from three."

Ohsawa called the two extremes that give rise to the finite world Yin and Yang. And he represents these with the following symbols: $\nabla$ (Yin) and $\triangle$ (Yang).

When I first saw these symbols, I thought of them as just that—merely symbols. But I soon realized that they have a profound meaning and an important function.

No method is as simple and clear as these symbols for understanding the order of the universe.

The following passage from *The Order of the Universe* describes how this world is made up in terms of the fundamental principle of Yin and Yang ($\nabla$ $\triangle$).

First, let's ponder where the life in this flesh and blood that we call ourselves comes from. . . .

Of course, we inherited this from our parents and ancestors, but how did our parents, our ancestors, and we ourselves come to have and inherit this moral body of ours? This is readily understandable. There are many, many things, but of these the largest and most important is food. We live by virtue of the food we eat, and it is because we partake of food that we are born and give birth, that we move and think. People who do not live by eating do not have the faculty to think. In order to understand this act of eating and the grand and mysterious force of food, one must by all means try fasting. I urge all those people who do not yet know and understand this to try fasting for a week or two.

In any case, for thousands of years it has been possible for us to be born, to give birth, to live, to act, to think and conceptualize, and to know God; we have been able to do all of this through food. From this, we know that life comes from food. In other words, we know that the precursor of the life of an organism, of the life in our own flesh and blood, our living and mortal body, is food. This food consists of such things as vegetation (plants), fish and fowl (animals), water and air, and sunlight.

Upon examining the animal and vegetable foods that represent the greatest

---

[1]  Japanese title: *Uchu no chitsujo.*

portion of this food as the first foothold in our quest for the source of life, it is apparent that these are the same. That is, we know that all animals—fish, fowl, and beast—live by feeding directly or indirectly upon vegetation. Man is one of these animals. So we know that the source of life of those organisms such as man and other animals which move about on their own are plants, which do not move about. Motile organisms thus come from immotile organisms. How interesting that motile organisms emerge from immotile organisms.

We must search then for what the source of the life of vegetation (plants) is. This is, first of all, the ground, the earth—which serves as the second foothold in our quest. The earth consists of soil and water. The soil contains many different minerals. In contrast with vegetation, which remains quiet and still, the earth moves constantly, staying still not even one brief second. How interesting that nonmoving organisms emerge from something that moves. However, it takes more than vegetation, soil, and water for man to live. Nor can vegetation live with just the ground. It needs also space, air (wind), sunlight (heat and fire), atmospheric pressure, voltage, magnetic forces, gravity, and so forth. To begin with, the ground does not exist entirely by itself. Something that is necessary and most important to man, vegetation, and the ground is the sky. This sky envelops the earth with several thick mantles. Of these, the mantle which directly envelops the earth is air. The earth was born from the sky. Without a sky, earth could not have been born. Unlike the earth, this sky is not characterized by vigorous movement. I discovered that here too, something that moves emerges from something that remains still. This sky is the third foothold for us explorers. Even with this vegetation, earth, and sky, man and animals need something more to live. They need light. This is the sun, heat, the source of fire. Without this light, the sky, the earth, the vegetation, and man cannot live. Moreover, this sky is a world that emerged from light. But light has incredible speed. How interesting that this rapid entity should have given birth to the quiet skies. This light is the fourth foothold of explorers in search of the root of life. Having followed to this point a progression toward greater weight and size in the search for the root of life, upon looking back, we find that the earth, water, wind, and fire envelope and create the world of organisms such as man, animals, and plants. There are signs that the sages of ancient Greece and India came this far in their explorations (the four elements).

Have we been able thus to grasp the source of the flow of life? Let us try now taking another look at our lives. Oh! There is still a great deal that is lacking. Although the body lives by virtue of the four elements earth, water, fire, and wind, what about spirit? From where is this inherited, and just how is it maintained and raised? Without spirit, we are just a corpse; just dead flesh. Moreover, without spirit, which does has not have the weight, length, life or "ability to see" of the flesh, and which is totally devoid of such characteristics as warmth, motion, action, we cannot even be born. We cannot emerge. Does this mean that we have pursued our search for the flow of life in the wrong direction? Or is it that we have given too much thought to what is heavy and large?

Or is there perhaps an origin from which the four large, heavy elements emerge? Do the four elements have parents? Could it be perhaps that the spirit which gives birth to the characteristics of these motile organisms, animals, and man is the parent and source of these four elements?

Ohsawa in this way traces the flow of life back to its source. If what moves is yang ($\triangle$), then what does not move is yin ($\triangledown$). In the above passage, Ohsawa states that what moves was born from what does not move, and what does not move is born from what moves. This certainly seems hard to understand.

Representing what Ohsawa writes above in as simple a form as possible, we get the following:

> Man (animals) → Vegetation (plants) → Earth → Sky → Light
>  moving              still                        moving    still    moving

This can be rearranged as follows:

> Darkness (emptiness, nothingness) → Two Extremes of Yin and Yang ✡
>                                                                          $\triangledown$      $\triangle$
>
> → Light → Sky → Earth → Vegetation (plants) → Man (animal)
>    $\triangle$    $\triangledown$    $\triangle$           $\triangledown$                   $\triangle$

Please note in particular the alternation of yin and yang in the above order.

Having arrived at this point, I succeeded in understanding the principle that this world (creation, the finite world) is made up of the two relative and complementary extremes of Yin and Yang. The order of the universe shows us what it is that enables man to live and nurture him; it tells us that eating plant-based foods is natural for man and that animal-based foods violate that order. Clearly, a vegetarian diet based on brown rice makes more sense than a meat diet.

## Switching from a Nutritional View to a Life View

When I began studying the marcobiotic principle of the order of the universe, the first thing I learned in terms of real-life problems was the harm caused by the *sanpaku*, "three whites"—white rice (or white bread), white sugar, and chemical seasonings (including also various food additives). Although this no longer is a new idea, refined products such as these are still very much a part of many people's lives.

At first, I simply understood refined products to be foods which are bad for the health. Having learned that these foods are harmful to the body, I resolved not to consume any. Now, it is one thing to talk of eliminating such foods from modern life, but quite another thing to actually do so. Unless one has a proper understanding of the harm these cause and makes a very careful and determined effort, they cannot be successfully removed and eliminated from one's diet. This is because we have lived for so long in close association with refined foods that it is very easy to compromise.

For instance, it is easy for one to think as follows. "Even though refined foods are harmful, we do not ingest just this. These foods don't cause such direct harm.

Because white rice is eaten together with various other foods, any nutrition lacking in the white rice is surely obtained from the accompanying dishes. As for white sugar, this is just used to flavor cooked food, and to sweeten coffee, tea, milk, and cakes and other confections. Finally, chemical seasonings (including food additives) are used in very small amounts for flavoring. Even though these may have adverse effects, such effects should be greatly diminished; unless used in great excess, they should not be harmful." It is with such justifications that we end up making compromises.

Common sense tells us that highly refined products such as the "three whites" are not natural foods. These are clearly foods that have been industrially processed by such technical operations as refining, polishing, and extraction. Since I was learning to view life as a flowing stream, it seemed to me that I could see in these refined foods a rejection of cosmic life through the division and destruction by industrial technology of the life and vitality that the plants serving as our food receive from the universe. The life and vitality that comes swiftly flowing toward us from the far reaches of the universe is stripped off, diluted, and eliminated by the food processing technology just before it reaches our mouths. The processing of food should be kept to a minimum so as not to mar the live-giving properties received from the universe; the use of more artificial processing than is necessary results in a technological product that disregards life. In this sense, refined products such as the "three whites" are technological foods that have been overprocessed.

White rice is more highly processed than half-milled rice, three-quarter-milled rice, and brown rice. Being so highly processed, it has been stripped of the original vitality it received from nature. Why is there any need to ruin the vitality and nutrition inherent to this rice by polishing it to such an extent that the resulting product is labeled "crystal rice," "pearl rice," or "diamond rice"?

The same thing can be said of sugar and salt. It is not necessary to refine these into virtually pure chemicals; taking in the vitality and nutrition of these foods as muscovado or natural salt is more natural. And in the case of seasonings, what real need is there to go to all the trouble of making synthetic chemical seasonings, and why do these predominate?

When we take the view that food is something we consume in order to receive nutrition or that food consists of nutrients, then refining, polishing, and otherwise processing food becomes essential. A high degree of ingredient purity is helpful when combining many different nutrients in a precise formulation, and high-purity ingredients are convenient in the cooking and preparation of nutritious food and food products. In order for dietetics to be recognized as a valid scientific discipline, it must be supported by evidence in the form of numerical data, and numerical data can only be acquired through analysis. Thus, nutritional science is necessarily focused on nutrients rather than on the inherent life-force or vitality of natural foods. Life and vitality are not entities that lend themselves to physicochemical analysis and measurement; hence, an understanding or validation of such concepts through scientific inquiry and analysis is impossible. It is reasons such as the above that have helped justify the industrialization of food and its conversion into processed food. From the standpoint of industrial capital seeking to enhance profits, this bias towards the scientific analysis and quantification of ingredients provided an ideal environment in which to develop food processing as an industrial field. The "three whites" are typical products of this industry.

I regard refined foods such as these as defective food because the order of life intrinsic to the original food has been for the most part destroyed and the food stripped of its vitality. In order to compensate for the deficiencies of refined foods, modern nutritional science has had to become even more precise and exacting. Even some pharmaceutical products have become fixtures at many dinner tables, not as medicine, but as food!

I had placed my entire trust in modern medicine, Western dietetics, and pharmacology, yet my body did not regain its proper order (health). I was always sickly, as was my entire family. After turning to a macrobiotic brown rice diet, however, I came to understand the vital and life-giving properties of food. It became possible for me to sense with my own body that industrial processed foods are almost devoid of natural vitality, and that even nutritional foods put together by combining nutrients have virtually none of the life and vitality that flows in from the universe. I eventually came to feel that injections, medications, dietetics, and nutritional foods impair the flow of cosmic life.

It was only when I learned and started practicing proper dietary habits and when I made a sincere effort to live in accordance with the universal order that I regained a sense of physical well-being and health. The order of my body became normal and my life began to join the flow of cosmic life. Defective foods and the science and technology that create these are unable to bring the order of our bodies—we who are the children of nature—entirely back to normal. Even when we do attempt to breathe life into refined and polished foods, there are limits to what is possible; we are unable to increase the basic vitality of the food. When we live a life involving compromise with highly refined foods, we adopt industrial technology-oriented dietary habits, forcing us to live a life of diminished vitality, a life in which we are unable to enjoy full health, a sickly life.

In addition to harming the body, refined foods also pose a great potential danger to the mind. There is no denying the truth of the equation: refinement of food = debilitation of man. The refinement of food to an unnecessary degree constitutes a stripping away of the life and vitality of that food, which enfeebles the body and renders it frail and delicate.

The elimination of refined foods from our home was the first concrete step my wife and I took toward a revolutionary change in our diet and our life; this led to the restoration of natural vitality (health) to our bodies. It was our first step toward a life style that reexamines life, and it changed our understanding of food from a view concerned solely with nutrition to one that holds vitality in greatest esteem.

## The Housewife and Toxic Chemicals

People often ask me, "You constantly stress the life and vitality of food, but how in the world can someone determine whether a food has vitality and measure how much of this it has?"

Another question constantly asked of me is this: "Except for raw foods, all foods pass through a series of processes such as washing, cutting, slicing, roasting, frying, boiling, baking, and—when the food is placed in the mouth—chewing. Although some difference exists in the speed of such processing, aren't these essentially identical with industrial processing? It's strange to arbitrarily decide that the former have vitality and the latter none. If you make the claim that industrially processed foods have no vitality, then doesn't it follow that the vitality of food also vanishes as a result of the former processes?"

Then there is the problem of contaminated natural foods. I am sometimes asked to respond to items such as the following.

> The intake of some contaminants by food type can be summarized thus: virtually all organochlorine compounds are known to originate from animal foods, 61% of BHC comes from fish and meat, 56% of DDT from fish and 32% from meat, 30% of dieldrin from animal-based foods and also vegetables, and 76% of PCBs from fish. As for harmful metals, 53% of the mercury is absorbed from fish and 25% from rice; 58% of arsenic comes from fish, and 53% of cadmium comes from rice. The manner in which these contaminants are assimilated through food varies considerably with the dietary habits of different countries. In the case of Japan, the majority of harmful contaminants originate from traditional foods such as rice and fish.[2]

Although macrobiotics teaches that natural and traditional foods have greater vitality, statements such as the above appear to indicate that processed foods are safer.

In response to such views, I would like to quote here from Ohsawa's essay, "The Housewife and Toxic Chemicals." This appeared in *Poisons in Five Colors* [Goshiki no doku] by Keisuke Tenno (published by Nippon C.I.), which was the first book to alert the public to the problem of food contamination in Japan.

> Housewives who don't know how to distinguish between proper and improper foods are committing suicide and murder by degrees!

> 1. All misfortunes (disease, crime, violence, war, accidents) arise from the poor judgment that causes people to unknowingly ingest poisons they think of as food products on a daily basis.
> Eternal happiness (absolute health, unlimited freedom, supreme justice, peace) springs from a supreme power of judgment that allows one to discern and select proper foods from the vast array of food products sold at the markets and shops, and properly prepare and eat these.
> This supreme power of judgment is innate in all people. What takes this power out and polishes it up is that womb of man's highest philosophy and religion, the physiological and biological educational process that instills the ancient oriental principle of life known as The Way: teaching and discipline.
> Don't we have to translate this principle of life into the scientific language of the twentieth century, then with this reexamine our real life and determine how to once again establish a bright, happy oriental world that is free and peaceful and has few wars and little crime?
> So that we may enjoy to our heart's desire a healthy (free) and happy (peaceful) life!

---

[2]   Excerpt from "Food contamination and the question of safety," by Masahiko Ueda, Director of the Food and Animal Quarantine Division at the Kochi Prefecture Institute of Health.

2.  I have spent forty years of my life distributing two million sheets of paper on which is written the secret to swimming out of the raging billows of the rough seas to people who, like me, have led pitiful and unhappy lives (I was sickly and weak; at about the age of ten, I became an orphan and was thrown into a world of violence—laws, authority, knowledge, ability, money. In the course of all this, I, who thought I would die at the age of eighteen, have reached 60 years of age).

Here is what I have learned in those forty years:

(1)  People are free. People are correct. People are love.
(2)  Anyone without limitless freedom, the most correct powers of judgment, and eternal and absolute love is either sick or has not yet fully developed.
(3)  A person becomes sick because there is no order to that person's diet.
(4)  Dietary order is merely one translation for the principle underlying all laws—the eternal Order of the Universe.
(5)  All misfortunes (all illnesses, all disputes, arrogance, poverty, deformity, disasters, lies, premature death, crime, wars, etc.) arise from a clouding of judgment.
(6)  The clouding of judgment is an ailment of the mind; like all ailments of the body, this is created by bad food.
(7)  No illness cannot be cured by correcting one's diet.

So, if some misfortune befalls you or you are faced with a perplexing problem, then this is either because your judgment is clouded or confused. The reason for this is that your judgment is borrowed and not your own. The time has come to use your own judgment, your own head. Only hardship and sorrow can shape one's own true judgment. In this world, nothing can be depended upon other than oneself. Yet even this is not easily understood. (Quite truthfully, I was unable to grasp why people have so much trouble understanding this.)

3.  In any case, I found the secret for overcoming all misfortune in the source that gives birth to and creates people, that induces them to thought and action—namely, discipline and order in their diet. I applied this myself, and had many tens of thousands of people try it; they were delighted with the results.

We must begin by discovering how to combine, prepare, and eat the proper foods. I have called the principle based upon which one judges what is proper the Order of the Universe (this consists of seven basic principles and twelve theorems). For forty years I have taught these through stories and fairy tales under such titles as "The Magic Spectacles" and "The Immortal Boy. "I have written also on how to cure illness, such as in my book *A New Theory of Nutrition and Its Therapeutic Effects*.

It is absolutely impossible for people unaware of these principles of correct diet to live a happy (free and peaceful) life. This is the physiological and biological foundation of absolute justice, limitless freedom, and eternal peace. That is why there can be no peace, freedom, or democracy without knowing these principles. The kitchen is the apothecary of life; the housewife is the pharmacist of happiness and unhappiness; the mother is the manager of peace.

4.   I urge you to read this book *Poisons in Five Colors* [Goshiki no doku]. You will soon see just how many opportunities for misfortune there are around you. Once you've read this book, you will become frightened to buy foods from the supermarkets and shops. Foods that cause cancer are everywhere. Everyday, you buy without the least forethought foods that kill your dear children with dread conditions such as infantile paralysis, deformity, dysentery, or ekiri; foods that make them feebleminded and retarded; foods that turn them into criminals.

Most important of all is the power of judgment to discern and select proper foods from the many deplorable and dishonest foods aimed only at making a profit; these latter only titillate your senses, eating away at health and happiness. After this, one must discover how to properly cook and eat proper foods. . . .

This is truly an age of homicidal mania. Countless people are killed in war. And yet the people killed by disease are far more numerous than those killed by war. Even doctors die from disease, unable to protect themselves; so each of us has no choice but to protect ourselves. . . .

Ohsawa wrote this thirty-five years ago, in 1953. What he wrote is as true today as it was back then for his words express truths that transcend time. How does one distinguish between and handle the life-giving forces and vitality of different foods? How far should we go in processing food as a product? What is proper food and what are proper food products? What are artificial and dishonest food products? The powers of judgment needed to make these distinctions are given to us by "the voyage to life."

## From Where Does Man Come and Whence Does He Go?

My journey to life resolved in a very simple and natural manner a great many perplexing questions and doubts I had had. One of these problems that made a particularly strong impression upon me was the question of where man comes from and where he goes.

I remember wondering once where I myself had come from and where I was headed. If one treats this as a hard question, it becomes impossibly hard. We would probably never arrive at a satisfactory answer if we attempted to solve this by running experiments, corroborating hypotheses, and theorizing. I wrestled with this problem by applying the method of practical dialectics and the principle of the Order of the Universe that I had learned. Making reference to the views and opinions of the many people I had learned from, I came up with the diagram shown in Fig. 5.1. Since this is the work of a rank amateur trying to schematically depict the order of the universe and the flow of life, those knowledgeable in this area will surely be appalled at the childishness and awkwardness of the diagram.

But my purpose here is not to aim for scholarly perfection or to publish a theory. All I have sought to accomplish here is to schematically depict in a clear and simple

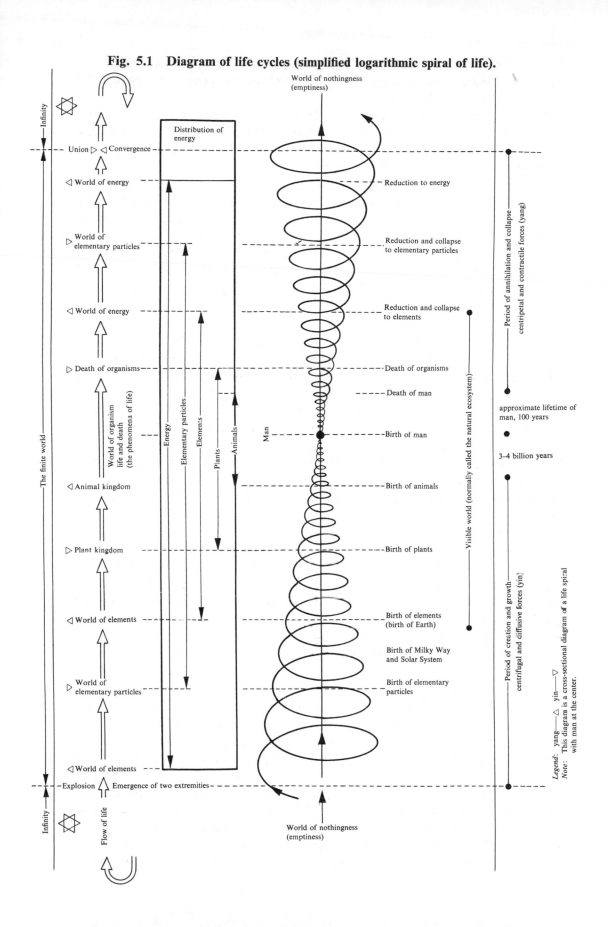

**Fig. 5.1  Diagram of life cycles (simplified logarithmic spiral of life).**

World of nothingness
(emptiness)

Infinity

Union ▷ ◁ Convergence

Distribution of energy

◁ World of energy — Reduction to energy

▷ World of elementary particles — Reduction and collapse to elementary particles

◁ World of energy — Reduction and collapse to elements

▷ Death of organisms — Death of organisms

Death of man

Birth of man

◁ Animal kingdom — Birth of animals

▷ Plant kingdom — Birth of plants

◁ World of elements — Birth of elements (birth of Earth)

Birth of Milky Way and Solar System

▷ World of elementary particles — Birth of elementary particles

◁ World of elements

Explosion ⩕ Emergence of two extremities

Infinity

Flow of life

World of nothingness
(emptiness)

The finite world

World of organism life and death (the phenomena of life)

Energy | Elementary particles | Elements | Plants | Animals | Man

Visible world (normally called the natural ecosystem)

Period of annihilation and collapse centripetal and contractile forces (yang)

approximate lifetime of man, 100 years

3–4 billion years

Period of creation and growth centrifugal and diffusive forces (yin)

*Legend:* yang——△ , yin——▷
*Note:* This diagram is a cross-sectional diagram of a life spiral with man at the center.

manner the order of the universe and the flow of life. Although such was not my intention, through this diagram, it became immediately apparent to me how I got here and where I am headed.

This was not the only discovery I made. Many things became easy to observe and consider. For instance, one can see at once that all organisms are born from the earth, and return from the earth to the sky. Passing back again through the same stages as when they came, organisms eventually return to the world of infinity, the world of nothingness. Although the time required when coming and when returning may appear to differ greatly, the changes and vicissitudes of Yin and Yang undoubtedly pass through the same process as when these first emerge. The sufferings of life and the serenity of death seem somehow to suggest the length of time and the breadth of space in this coming and going.

Examining closely this Life Cycle Diagram forced me to consider also the life view of modern man. When modern man ponders the connection between his own life and the universe, he is interested only in when space rockets will become a reality and where and how far into space man will be able to travel. Thoughts of the universe tend to be limited to the Solar System or the Milky Way.

Formerly, I had a shallow understanding of life that could be described thus: "Because I am alive, I am able to see and think about the lives of other people and the lives of animals and plants." Similarly, the strong can, according to the strength of their vitality, polish rice and wheat to make white rice and white bread that is easy to eat, and by making these foods easy to eat, strip off and shed life and vitality without concern. This is all they think of life. If an awareness that the life and vitality of all living things are one with cosmic life were the generally accepted life view, I am certain that man would not treat the life and vitality of the heavens, the life and vitality of the earth, the life and vitality of plants, and the life and vitality of animals and people as carelessly as he does today.

People believe that they have developed their own life and sphere of life through their own efforts. Because we hold to the view that other life is predicated upon our own existence, we think that we must do something with our lives. We conquer nature for our own lives, and for our own lives prepare to jump into outer space. Man has his world, animals have their world, plants have their world, the earth has its world, and the atmosphere has its world; yet, although everything has its proper world, only man is captivated by eager illusions that he may invade and conquer other worlds. This leads him to disrupt and destroy the natural ecosystem, gradually setting in place the conditions for his own destruction. We are not now trying to calmly and correctly contemplate where man came from and where he is headed. This single human being that I represent has already journeyed at some time through the world of plants, and through the worlds of the earth, the sky, light, and darkness; it is only after these travels that this "I" has at last emerged here as a human being. The various worlds are embodied in the person of people; they are you and me.

Yet, in spite of this, we are laboring under a delusion. Under the pretext of acting for the sake of humanity, for our descendants, or for a just cause, we are night and day polluting, destroying, and overrunning those worlds that gave birth to our own life. In the process, we are disrupting the natural ecosystem.

The body (vessel) that is me was born from my parents. However, life did not emerge from my parents. Life and vitality flows from a source at the far corner of the universe, at the far reaches of the cosmos, in the world of emptiness (nothingness, absoluteness, ultimate extremity, infinity). Not only, then, am I a child of my parents, I am also a child of the universe; I am a particle, a molecule if you will, born from emptiness and destined to return to emptiness.

## Cosmic Life and Human Life

In Japan, one often hears the expression "a person's life is more precious than the earth." True, if I lose my life, then that essentially is the end of the world for me. However, this is ultimately a problem concerning only one individual—me. The universe is oblivious to whether or not I exist. Until I experienced the journey toward life, I was moved whenever I heard someone say something to the effect that a human life is more precious than the earth; I was moved by the great humanity and love for people expressed in these words. But it is in the name of such noble sentiments that we zealously carry out deeds and behavior which destroys and ruins life each day. By stripping food of its life and vitality, and turning it into nutrients or medicine, we impoverish the body and the earth. We scatter nuclear materials in the atmosphere, seas, and land in a race that will someday destroy man and other organisms.

Why the large contradictions between what we say and what we do? We tend to interpret in a sense favorable to ourselves the verbal pieties offered up to underscore the preciousness of human life. What stands out clearest of all in the true image of modern man is the egoism that makes him willing to consume the earth's resources and contaminate the atmosphere with radiation provided it serves human purposes. "As long as I survive, I will worry about everything else later on"—that is what we seem to be saying. Holding as we do only a self-centered life view, a life view that holds humanity supreme, we have become incapable of contemplating, taking into account, or acting properly in regard to life other than our own.

The great importance that man places on his own life has the actual effect of causing him to treat his life carelessly. Unless we see cosmic life as the source of our lives and recognize that a macrocosmic life view fosters our own life and vitality, we risk inviting upon ourselves a cure that is worse than the disease. By continuing unchecked today's scientifically and industrially oriented life style, humanity is in essence devoting itself to the destruction and collapse of life.

I wish everyone would get on the Order of the Universe rocket, and set off on a journey to life. Anyone anywhere can go on a journey to life. Whether one goes on this trip or not makes an enormous difference in one's view of existence and in existence itself, in one's view of life and in life itself. Journeys make our life rich and meaningful, but no trip costs as little money, takes as little time, and involves as little danger while promising such great rewards as this. All you have to do is quietly close your eyes, trace the Life Cycle Diagram in your heart, and set off for cosmic space along the course pointed out by the spiral.

Why must we protect nature? Why shouldn't we destroy natural ecosystems? Why is it necessary for us to abandon nuclear weapons and nuclear industry in general? Why do we have to revegetate the earth? Why must we practice a natural diet?... These questions reflect very natural and instinctive concerns toward life that arise from the fact that human life is united with cosmic life and that cosmic life is received through human life. We are approaching an age in which we must open our eyes and heart further to cosmic life.

## Looking at Things Based on Yin and Yang

Thinking and looking at things based on the Principle of Yin and Yang opened up a new world for me. The journey to life showed me the universe. That universe is formed by the order of Yin and Yang. Even that microcosm we know as the human body and mind is formed and controlled by the order of Yin and Yang.

There is no special school for learning about Yin and Yang. The place of daily life is itself the classroom, and the only way to learn is to study on one's own. I'd like to mention here several ways of thinking and looking at things based on Yin and Yang that made an impression on me during my period of self-study.

Before doing so, I will quote the theorems and borrow the Yin-Yang table (which also appears in Chapter 4 as Table 4.1) from George Ohsawa's *The Order of the Universe* and *The Unifying Principle*.[3] Please continue to refer to the table and theorems as you read on. For a more detailed presentation, please consult the above books directly. Even if this is not entirely clear at first, with continued effort you should be able to gain a good understanding of Yin and Yang.

> *The Twelve Theorems of the Unifying Principle:* The Unifying Principle is a world view that demonstrates that the universe is composed of a Yin-Yang order having correspondence, rapport, complementarity, and affinity.
>
> (1) The universe unfolds and evolves with a Yin-Yang order.
> (2) The Yin-Yang order is infinite, arising constantly at all places; it is mutual exchange and vicissitudes.
> (3) Those things having a nature that is centripetal, compressive, and falling are called Yang, while those things having a nature that is centrifugal, diffusive, and rising are called Yin.
> (4) Yang attracts Yin, and Yin attracts Yang.
> (5) All things are a complex high-order aggregation of electronic particles of the universe in itself that bear both yinness and yangness in all proportions.
> (6) All things are merely aggregations of Yin and Yang with varying degrees of dynamic equilibrium.
> (7) Nothing is purely Yin or Yang; all things are relative.
> (8) Nothing is neutral or balanced; there is always an unequal proportion of Yin and Yang.
> (9) The mutual attraction between all things is proportional to their respective Yin-Yang differences.
> (10) Yin repels Yin and Yang repels Yang. The force of repulsion is inversely proportional to the difference therebetween.

---

[3] See also *The Book of Macrobiotics: The Universal Way of Health, Happiness and Peace* by Michio Kushi with Alex Jack (Japan Publications, 1987).

(11)    Extreme Yin produces Yang, and extreme Yang produces Yin.

(12)    All things are Yang at the center and Yin on the surface.

## On Sickness and Health

Is this person I call myself yin or yang? I am already well aware that I am a yin person. Let us take a look at this using the Yin-Yang chart in Table 4.1. I will start at the top of the chart.

I have a naturally white complexion. At times, it even appears pale. I have a low body temperature, which makes me sensitive to the cold; I don't fare well in winter. With regard to taste, I love sweet foods and am also fond of sour foods. I have flabby muscles and a quiet comportment; I am non-energetic and have a long, thin build. As for temperament, rather than getting angry, I tend to become moody. Such details are apparent from just a quick look at someone. If, in addition to this, the dietary history, physical constitution, and life style of a person's parents, as well as what he or she was fed after birth and how he/she was raised are all taken into account, then it is possible to make an even more accurate Yin-Yang judgment.

From this, I know that I am clearly yin. Although it is important also to determine just how yin or yang someone is, the first step is to find out whether one is generally yin or yang. For people like me who are yin, adopting a yin life style or yin therapy in response to illness is ineffective. As indicated in Theorem 10 above, Yin and Yang repel each other. Administering yin therapy for a yin ailment or advising someone who is yin to live a yin life style will not provide the proper and desired effects. Not only is this ineffective, it intensifies the degree of yinness and, in addition to aggravating the symptoms, predisposes that person's life toward tragic misfortune.

The modern medicine practiced in Japan is Western medicine. Western medicine arose in the West as a school of therapy suited to the physical constitution of Westerners, whose food staple is meat and who therefore have a yang constitution. Western medicine has advanced in a way that is suited to people of yang constitutions. Because this a form of medicine suited to people of yang constitution, the therapy is primarily yin. Hence, Western medicine is essentially yin. The essence of Western medicine becomes even clearer by looking at climate, physiography, life styles, and customs while referring to the twelve theorems above.

I had been totally reliant upon Western medicine, doctors, hospitals, and drugs without knowing this principle. What chance was there that Western medicine, which is basically yin, would have a salutary effect on such a strongly yin person as myself? It only stood to reason that the more I depended upon doctors and medicines, the more this aggravated the condition of my body, causing chronic illness.

Yang prescriptions and medicines containing yang principles were what I needed. The reason a brown rice diet suited my daughter and me so well was that the yang components of brown rice matched our physical constitutions well; a life style based on a brown rice diet was highly effective in making us more yang.

In Oriental medicine, a diagnosis is rendered through an evaluation of key symptoms based on the yin or yang character of the patient's physical constitution, temperament, and disposition. In addition, Oriental medicine is basically yang in character. This is not to say that Western medicine fails to look at the nature of the patient's physical constitution, but it is undeniable that Western and Oriental medicine each have certain properties inextricably associated with themselves.

From the bitter experiences of my family and myself and the countless examples in which people have been cured of illness and restored to health through nutritional therapy, I was able to grasp the basic features of both Western and Oriental medicine. Most disease arises from a yin-yang imbalance in the body and mind. Depending on how this imbalance is treated, the illness is either aggravated or alleviated. As one gets better at examining the Yin-Yang state of the body and becomes able to discern whether there is too much or too little Yang and too much or too little Yin, mistakes in care and treatment diminish. If there is a surplus of Yin, then the yin principle is either reduced or Yang is added, while a surplus of Yang calls for a reduction in yangness or the addition of yinness. By returning the overall balance of Yin and Yang to moderation, the flow of life energy or vitality improves.

In the past, while I knew disease to be a problem of the body, I could not help thinking of it as a difficult problem. That's why I rushed off at once to the doctor or hospital and relied entirely on them. But hospitals and medical practitioners are not as omnipotent as patients and the ill would like to believe. I learned with my body that disease is a signal of an imbalance in Yin and Yang, and came to realize that the true nature of disease is really quite simple and clear. In almost all cases, disease is something we create ourselves in our own bodies. Although some diseases are due to causes such as pollution that cannot be avoided by individuals, if one traces each of these causes back to their roots, we find that we (man) are the ones who created them. Since we caused and invited these ailments upon ourselves, we must cure them by ourselves.

Yet, in spite of this, we cram ourselves full of learning through scientific education that just fragments and complicates things while at the same time turning away from opportunities to learn about truth and wisdom that simplifies and clarifies the world about us. Wisdom ceases to function in our minds. We have lost the habit of judging things concerning us by ourselves, and rely increasingly on others and even machines (computers) to do this for us. We have become a people who are easily startled by little things, who blackout in a pinch, and who shift the burden of responsibility to others while at the same time claiming rights for oneself. I myself was a typical example of this.

While in this state, I learned about Yin and Yang and became able to cure myself of my own diseases. I was able also to cure my family of its ailments. Actually, it might be more accurate to say that I was able to prevent us from becoming ill. If I were at some future time to come down with a new illness and were unable to heal myself, since the cause of this condition would be a grave error or sin I had committed in my way of life, I would want to entrust my body to the will of God—like all animals and organisms. When there is no way to cure oneself of a self-inflicted illness, this is the same as saying that one has lost the ability to live. I do not think or advocate that everything has to be done entirely through one's own efforts, but I do believe that we must all choose for ourselves our own basic way of life.

The ancient and seemingly outmoded principles and theory of Yin and Yang cast an odd figure in our age of rapidly advancing science and technology. I too thought it eccentric at first. However, I now believe that the practical utility of the simple principle of Yin and Yang is nowhere more useful than in a complex, diversified scientific age.

## Science Has Weakened Man

Science has weakened man. Modern man in particular has become weak. The fact that modern man is frailer than his forbears has even been demonstrated scientifically. I do not set out here to prove these facts, particularly as they are evident to everyone. Children in Japan today are called "bean sprout kids"; bean sprouts are a symbol of frailty and delicacy.

Thanks to science, we lead lives of convenience and plenty. This has made people frail and weak. The protection afforded by science has made us into the fragile creatures we are today.

The opposite of frailty is sturdiness. People living in earlier ages in which science was not as advanced as it is today were sturdier and more robust than people are today, not only physically but in all aspects.

Characterizing frailty and robustness in terms of Yin and Yang, frailty is yin and robustness is yang. I was born frail. I was an early example of today's "bean sprout kids," so I know what it is to be a "bean sprout kid."

I wanted to become strong and healthy. Even as a child, whenever I fell ill I wished with all my heart that my body would become stronger. As I think back on it now, because I was yin, I instinctively sought to become yang. Yin is attracted to Yang, and Yang is attracted to Yin (Theorem 4). That is instinctive. Although I ought to have lived in accordance with my instincts, I sought ways of becoming stronger through modern science, from drugs and doctors. But because science makes man weak (yin), there was no chance of my becoming stronger and more robust in this way. I had no knowledge of the Yin-Yang way of looking at the world, so I sought help in yin solutions that were of no use to me.

Modern scientific notions and life styles are useless for making a frail person sturdy. In order for a frail yin person to become a sturdy yang person, the body and heart must be given yangness. How can this be done?

The principle of Yin and Yang provides a simple and clear answer. One large problem we face today is how to raise and educate frail kids to make them strong and sturdy. A correct response will never be forthcoming if we stick solely to science. Not only will we fail to obtain a solution, but our insistence on sticking to a modern scientific approach will have the ultimate effect of turning those frail children into truly weak humans or even living corpses. If we bear in mind both that the nature of science is such that it renders people weaker (Yin) and that science has in fact made people weaker (Yin), then an answer to the above question can easily be obtained by applying Yin-Yang judgment.

If science makes man weak (Yin), then a method other than science must be sought for escaping this state of weakness. What things and phenomena outside of science will impart yangness to us? Because the source of Yang in our Solar System is the sun itself, weak people need only live together with the sun. Living with the sun means living with nature. The most immediately accessible way of doing this is a diet that contains the greatest amount of the sun's life-energy and vitality. Because the processed foods created by the food processing industry are intrinsically yin, they are not appropriate for frail (Yin) modern man.

Even though, as a general rule, yangness should be sought for a yin constitution, there are various stages to the search for yangness. When bean sprouts are placed suddenly under the scorching heat of the blazing sun, the yinness of the sprouts shrivels up in a moment. One aspect of the proper knowledge and use of Yin and Yang consists of adjusting the degree of Yang according to the degree of Yin.

## What Is Science to Man?

I first experienced surprise upon coming into contact with the words Yin and Yang, then again upon learning the principle of Yin and Yang. Having thought the purpose of this principle to be divination, as symbolized by the phenomena of the ancient world and the eight signs of divination, I initially felt a mixed sense of astonishment and hesitation. Had I not directly experienced the benefits of a macrobiotic brown rice diet, I would have kept my distance from Yin and Yang as an old, outmoded concept of the ancients. However, because the theory of Yin and Yang is indispensable for properly practicing a brown rice diet, I today live hand in hand with Yin and Yang.

At the time, I thought of atomic energy as the energy resource of the future. Although I was absolutely opposed to the development and deployment of nuclear arms, I felt that the peaceful use of atomic power as an energy source or in industry was an excellent way to preserve earth's limited resources. In a resource-poor country such as Japan, atomic energy was generally thought to be a highly appropriate energy resource. A very aggressive program of nuclear power development has in fact been pursued in Japan.

It took me awhile, but I gradually came to understand the theory of Yin and Yang. All things in the universe exist in a proper order based on the principle of Yin and Yang. The universe and the natural world both operate according to the universal order and the laws of nature. While illustrating this after my own fashion in the Life Cycle Diagram (Fig. 5.1), I have given some thought to humanity and the use of nuclear power.

I have studied such questions as: "To what world do atoms belong?" "What does it mean for man to use the atom?" and "Does man's use of the atom constitute a violation of the universal order?" By applying Yin and Yang to these questions I have sought answers.

Looking at the Life Cycle Diagram (see Fig. 5.1), I ponder the question, "To what world does an atom belong?" According to the diagram, the world of elementary particles lies in both the period of creation and growth (the process of life) and in the period of annihilation and collapse (the process of death). Insofar as the use of the atom by mankind as an energy resource and in nuclear weapons involves the conversion of the atom to nuclear weapons and nuclear energy by a human agency, this corresponds to the stage of elementary particles in the process of annihilation and collapse back toward energy. Man is attempting to turn atoms

—which are transformed into energy in the universe—into energy right here on earth.

Mankind is attempting to perform here on earth the work of life that is normally conducted in the vast nuclear reactor of the cosmos at a great remove from the biosphere. The biosphere, of which mankind is a part, is but an infinitesimal part of the great life system of the universe, a very tiny ecosystem. Even the terrestrial ecosystem within our solar system is but a single tiny world. In this infinitesimally small terrestrial ecosystem, we are attempting to usurp a process that properly occurs in a vast and distant corner of the universe. This act of mankind represents immoderation and excess that is beyond the power of words to describe.

The proof of this can be seen in nuclear wastes. Mankind is at a loss now as to how to dispose of its nuclear wastes. The fact that these wastes cannot be reduced to its components in the natural world on earth without imparting some harm or other is clear proof that such wastes have no place in the terrestrial ecosystem. Both nuclear energy and nuclear wastes belong to a world different from the natural ecosystem that includes the earth. Let us verify this here.

In the Life Cycle Diagram, I indicate the flow of life as follows: (1) the world of nothingness (emptiness) → (2) the bipolar world of Yin and Yang → (3) the world of energy → (4) the world of elementary particles → (5) the world of atoms → (6) the plant kingdom → (7) the animal kingdom. Rewriting this in terms of dimensions, the first dimension becomes the animal kingdom, the second dimension is the plant kingdom, the third dimension is the world of the atom, the fourth dimension is the world of elementary particles, the fifth dimension is the world of energy, the sixth dimension is the bipolar world of Yin and Yang, and the seventh dimension is the world of nothingness (emptiness).

As is apparent above, the dimension in which elementary particles that were formerly atoms are reduced to energy differs entirely from the dimension in which animals live. The introduction through human artifice of phenomena from a different dimension into the dimension of the plant and animal kingdoms is clearly in violation of the universal order. In fact, it is more than a violation; it is a crime.

The sacrifices and losses accompanying such acts are thus tragic and immeasurable by ordinary standards. The reason that the atomic bomb exerts such a formidable and improper influence in this world is that it explosively releases energy that does not belong to our world, and because radiation and radioactive fallout continues to visit upon the survivors of Hiroshima and Nagasaki tragedy that has no place in our world.

The atomic bomb speaks clearly of the power and influence of a different dimension and of its evil and criminality. Acts that disregard differences in dimension induce reactions and forces of ruin and destruction proportional to the distance between the differing dimensions.

Is the peaceful use of the atom really desirable? Is it really possible to peacefully use phenomena from a different and distant dimension in the dimension of the plant and animal kingdoms? Even the use of pharmaceuticals, food additives, pesticides, chemical fertilizers, and compound feeds; the discharge of exhaust emissions and chemical waste fluids; and the use of laser in medical therapy have increased the incidence of strange and intractable diseases, newborn infants with anencephaly or gross deformations, and mentally deranged individuals. The world of man presents a map of hell. Such have been the consequences of violations within the natural ecosystem of this earth. What then will happen when man insists on performing on this earth the work of life from a dimension far removed from the natural terrestrial ecosystem? Is the peaceful use of the atom really possible? Man deludes himself by thinking and arguing that something which is not a peaceful act within the cosmic ecosystem can be put to a peaceful use.

Aren't we openly embracing those facets of nuclear power technology that we believe to be beneficial and useful, while at the same time shutting our eyes to the fact that the energy of reaction latent within nuclear power is something beyond the scope of human power? When we consider merely the term "energy" here, there exist many different types of energy from different sources, such as solar energy, hydraulic energy, wind energy, geothermal energy, thermal energy, and atomic energy. Each has its own properties and features. We have yet to achieve the requisite knowledge and ability to fully utilize even those forms of energy found in the natural terrestrial ecosystem.

The same is true of what we call the "calorie." Some foods have calories that activate the intestinal flora and become life energy, while other foods have calories that deactivate the intestinal flora and lead toward death. Isn't it more important that we first conduct basic research and studies to determine whether the foods we eat are in harmony with the ecosystem of our bodies and whether the forms of energy we use are in harmony with the terrestrial ecosystem?

We Japanese have experienced something very important. Even among the frenzy and excesses of World War Two, the bombing of Hiroshima and Nagasaki was a scene from hell that had no place in this world of ours. The idea that it is legitimate to develop the same atom for peaceful, nonmilitary uses shows that we have not yet understood that handling the atom in this terrestrial ecosystem of ours is itself a criminal act.

Beginning with the first nuclear test blast conducted in July 1945 at Los Alamos, the United States, the Soviet Union, Great Britain, France, China, India, and other nations have conducted a total of several thousand nuclear tests. Although each test was conducted with full safeguards to avoid accidents and dangerous levels of radiation exposure, individuals working at the test sites have developed unexpected symptoms twenty, thirty, and in some cases almost forty years after exposure. Poor physical conditions of unknown cause, leukemia, malignant tumors, autonomic ataxia, mental disorders, and other unfortunate and unanticipated effects have appeared.

Nuclear power plants have been built in many countries around the world. Although these are always claimed to be absolutely safe, in case after case even very minor accidents have continued to result in damage of totally unexpected proportion and irreversible effects. Not only are these accidents speeding up the march of living things toward death, even the soil and ecosystems in the vicinity of the nuclear power plants have been drawn into a cycle of death.

Although the public is assured of the safety of disposal practices for radioactive wastes, events indicating that such disposal is less than absolutely safe have emerged. Nuclear power development, which has proceeded under the conviction that every precaution is being taken and every possibility weighed, has arrived today at a point where we are seeing evidence of incalculable, unanticipated, and unforeseeable damage on almost a daily basis.

Whether one is talking of nuclear weapons, nuclear power plants, or nuclear materials for industrial or other uses, scientists and policy-makers insist that proper caution is being exercised in the development and the use or deployment of these. However, we are committing a grave error. Absolute safety measures cannot possibly be instituted with man's meager capabilities in an affair involving the violation of the universal order in a different dimension. Full precautions can be taken only when something occurs within its proper dimension, within the space and time to which it belongs. To confine and utilize phenomena that belong to another domain of the universe within the plant and animal kingdom in our terrestrial ecosystem is a very serious mistake, a grave crime.

Is science a weapon and tool for invading the universe and plundering substances from other dimensions and other orders of time and space so that we may live? If it is, then modern science is nothing other than a tool for killing ourselves.

As our expectations with regard to atomic energy symbolically demonstrate, we appear to have mistaken science as the parent or guardian of life. Is this what science really is? We appear to be making a grave mistake in our attitude toward science. Isn't science supposed to serve man as a tool for discovery and a better understanding of his place in the universe?

I have learned how to see and think of things in terms of Yin and Yang. A way of observing and thinking based on the principle of Yin and Yang serves as a tool for living. This ancient tool has shown me the universe and its order. It will show these not only to me, but to anyone who cares to look.

## Yin and Yang as a Principle of Relativity

I started a brown rice diet in 1965. The 1960s and 1970s were a period of high growth for Japan. We in Japan saw a rapid rise in our incomes, and mass production ushered in mass consumption. Some even referred to this period as a "throwaway" age. It was a time of unsurpassed economic prosperity in which the quality of life and the sheer abundance of goods rose rapidly to new heights; a state of luxury was achieved almost overnight in food, clothing, and shelter. Abundance and luxury became the rule, particularly in food and drink. People who continued to eat brown rice were looked down upon as eccentrics and oddballs. I don't know how many times my parents grumbled that there was no need to eat brown rice in this age of plenty when one could eat anything nutritious one desired.

Because many aspects of a macrobiotic brown rice diet run counter to the notions of Western dietetics, it is basically incompatible with modern diets that stress nutrition above all else. This was the source of the friction that arose in my family over our diet and way of life. I received plenty of cold stares, complaints, and unkind comments even from my brothers, relatives, and friends. Moreover, because the brown rice diet that I was following was based on Ohsawa's Principle of Yin and Yang, people kept me at a distance. Both this primitive food called brown rice that I was eating and all my talk of Yin and Yang were felt to be out of place in modern Japan.

But new truths exist in old things. The Principle of Yin and Yang that I learned as the practical dialectic taught as the Unifying Principle by George Ohsawa is originally derived from the teachings of the Chinese sage Fu-Hi around 2500 B.C. This is a "practical principle of relativity" for rendering simpler and clearer things in modern life and society that are becoming increasingly complex and diversified, making judgments based upon this simpler and clear view, and conducting modern life with greater simplicity and harmony. Einstein's theory of relativity is too difficult for me to tackle, but the Principle of Yin and Yang is a principle of relativity that anyone with ordinary common sense can apply to his or her own life. Ohsawa delves into this in greater detail in his *The Unifying Principle*, *The Magic Spectacles*, and other writings.

When I began eating brown rice, I had no idea what bearing Yin and Yang had on eating brown rice. All that was necessary, I thought, was to become strong and healthy. The theory of Yin and Yang and all reasoning of that sort seemed extraneous and irrelevant. But after a while I came to understand the importance and necessity of a way of thinking and seeing based on Yin and Yang. True, when you faithfully practice a brown rice diet, your physical condition does improve. You recover from illness and regain health and vitality. However a brown rice diet is not a panacea. One's body does not always remain in peak physical condition. Moreover, the spirit and emotions are constantly beset by anxieties and concerns. If one is able to perceive and understand the constant shifts and changes that occur in one's body and heart, then it becomes easier to cope with the changes that follow.

The Principle of Yin and Yang served as a compass for reading the direction of events and things in constant flux. I ate brown rice and studied Yin and Yang. Also, because I wanted to live better, I began at the outset by contemplating how my own "life and death" can be viewed in terms of Yin and Yang.

While preparing the Life Cycle Diagram that appears earlier in this chapter and by pondering life and death in terms of Yin and Yang, I initially came upon the following realizations.

(1) The world of substance (the finite world, the world of relativity) arose from the world of emptiness (the world of nothingness, the world of infinity, the world of ultimate extremity).

(2) The finite world (relative world) originally arose from the two opposite extremes or poles of Yin and Yang.

(3) From the two extremes of Yin and Yang emerged energy, and after passing through the Yin-Yang journey of life from energy to elementary particles ($\bigtriangledown$) to elements ($\bigtriangleup$) to plants ($\bigtriangledown$) to animals (including man) ($\bigtriangleup$), came the birth of man.

(4) When determining the Yin and Yang of life and death, it is clear that the process of life is a journey from nothingness to somethingness. Similarly, the process of death may be regarded as a journey from somethingness to nothingness. A simple graphical representation of this is given in Fig. 5.2.

(5) Life can be seen broadly as the emergence of a living body as a result of the centripetal occurrence of a process based on two extremes, such as explosion and fusion or division and union, from space and time of

limitless expanse. Death may be similarly regarded as the phenomenon whereby an individual returns to infinite space and time by centrifugally carrying out such processes as division and union or explosion and fusion.

(6) One theorem of the Unifying Principle states that centrifugal forces (centrifugality) are yin and centripetal forces (centripetality) are yang.

**Fig. 5.2   A Simple graphical presentation of Yin and Yang of life and death.**

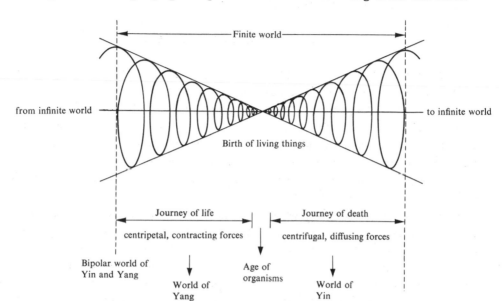

From the above considerations taken as a whole, I tried looking at life as a Yang phenomenon and death as a Yin phenomenon. I found that in this way it is easy to determine the conditions that serve to maintain health and longevity in living organisms. What has life begins walking toward death from the moment of birth. No, in fact, from the moment of conception—this being the union of a sperm (Yin) with an ovum (Yang). We set out on a journey of death in which the forces of division and diffusion hold sway. One can even say that man lives in a world controlled by Yin. Therefore, our longevity and fate are determined by how we select and practice a Yang life style and way of living in harmony with this Yin world.

One of the most salient features of modern science is the manner in which it tirelessly analyzes, fragments, and reduces things and phenomena. Our busy modern way of life has been created by the specialization, diversification, and complexification of all things out to the very periphery of everyday life. Analyzing, fragmenting, and investigating things on a microscopic scale may appear at first glance to be a Yang process, but it is in fact a diffusive and divisive Yin process. What it does is further accelerate the yinnization of the modern world, which is already predominantly yin. This has the effect of geometrically accelerating yinnizing tendencies. Symptoms that man is accelerating the speed of his own self-destruction are starting to appear in many different phenomena; this is an indication that the defects of modern science's analytic and reductive approach are rising to the surface.

The Yin-Yang approach to seeing and thinking of things is a comprehensive science of the macrocosmic and the microcosmic. Not only is it able to clearly put its finger on the failings of modern science, it can compensate for those failings and point out the way we must go. The reason why the Principle of Yin and Yang is called the practical principle of relativity is that it can be used to immediately and precisely render a comprehensive and all-embracing judgment on both a macro-cosmic and a microcosmic level.

## The Ecosystem Within Us

After the above ruminations of life and death as seen in terms of Yin and Yang, I would like to turn now to the ecosystem.

First of all, can't the region of the ecosystem be thought of as indicating the boundary lines of life and death, within the range of which the balance of life and death swings about the time of birth of organisms as the fulcrum (see the Life Cycle Diagram)? The cosmic ecosystem, the terrestrial ecosystem (what we call the natural ecosystem), the ecosystem within the body—each of these equally divide life and death in the respective worlds.

We all want to live long healthy lives. In order for this to be possible, the ecosystem within our bodies must first be healthy. In order to make the ecosystem within the body healthy, the natural ecosystem (terrestrial ecosystem) which is our living environment must be healthy. To this end, we must take care not to assault the natural ecosystem. In order to correctly judge whether something constitutes an assault on the natural ecosystem, we must have in our minds a notion of the cosmic ecosystem. What this means, in other words, is that we must correctly grasp and recognize the universal order. I believe that the universal order is none other than the principle of Yin and Yang; it is the wellspring of science.

The principle of Yin and Yang enables me to understand my own physical constitution. Unless one has at least a basic grasp of whether one's physical con-stitution is yin or yang, it is impossible to normally maintain and develop the ecosystem within one's own body. If someone who is yin eats a yin diet, undergoes yin treatment, lives a yin life, and does yin work, then he becomes increasingly yin, speeding the progression toward death. The outcome is the same when someone who is basically yang is biased toward yang. Someone who is yin should lead a life that is yang in proportion to his degree of yinness, while someone who is yang should lead a life that is yin in proportion to his yangness.

My body's ecosystem, which tended strongly to Yin, was neutralized by the yang nature of brown rice. A balance between Yin and Yang established itself. I became cured of illness and my physical condition improved. This improvement that doctors and drugs had been unable to achieve in the course of more than ten years was achieved with the greatest of ease through a Yin-Yang life style.

I realized that in the body's ecosystem, it is the stomach and bowels that serve as the real temple symbolizing health or lack of health. When the condition of the stomach and bowels is good, then one is in good health. When the stomach and bowels are in a poor condition, various problems and illnesses arise. The most important way to make the body's ecosystem sound and healthy is to make the ecosystem within the stomach and bowels sound and healthy.

This is why the ecosystem within the bowels must be made sound. In order for this to be possible, the intestinal flora must live healthy lives. This is why we must choose a diet and way of life that assures the health of the intestinal flora. Putting this in cruder terms, unless we choose a life and a life style that enables us to pass wonderfully healthy stools, the ecosystem within our body cannot be healthy and sound.

We live in an age today in which what leaves the body is already foul and dirty. This is an age in which human excrement must be flushed away with water or treated with chemicals. We have come to accept foreign substances that are poorly suited to the ecosystem within our bodies as food, and so must wash away our excrement with water or chemicals. In the same way that our intestinal system flushes out foreign matter as diarrhea, we have developed wastewater systems that treat our excrement as waste by washing it away with water. This today is an inseparable part of our daily lives.

When one adopts a brown rice diet, the activity of the intestinal bacteria increases. Intestinal gases are often discharged. One often gets diarrhea or constipation. Old matter and even stercoromas are eliminated. By then also making effective use of Yin-Yang judgment and, even if this seems a roundabout way, patiently chewing each bite of food without rushing or giving up, the living environment within the intestines gradually becomes orderly, allowing healthy intestinal flora to thrive and restoring the intestinal ecosystem to a normal state. I have observed that the very first effect of a brown rice diet is that it renders the intestinal ecosystem normal. Once you become better acquainted with the method of making Yin-Yang judgments, you learn how to tell, merely by examining your daily stools, if your life style and diet are having an unbalancing influence on your physical condition.

What should be done to convert weak, feeble people into strong, sturdy individuals within the constraints of our modern culture and way of life? It is clearly impossible to revert to the life style of the past. Nor can we all simply pick up and move to an environment in which there still exists a natural ecosystem free of all pollution. Whatever we do, it must obviously be something that we can do here and now.

Although passive, one method I would propose is to begin first by eating a diet and living a life that enables one to pass healthy stools. The very least we wish to do is to restore to our stomach and bowels a robust and healthy nature.

Driven by a desire to cure my daughter's and my illness, I made my family change its diet. That illness was a sign of God's love served to compel me to change our diet. Uncertain as to how to change my diet and what to eat, I clung blindly to brown rice as a drowning man grasps for a straw. But there is no need for anyone to change their diet blindly. By considering what type of food is most natural to the internal ecosystem and the intestinal flora, anyone ought to be able to change their diet naturally. The Yin-Yang approach to viewing and thinking of the world is a stethoscope for catching and listening in on the anger and joy of the intestinal bacteria. We are in an age where we must all change the way we eat. The ecosystems within each of us are furiously signaling this message out to us.

# The Yin and Yang of Macro and Micro

"Macro" is usually understood to mean very large, and "micro" to mean very small. Macro is yin and micro is yang.

I visited the macrocosmic world by undertaking "my voyage to life," and I visited the microcosmic world of the intestinal bacteria by journeying to the "ecosystem within the intestines." Modern science advances toward the macrocosmic world and toward the microcosmic world by expanding the fields of inquiry and development. There is no telling how far science will advance in the future. Because the fragmentation of science continues to narrow the purview of scientists to increasingly small areas of expertise, they don't appear to have a very good idea of where science is headed. This fragmentation has progressed to such an extent that mankind no longer is capable of properly controlling and integrating his inquiries. This function is being relegated to machines and, more specifically, computers. What this essentially amounts to is a renunciation of human ability.

We have invented the computer and put it to practical use. Some hold the view, which is quite understandable, that since this is a technology that we have invented and learned to utilize, what is wrong with using it to replace some of our own faculties? But substituting machinery for human faculties causes our primitive life faculties as organisms to regress. Impelled onward by their curiosity and ambition, scholars and scientists have eagerly set to work investigating and developing the world of the unknown. Devoting themselves entirely to the race at the leading edge of science, they leave it to the machines to bear the consequences of what they have done. I can't help feeling that today's technicians and scientists have become nothing more than machines for fabricating new data.

The reason that scientists have been praised to the skies up until now is that their inventions and discoveries have played a vital role in killing people and making money; their work has been invaluable to the military, to politicians, and to capitalists. However, scientists have almost always been tormented by a sense of regret. As one would have expected, scientists cried bitter tears of shame at the creation and proliferation of nuclear weapons, protesting that theoretical physics was never intended to be a discipline that creates atomic bombs and neutron bombs. But it was too late.

The day will come when scientists will again shed tears of shame, saying that all the test tube baby should have done was bring welcome tidings to infertile people. Although scientists anticipated that nuclear wastes might have somewhat of a detrimental effect on the natural ecosystem, they never thought that they would be handing down a terrestrial inferno to future generations; but here too, they are in for a rude awakening. Maybe I'm being a little blunt in saying so, but in view of all this one is left with the feeling that scientists have done nothing more than serve as tools for advancing human destruction and hastening the degradation of human faculties.

I can't help feeling that groups of scholars and scientists in the past have blurred the boundaries of the ecosystem and, giving full play to their curiosity and ambitions, have galloped ahead to these worlds of "macro" and "micro." They have consoled and flattered themselves with thoughts of their contributions to the advance of the human race, but in fact they have served as nothing more than temporary tools and cogs. Today, at last, scientists who understand this are emerging. New scientists are appearing whose greatest goal is to get a clear view of the world that man must not violate.

## Peace through an Exchange of Bodies and Hearts

Yesterday's and today's science has been largely a discipline devoted to making stronger weapons. The science of tomorrow is developing into a discipline that makes the heart a stronger weapon. I believe that the cosmic significance that the computer has given birth to is the potential for a state of preparedness in which the heart is turned into a weapon. Strategy in which nuclear missiles are deployed throughout the world is already passé. It is an old strategy that does nothing but disseminate waste, distrust, and fear. The new strategy of a new age should be one in which the heart serves as the weapon in place of nuclear arms. People themselves will serve as the missiles. I would like to call this *taishin heiki* (body and heart weapons). Let me give here one example of a *taishin heiki* strategy.

In our world today, a superficial state of peace is being maintained through the nuclear parity achieved by the two superpowers—the United States and the Soviet Union. However, this is only a semblance of peace achieved through suspicion, anxiety, and fear; it is not a peace attained through mutual trust and a sense of security. I believe that instead of deploying nuclear weapons, the U.S. should move the White House to Moscow and the U.S.S.R. should move the Kremlin to Washington, D.C. The top-ranking staff of both governments, including of course the respective heads of state and the national representatives, as well as the leading politicians and administrative officials, should become "human missiles" by being based within the other country and there performing their political and administrative functions. They would place themselves in the care of the other country, and there carry out their political and government work. In a sense, these would be voluntary hostages. Isn't this the best possible way of using the heart as a weapon for peace? Our computer and other state-of-the-art technology has been developed to a stage where this would be possible. Isn't it through God's will in fashioning the heart into a weapon for peace that modern science has advanced this far? Hasn't God allowed the material sciences to advance first in order that the preparations be made for achieving the highest mutual trust between peoples, and isn't he now imparting to humanity the ability to turn the heart into a weapon for peace? I believe that the day has come when man himself will become a missile. The age of a *taishin heiki* peace is here. I wish to correctly understand the significance of the advent of an age of material science in which someone can be anywhere at all in the world and still obtain news from around the world, issue orders, and carry out one's work. Are not we greeting a new age in which we shall all become naked and offer our hearts and bodies as missiles?

We should look forward to an age in which we shall see the birth of new scientists and, with this, the birth also of new political leaders. This is what I hope for.

# 6

## Brown Rice Macrobiotics

# Reading Your Own Fortune

In order to help you succeed with your brown rice diet, I must again turn to George Ohsawa for assistance. What I refer to here is his *Reading One's Own Life Fortune* (Japanese title: *Issho no unsei no hitori uranai*). This was the product of his sixty years of personal experience with the Unifying Principle and macrobiotics, and his forty years of experience in teaching people how to attain health and happiness. Why don't you read your own life's fortune by taking the Health and Happiness Test below? You should try taking the test first when you begin a brown rice diet, then once more after you've been on a brown rice diet for a month. I am certain that you will be amazed by the results when you again take the test a year, three years, and ten years after commencing this diet. The test can determine whether your macrobiotic diet is succeeding or not and if indeed your luck has turned for the better. In my case, the results were very negative when I began a brown rice diet. I was in a totally pessimistic state. The score was so low that I'm ashamed to report it here. But as time passed, I was amazed at the good turn that my fortune was taking. My luck and degree of happiness improved in proportion with my health. Unless one's physical and mental health both improve and lead in turn to good fortune and happiness, then what one practices is not a true way to attain health. It will not do for just the body to be strong while the mind is poor and sick. Both the body and mind must be healthy and happy. Ohsawa's Health and Happiness Test measures the current level of physical and mental well-being and predicts the future.

Well then, please grab a pen and fill in the answers below while keeping an eye on the clock.

---

### P.U. Health and Happiness Test
### —How to Read Your Own Fortune in 40 Minutes—

---

*Directions:*   Spend 10 minutes each on parts A, B, C, and D.

A.   Worth up to 20 points.
   (1)   Circle one of items 1 through 13.
   (2)   Write out a one- or two-line response to (2), (3), and (4).
   Each of the above four items is worth 5 points.

B.   30 points.
   Items 1–3 are worth 2 points each.
   Items 4–6 are worth 3 points each.
   Item 7 is worth 15 points.

C.   30 points.
   Give yourself a half-point each for the first 20 "yes" answers and one point for each additional "yes" answer.

D.   20 points.
   A perfect score is 100 points. Take a look at the time and begin at once.

## A. Outlook on Life

(1)  Which of the following best characterizes your outlook on life? Circle the most appropriate answer.

1.  I wish to devote my life to the world and to people.
2.  Life is a mystery. What will be will be.
3.  Life is like traveling a long road laden with a heavy burden. Want and deprivation are constant companions.
4.  Set your mind to something and you will succeed.
5.  Live a short, rich, and happy life.
6.  Walk a straight and proper road as a person.
7.  Live a good life filled with joy and wonder.
8.  Strive for the happiness of one's parents, husband, wife, and children.
9.  Be a good wife and wise mother.
10.  Rise up in the world and become a prominent person.
11.  Become a millionaire or billionaire.
12.  Live a life free of want.
13.  God helps those who help themselves.

(2)  What do you wish to accomplish in this world?
(3)  What is the most difficult thing that you have ever dealt with alone?
(4)  What was the happiest thing that ever happened to you?

## B. Health

Grade yourself on the seven conditions of health:

1.  No fatigue (2 points)
2.  Good appetite (2)
3.  Sound sleep (2)
4.  Good memory (2)
5.  Incredibly good humor (2)
6.  Precision in thought and action (2)
7.  Never tell a lie (2)

## C. Life style

1.  Do you keep your promises?
2.  Do you avoid giving excuses and justifying yourself?
3.  Are you trusted by many people?
4.  Are you loved by many people?
5.  Are you punctual?
6.  Do you enjoy doing things for others?
7.  Do you enjoy speeding up everything that you do?
8.  Are you good at finding things?
9.  Do you keep calm and cool?
10.  Do you enjoy reading and seeing movies?
11.  Do you like poetry and songs?

12. Do you like to keep things neat and clean?
13. Do you keep from damaging or breaking things?
14. Are you one who doesn't complain or whine?
15. Are you free of preferences?
16. Do you enjoy tackling difficult problems?
17. Do you enjoy traveling?
18. Do you like meeting people?
19. Do you enjoy taking care of sick people?
20. Are you afraid of few things?
21. Are many people receptive to what you have to say?
22. Have you been able to inspire those about you first?
23. Are you free of capriciousness?
24. Do you enjoy talking?
25. Are you good at listening?
26. Do you have a faith?
27. Was your father strict?
28. Was your mother a hard worker?
29. Do you have many siblings?
30. Do you take part in any social movements?
31. Do you answer at once when spoken to?
32. Does your answer have a pleasant rhythm to it?
33. Does your voice have a pleasant ring to it?
34. Do you immediately carry out what you think is good?
35. Do you always check things first-hand before making a decision?
36. Can you successfully grasp, use, and cultivate new thinking, technology, people, and issues?
37. Do you have a sense of humor?
38. Are you free of bad habits?
39. Do you worry needlessly over the future?
40. Are you free of discontent, regrets, the habit of cursing, and hatred?

## D.  Insight

$$C/B = ?$$

So what's your score? Go ahead and announce your score without being ashamed. Of course, because I myself lacked a sense of self-respect, I cannot compel you to do so. But George Ohsawa is impatient to see what you got. Look how he awaits with bated breath:

> "What? You mean you didn't give yourself a score? You're a person who lives a dry, humorless existence.
> "You think this is a boring exercise? You must be someone who has passed a life without experiencing youth.
> "You got a score of 0? Do you mean to say that you flunked? You're living a gloomy life. You've been eating too much fruit, sugar, sweets, drinks, potatoes.

154

"You're not going to take part? My God! What a proud, arrogant person you are. I see that you don't believe in self-criticism, introspection, self-improvement, and dedicated do-or-die effort. You have never experienced burning passion or maddening love; you have never found work or a lover to which you would devote your entire life. How sorry I feel for you!

"Everyone now, come along! Let me sing you a song of Walt Whitman's. Then let me take you to 'The World of Freedom and Happiness' of which Whitman sings."

George Ohsawa has devoted his entire life to leading others to this "world of freedom and happiness." I am but one person who was saved by him. This road to salvation was not filled only with tranquil, pleasure-filled days. There were also days of hardship and pain, days of sorrow and sadness, days in which I had no idea what I should do. On days like this, I would always hum Ohsawa's Whitman-inspired song below. Why don't you try singing it too. It's a song toward a world of freedom and happiness.

Song of the Open Road (inspired by poem of same title by Walt Whitman)

It's a wide open road that goes on
Without right or left and without end.
Let us start off, then.
Yes, let's be on our way!

Do not cry or whimper.
We have no need for books or work.
And money is immaterial.
Money is immaterial!

Everyone, come follow me.
See how many stars there are!
And look at the mountains and the seas.
Just look at the mountains and the seas!

The birds are singing. The sky is blue.
How can we complain?
We are all children.
We are all children!

It's a wide open road without end.
God and life and strength,
Wisdom and freedom are all mine!

Well, in order to set out on the road to "a world of freedom and happiness" full of confidence and conviction, let me comment here on how to interpret the Health and Happiness Test.

# Interpreting the Health and Happiness Test (HHT)

(1) Any one of parts A, B, C, and D can determine one's fortune. A and D are worth a maximum of 20 points each, while B and C are worth a maximum of 30 points each. Even just one of items (1)–(4) in part A is enough to determine one's fortune. Those people whose life view is not expressed in one of choices 1–13 may write in a more appropriate response.

(2) You can score part B by yourself. The criteria for doing so are as follows.

*Condition 1:* If you always have the energy of a lion about to pounce on its prey, and if you are able to continue doing close, detailed work hour after hour, day after day, year after year without getting a stiff neck, then you get 2 points. Those who catch colds and those under 50 years of age who wear glasses get 0 points. Women between the ages of 14 and 49 whose periods don't come exactly on the 28th day and who experience discharge for more than 3 days running or suffer menstrual pain or other complications get no points. No points for people under 50 years of age with white hair, people who are married but have no children, and people who were unable to marry until age 30. Anyone who claims that it is impossible for anyone never to get tired also receives no points here.

*Condition 2:* Two points for anyone who finds rice delicious and who does not care what the side dishes are. People who, in the absence of side dishes, would be content to have just salt and water with their rice also get 2 points.

*Conditions 3:* Two points for those who are sound asleep within 3 minutes after they turn in, those whose heads remain on the pillow while asleep, those who do not awake to go to the bathroom, those who have no dreams, those who awake easily (and who don't oversleep more than 5 minutes), those who don't talk in their sleep, those who wake up exactly at the time they want to and are done washing their face within 3 minutes, those who are still in the same position when they wake up as they were when they fell asleep, those who do not doze off during the day, those who do not feel sleepy while driving, and those over twenty years of age for whom four hours of sleep each night is enough.

*Condition 4:* No points for those who are forgetful.

*Condition 5:* Three points for those who make others happy and give them feelings of pleasure.

*Condition 6:* Three points for people who are always neatly dressed, stylishly attired or chic, whose underwear is clean, whose hands and feet are clean, whose beard and moustache are neatly trimmed (men), whose hair is neatly combed or arranged, whose minds are clear, whose closets, drawers, desktops, pockets, and bookcases are orderly and well arranged, who do not leave things on the top of their desks, who keep the house clean, who keep things polished (not from long use), who keep the windows clean, who must keep things in order whether at someone else's house or in a vehicle (wherever they go or stop for the night). All other people, such as those who are unable to budget or plan, housewives whose personal accounts at the end of the month are two days late or more—in short, all individuals who are not neat and precise in thought and action receive no points.

*Condition 7:* Become a miracle worker. Play the Universal Principle game. That is, acquire the habit of applying the ▽ △ formula at once to all problems and puzzles by carrying out macrobiotics. This is the manifestation to absolute justice; the secret for enjoying unlimited freedom and everlasting happiness, and for living one's life to the utmost. This the key condition for those who embody justice. Justice is the order of the universe; there are no lies or falsehood in the universal order. Fifteen points for the above.

(3)  You can grade part C by yourself. However, all those who gave themselves a half point each for items 1–20 and one point each for items 21–40 get 0 points for not following directions. Those with up to 20 "yes" responses get a half point each; those with 21 to 30 "yes" responses get 10 points for 20 of the "yes" answers and 1 point for each additional "yes" response starting with the 21st (thus, someone with 28 "yes" answers gets 18 points). Those with more than 30 "yes" responses get 20 points for the first thirty "yes" answers and 1 point for each additional "yes." Those with 40 "yes" answers get all 30 points for this part of the test.

(4)  Part D is the most difficult portion of the test. Ohsawa says that anyone able to do just this will do okay on parts A, B, and C as well. In order to solve this problem, you will have to keep a macrobiotic brown rice diet and read all of Ohsawa's writings. The answer can be found somewhere in his works. Good luck!

## First Begin by Gaining Health and Freedom

The aim of democracy and the physiological basis of freedom is physical and mental health. This is extremely important, so I shall quote directly from Ohsawa here.

> Those people who did not get 100 points on the HHT must begin by finding the principle of health, freedom, and happiness. However, one must not speak of health, freedom, and happiness in visionary or utopian tones; it is all a lie unless one actually acquires these.
>
>   Democracy is a social arrangement whereby people carefully protect each other's freedom and happiness. At first, this may seem at odds with such notions as the law of the jungle and the struggle for survival, but such is not the case. Democracy is like a rule of fair play, according to which everyone is given an equal opportunity; the struggle for survival and the law of the jungle take place on top of this. That is why, if one fails to first acquire the principles of freedom, health, and happiness, one is unable to live idly no matter how democratic the society in which one lives.
>
>   I can assure you that, no matter how happy and free they may now appear to be, those people who scored below 100 on the HHT, and especially those who scored about 40 or less, will soon experience misery. At the same time, allow me to show those people who aspire to reach 100 points, or at least 80 points, how they can do so as soon as possible....

First there is health. What I mean by health is someone who fulfills the 7 conditions for health given in part B of the HHT. It is possible to identify someone who fulfills these 7 conditions by looking at the soles of their shoes or sandals. The amount of wear in the soles should be horizontally balanced across the surface of the sole. Such a person would score at least 80 points on the HHT. Those whose soles are worn down more toward the heel or toe of the shoes underwent a decline in health at least ten years ago. In people whose soles are worn unequally across the width of the shoe and those in which the front and back of the sole are worn on opposite (right and left) sides of the foot, this is a sign that they lost their health at least 15 years ago. People who walk noisily are indisposed in some way.

Let me show you then how to get perfect scores on parts A, B, C, and D of the HHT. Even the doubting Thomases must persevere for at least 10 days. In no way will doing so be to your detriment. If you stick with the simple rules I outline below for even one month, you will surely come to realize the importance of what I have done for these forty years. To satisfy these conditions and obtain a perfect score, I do not use expensive medications, painful operations, unpleasant hospital stays, or difficult and demanding ascetic practices. All that is required is that the diet be corrected. This will not raise the food costs; in fact, food costs will come down. . . .

Chew your food properly. Keep your fluid intake down to a level where you pass urine about 3–5 times a day (24 hours). Make your food staple whole grains and keep your non-staple secondary foods to a minimum. Cut out all between-meal snacks. Take no white sugar. You will feel for yourself the amazing results that can be had by following these few simple rules.

(The above excerpts are taken from Ohsawa's *A New Theory of Nutrition and Its Therapeutic Effects*; Japanese title: *Shin-shokuyo ryoho*.)

## What Is Genmai?

The character 'gen' (玄) in "genmai" has a number of meanings in Japanese, including "black," "the color of the heavens," a "reddish-black color," "the heavens," "profound truth" and "something that is subtle and profound." Additional meanings ascribed to this character include "first" and "source."

The character 'mai' (米) in "genmai" is generally rendered in dictionaries as: rice itself and the seed or fruit of the rice plant.

Based on these explanations, "genmai" means "black rice," "rice that has not been polished," "unpolished rice from which only the hull has been removed." This understanding of genmai when perceived as a substance should be adequate.

But genmai is far more than just this; it is more than what is described in the dictionaries. Referring to my own personal experiences, I will show now the awesome mystical powers with which genmai is endowed.

I offer my own personal interpretation here, although this is based, of course, on the definitions given in the dictionaries. After eating genmai, I arrived at a new and greater understanding of this food.

I shall describe genmai here as "a food within which lies concealed the energy and vitality of a chaotic universe." I use the expression "chaotic universe" here to refer to the infinite, dark world of nothingness; the world in which Yin and Yang are united as one; the world that gave birth to our finite world. The ancients may perhaps have endowed "genmai" with a deeper meaning. Let me describe now how I arrived at this understanding of genmai.

"Genmai" is more than just a title conferred as a symbol to the seed of the rice plant from which only the hull has been removed. You will surely come to understand this if you eat genmai correctly. If at the same time you earnestly and enthusiastically study Ohsawa's *The Universal Principle* and *The Order of the Universe*, you will come away convinced that genmai is more than just a foodstuff.

I understand "rice" in the following sense. I shall explain this using only the concepts of Yin ($\nabla$) and Yang ($\triangle$) that one learns from the Universal Principle.

(1)   Heaven and Earth, Up and Down:

$$\frac{\uparrow \text{ Heaven}=\text{Up}=\text{Yin } (\nabla)}{\downarrow \text{ Earth}=\text{Down}=\text{Yang } (\triangle)}$$

*Note:*   Some schools of thought interpret Heaven as being Yang and Earth as being Yin. This is a difference of opinion; please investigate for yourself which interpretation is more valid.

(2)   Left and Right:

$$\begin{array}{c|c} \longleftarrow & \longrightarrow \\ \text{left} & \text{right} \\ \| & \| \\ \text{Yin} & \text{Yang} \\ \nabla & \triangle \end{array}$$

(3)   Up and Down, Left and Right:

$$\begin{array}{c|c} \begin{array}{c}\text{Yin}\\ \times\\ \text{Yin}\end{array} & \begin{array}{c}\text{Yang}\\ \times\\ \text{Yin}\end{array} \\ \hline \begin{array}{c}\text{Yang}\\ \times\\ \text{Yin}\end{array} & \begin{array}{c}\text{Yang}\\ \times\\ \text{Yang}\end{array} \end{array} \rightarrow \begin{array}{c|c} \nabla\times\nabla & \nabla\times\triangle \\ \hline \triangle\times\nabla & \triangle\times\triangle \end{array}$$

(1), (2), and (3) above are two-dimensional representations. Let us now rearrange these as follows:

$$\begin{array}{ccc|cc} \nabla\times\nabla \rightarrow \blacktriangledown & \nabla\!\!\!\triangledown & \leftarrow \nabla\times\triangle \\ \hline \triangle\times\nabla \rightarrow \triangle\!\!\!\triangledown & \blacktriangle & \leftarrow \triangle\times\triangle \end{array}$$

By simply dividing a flat, blank surface into up and down, left and right with two straight lines, we get four different regions. If we do the same with a solid such as a sphere, what shapes can we imagine will result? And what will happen if we then try blowing some *ki* into this?

(4)

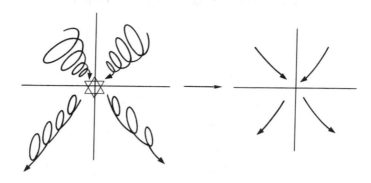

Although I am unable to graphically represent the phenomenon of *ki* in a solid or sphere, I can imagine in my mind how the "ki" of Yin and Yang interact and flow. If one considers centripetal forces as acting at the core of the sphere and centrifugal forces as acting at the periphery, then one can imagine the flow of *ki* as occurring in the manner shown in (4) above. If the nature of yin *ki* and yang *ki* are included, then not only the movement of *ki* within each of the four divided regions, but the direction of the united flow of this *ki* can also be perceived.

(5)   The Chinese character for rice, 米, is written starting with Yin and ending with Yang.

|   1   |   2   |   3   |   4   |   5   |   6   |
|-------|-------|-------|-------|-------|-------|
|   丶   |   ⺍   |   ⺞   |   半   |   米   |   米   |

I am convinced that the character for rice (米) symbolizes the universe and the flow of *ki*. Why should I feel this way? Because genmai has an incredible vitality. If the great *ki* of the universe were not concentrated in genmai, then genmai would certainly not have the amazing power it has. It is surely because the ancients understood this that they assigned the symbol to the fruit of the gramineous rice plant.

Let us explore now whether genmai truly has an awesome and mysterious power.

Through my own meager experiences, I was able to learn just how wonderful genmai is. But for a long time I had no way of knowing how and from where the life and vitality of genmai came. It was George Ohsawa who finally taught me this through his writings. He gave me a ticket for a journey toward life. This may have been in part a reward for the earnestness with which I continued to eat genmai. Ohsawa bestows lots of unexpected jewels upon everyone. The presents he gives seem to change in proportion to the degree with which one continues to properly eat genmai. He gave me a ticket for a journey.

## The Internal Structure of Brown Rice

Fig. 6.1 is a longitudinal cross-section of a grain of rice. Fine starch granules are present at the periphery and center of the rice, making for a structure that is truly superb even in an architectural sense.

## Fig. 6.1  Longitudinal cross-section of genmai.

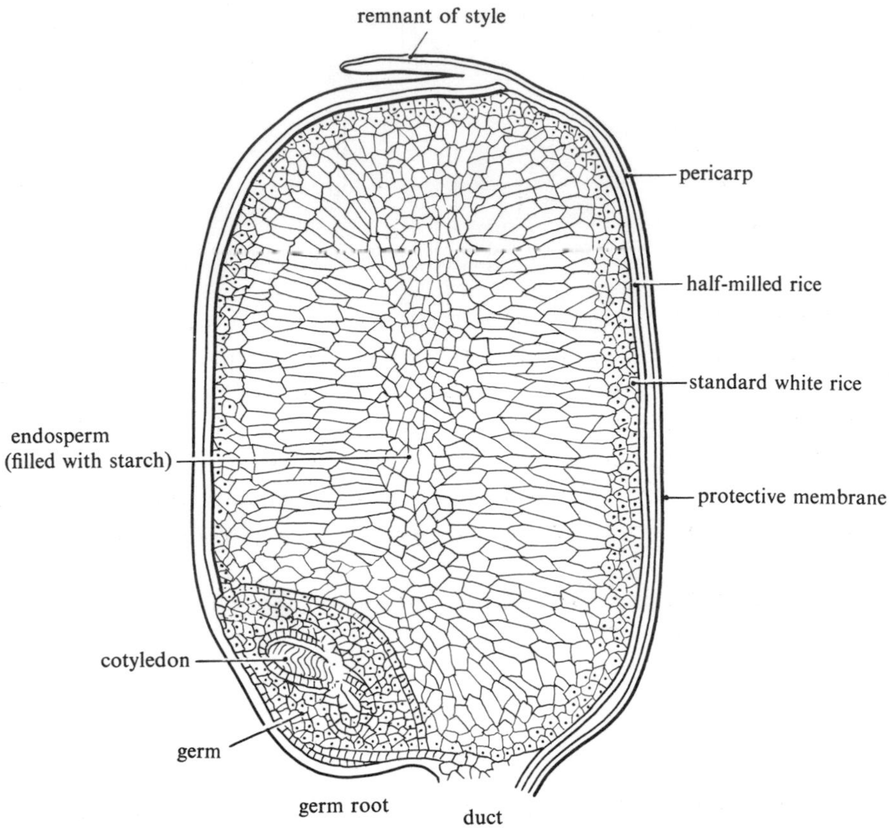

As shown in this illustration, rice ("kome" in Japanese) consists mostly of a starch ("ko") portion; off to one side there is also a germ ("me") portion. The combination of the two ("ko"+"me") gives "kome," which is carefully wrapped in six layers.

The outermost layer is the protective layer discovered by Chohei Sato. This has an extraordinary chemical composition that resists attack even by sulfuric acid, nitric acid, hydrochloric acid, caustic soda, benzene, and hydrofluoric acid. When this layer is marred or ruptured, the underlying layer comes into contact with air. As a result, in the summer, the color of the rice turns bad, the quality degenerates, and the rice becomes unpalatable and loses its nutritional value.

The region between the epicarp and the Klebel layer contains protein, fat, vitamins, and the exceedingly important inorganic salts. Indeed, this portion contains what could be called "the source of life."

## The Seven Stages of Rice

In order to better understand where genmai stands in relation to other rice, I have divided rice into the following seven stages according to the degree of polishing.

As is clear from Fig. 2.4 in chapter 2, genmai is unpolished rice from which only the hull has been removed.

In Fig. 2.4, genmai can be seen to have a hard pericarp on the exterior; this is then followed on the inside by a seed coat and an aleurone layer. At the very interior is the endosperm, to which is attached the germ.

The pericarp, seed coat, and aleurone layer together comprise the bran layers. This portion of the rice grain contains various nutrients of inestimable value.

Rice bran is used in many ways. Among its primary applications are drugs, edible oils, fertilizers, animal feeds, detergents, and cosmetics, but its uses extend far beyond just these. Rice bran oil in particular is a very high-grade oil that is rich in linolic acid. Drug components such as vitamins extracted from bran are of excellent quality, demonstrating that rice bran truly excels in nutrients.

What eating milled rice essentially boils down to is the throwing away of the precious and irreplaceable nutrients in the bran and the germ.

The first time that I heard the word 'genmai,' I asked what it meant. I thought that all rice was white rice. I suspect that many people feel this way because people usually ask the same question as I did.

"What's genmai?"

"Is genmai a kind of rice?"

"Can you eat genmai?"

It's really not surprising. Because people have been eating white rice for so long, they've got a fixed notion of rice as being white rice. Moreover, with the establishment of a food distribution system that has made it almost impossible to purchase anything but white rice and the treatment of rice in nutritional theory as nutrient-depleted white rice rather than nutrient-rich brown rice, a life style according to which rice was properly eaten vanished at some point.

Today, we are at last being awakened to real life. We are starting to see for ourselves the amazing vigor and power of brown rice. Through personal experience, people are beginning to realize that genmai has the life-force or vitality that is lost in polishing rice, and that this vitality greatly strengthens the vitality of the human body.

It is said that the value of genmai lies in the bran and the germ portions of the rice kernel. This has given rise to unfortunate misunderstandings. Many people reason that if most of the nutrients in rice exist in the bran and germ, then why not eat white rice as white rice and prepare the bran and germ in a form that readily lends itself to consumption? By so doing, they claim, the bran and germ can be eaten much as if one had eaten genmai in the first place. True, if one thinks only in terms of nutritional value, this argument is generally sound. However, from the standpoint of vitality, this is clearly mistaken.

Genmai must be eaten as genmai.

It should be clear from the above table just where genmai stands in relation to milled rice.

There is something else of great importance that I would like you to know about: the practice of eating just-hulled genmai. This consists of taking genmai that has been stored with the hulls intact and removing the hulls from the grains just before use, then cooking the freshly hulled genmai.

The nutritive value and vitality of rice varies greatly depending on how the rice is stored. Rice that has been stored in its hulls can be preserved for over ten years without losing its flavor, nutritional value, or vitality. In fact, the claim has been made that rice can be stored in this fashion for decades.

The length of time that genmai can be stored is greatly shortened when the hulls are removed. Even so, because the rice grains themselves have not been damaged or treated, the nutritional value and vitality of the rice can still be maintained for quite a long time. When stored at a cool temperature and under conditions conducive to the preservation of genmai, the rice remains alive.

The question of why storage with the bran intact is desirable is an important one for the Universal Principle. Why don't you try solving this problem yourself based on what you have learned already?

In addition to unhulled rice and brown rice, of course, quarter-milled rice, half-milled rice, and even white rice all respire. In fact, they do more than just respire. They constantly carry out an exchange of electrical and magnetic signals. All things in this world are connected with the cosmic *ki* (the energy or life-force of Yin and Yang).

What sort of signal exchange does unhulled rice have with the cosmic *ki*? And what about brown rice? Quarter-milled rice? Half-milled rice? Three-quarter-milled rice? Milled rice with the germ attached? White rice? Try pondering and experimenting with rice at each of these levels. Although it is certainly useful to know the differences in the nutrients of rice at all these levels, the most important question is that of vitality or life-force. Which type of rice is endowed with the greatest amount of cosmic vitality? Rice at which of these levels has the structure and mechanisms allowing it to possess and preserve the most vitality? It should be clear at once from this that just-hulled genmai which has been protected by the hull is the ultimate food.

**Fig. 6.2  Structure of an unhulled rice grain.**

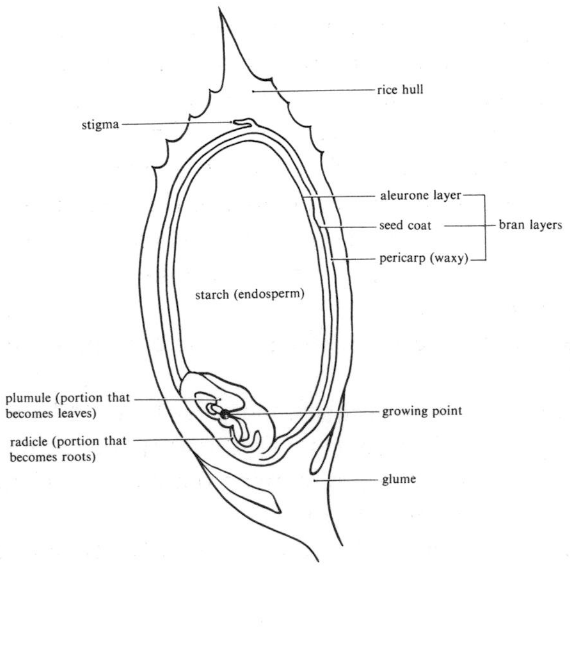

# American Rice and Japanese Rice

Today, rice is grown in all parts of the world. Rice and wheat are the leading cereal grains. Although both are cereal grains, rice and wheat differ radically in their properties and components. Let us examine how they differ by applying the Universal Principle.

There even exist subtle differences in the composition and flavor of rice depending on such factors as where it is grown, the climate and terrain, the variant, and the method of culvitation. Rice apparently is divided into two broad types: *indica* and *japonica*. Indica rice has long, slender grains that are not very glutinuous, whereas japonica rice is rounder and highly glutinous. These are the major differences. Differences in the climate and terrain of the producing area are manifested in these two widely differing characteristics, but the people indigenous to those areas are accustomed to eating the rice that grows there and find it delicious. What is true here for humans applies as well to organisms in general: the consumption as food of products grown in one's area or habitat is most fitting physically and mentally, tastes best, and is best for the health. That is why it makes no sense to ask which type of rice is better and which is worse. Each type of rice is extremely valuable in its own right as a food for the area where it is cultivated and the people who grow it.

Although rice can be broadly divided into these two subspecies, indica and japonica, countless cultivars have emerged from each. Because rice is such an outstanding foodstuff, man has constantly sought to genetically improve the rice plant; today, an enormous number of different rice varieties exist throughout the world. It is astonishing that, in spite of the presence of such a large number of varieties, no extreme differences exist in the composition or taste of the rice itself. This may very well be one reason why rice is a major foodstuff of man.

In 1973, I took a trip to the United States. I ate brown rice throughout my travels there, and found the brown rice in all these places delicious. California-grown rice in particular tasted just as delicious as the Japanese rice that I was used to. Compared with rice grown by natural farming or organic farming, rice grown with the use of lots of pesticides and chemical fertilizers is inferior in taste and has a less salubrious effect on the body, regardless of whether the rice is grown in Japan, the United States, or anywhere else in the world.

The largest problem we face today is the question of how environmental pollution resulting from industrial contaminants and the widespread use of chemical pesticides and fertilizers is affecting the quality of rice. Depending on the degree of such contamination, there arises the concern that some of the rice grown may not be fit for consumption. We have reached an age in which we must assure with the greatest of care the suitability of the growing environment and method of cultivation for the food that we eat. This is how I see things.

I have before me now a U.S. Food Composition Chart, which is edited and put out by the U.S. Department of Agriculture's Office of Agricultural Research, and the Fourth Revised Chart of Standard Ingredients in Japanese Foods, edited and published by the Japanese Science and Technology Agency's National Institute of Resources. Nothing is indicated concerning where the rice for which data is given in these tables was grown in each country and the method of cultivation used. It is

Table 6.1  Composition of U.S. and Japanese rice.

| Food product | | Moisture content % | Energy kcal | Protein g | Lipids g | Carbo-hydrates Total g | Fiber g | Ash g | Calcium mg | Phosphorus mg | Iron mg | Sodium mg | Potassium mg | Vitamin A I.U. | Thiamine mg | Riboflavin mg | Niacin mg | Ascorbic acid mg |
|---|---|---|---|---|---|---|---|---|---|---|---|---|---|---|---|---|---|---|
| U.S. | Brown rice (raw) | 12.0 | 360 | 7.5 | 1.9 | 77.4 | 0.9 | 1.2 | 32 | 221 | 1.6 | 9 | 214 | (0) | 0.34 | 0.05 | 4.7 | (0) |
| Japan | Brown rice (raw) | 15.5 | 351 | 7.4 | 3.0 | 71.8 | 1.0 | 1.3 | 10 | 300 | 1.1 | 2 | 250 | (0) | / | / | / | (0) |
| U.S. | Brown rice (cooked) | 70.3 | 119 | 2.5 | 0.6 | 25.5 | 0.3 | 1.1 | 12 | 73 | 0.5 | 282 | 70 | (0) | 0.09 | 0.02 | 1.4 | (0) |
| Japan | Brown rice (cooked) | 63.0 | 153 | 3.3 | 1.3 | 31.4 | 0.4 | 0.6 | 4 | 130 | 0.5 | 2 | 110 | (0) | / | / | / | (0) |
| U.S. | White rice (fully milled, unenriched and raw) | 12.0 | 363 | 6.7 | 0.4 | 80.4 | 0.3 | 0.5 | 24 | 94 | 0.8 | 5 | 92 | (0) | 0.07 | 0.03 | 1.6 | (0) |
| Japan | White rice (unenriched and raw) | 15.5 | 356 | 6.8 | 1.3 | 75.5 | 0.3 | 0.6 | 6 | 140 | 0.5 | 2 | 110 | (0) | / | / | / | (0) |
| U.S. | White rice (fully milled, unenriched and cooked) | 72.6 | 109 | 2.0 | 0.1 | 24.2 | 0.1 | 1.1 | 10 | 28 | 0.2 | 374 | 28 | (0) | 0.02 | 0.01 | 0.4 | (0) |
| Japan | White rice (milled white rice, cooked) | 65.0 | 148 | 2.6 | 0.5 | 31.7 | 0.1 | 0.1 | 2 | 30 | 0.1 | 2 | 27 | (0) | / | / | / | (0) |
| Japan | Diluted rice gruel Brown rice | 91.5 | 35 | 0.7 | 0.3 | 7.3 | 0.1 | 0.1 | 1 | 30 | 0.1 | 2 | 25 | (0) | / | / | / | 0 |
| | Half-milled rice | 91.5 | 36 | 0.7 | 0.2 | 7.4 | 0.1 | 0.1 | 0 | 12 | 0 | 2 | 10 | (0) | / | / | / | 0 |
| | Three-quarter-milled rice | 91.5 | 36 | 0.7 | 0.2 | 7.5 | 0 | 0.1 | 0 | 10 | 0 | 2 | 9 | (0) | / | / | / | 0 |
| Japan | Rice gruel soup Brown rice | 93.5 | 27 | 0.5 | 0.2 | 5.7 | 0 | 0.1 | 0 | 20 | 0 | 2 | 19 | (0) | / | / | / | 0 |
| | Half-milled rice | 93.5 | 27 | 0.5 | 0.1 | 5.8 | 0 | 0.1 | 0 | 9 | 0 | 2 | 8 | (0) | / | / | / | 0 |
| | Three-quarter-milled rice | 93.5 | 27 | 0.5 | 0.1 | 5.8 | 0 | 0.1 | 0 | 7 | 0 | 2 | 7 | (0) | / | / | / | 0 |

not clear whether this is rice grown by natural farming methods, whether it is organically grown rice, or whether it is rice grown with pesticides, chemical fertilizers, and heavy equipment. One cannot determine from this data alone the differences in components resulting from different farming methods. Hence, I decided to study American rice and Japanese rice based only on the values given in these tables, without taking into consideration the respective growing methods or conditions.

Let us begin first by examining the raw brown rice (rows A and B). Since we are studying the Universal Principle of Yin and Yang, please take an especially close look at the sodium and potassium columns that best represent these properties.

Now look at the entries under "cooked brown rice." "Cooked rice," of course, means rice that has been cooked for consumption. We can see here that an astonishingly large difference emerges between raw and cooked brown rice. Especially remarkable is the discrepancy in the levels of sodium (Na) and potassium (K) before and after cooking. In fact, the changes are so large that one is tempted to ask whether these values aren't mistaken. I myself thought at first that this was due to misprints in the data.

| Sodium | Raw brown rice | Cooked brown rice |
|---|---|---|
| U.S. | 9 mg | 282 mg |
| Japan | 2 mg | 2 mg |

| Potassium | Raw brown rice | Cooked brown rice |
|---|---|---|
| U.S. | 9 mg | 282 mg |
| Japan | 2 mg | 2 mg |

Now let us take a look at the sodium-potassium ratios of each.

Na: K Ratio of Raw Brown Rice

| | Na | K | Na: K |
|---|---|---|---|
| U.S. rice | 9 mg | 214 mg | 1: 24 |
| Japanese rice | 2 mg | 250 mg | 1: 125 |

So the ratio of sodium to potassium is 1: 24 in U.S. rice and 1: 125 in Japanese rice. Although this is only a simple comparison, one could say that U.S. rice has a more yang composition. What about cooked brown rice?

Na: K Ratio of Cooked Brown Rice

| | Na | K | Na: K |
|---|---|---|---|
| U.S. rice | 282 mg | 70 mg | 1: 0.24 |
| Japanese rice | 2 mg | 110 mg | 1: 55 |

Judging from these numbers alone, when U.S. rice is cooked, the level of sodium rises enormously. This large increase with respect to raw rice can only be due to the addition of sodium during cooking. Merely adding water to raw brown rice

166

and heating and cooking the rice could not possibly result in an increase in just the sodium content. This value can only be explained by the addition, for whatever reason, of sodium or some substance that changes into sodium during cooking.

The same is true of white rice. Please look now at rows E through H.

| Sodium | Raw white rice | Cooked white rice |
|---|---|---|
| U.S. | 5 mg | 374 mg |
| Japan | 2 mg | 2 mg |

The sodium content of Japanese white rice is the same as that of Japanese brown rice. What can the significance of this be? In the case of U.S. rice, the sodium content in raw brown rice is 9 mg. This is 5 mg in completely milled white rice, but rises to 374 mg in cooked rice. The only possible explanation for such a rise is the addition of something when the rice is cooked.

What about the potassium level and the Na: K ratio? Let us examine these for white rice as we did above for brown rice.

| Potassium | Raw white rice | Cooked white rice |
|---|---|---|
| U.S. | 92 mg | 28 mg |
| Japan | 110 mg | 27 mg |

Na: K Ratio of Raw White Rice

| | Na | K | Na: K |
|---|---|---|---|
| U.S. rice | 5 mg | 92 mg | 1: 18.4 |
| Japanese rice | 2 mg | 110 mg | 1: 55 |

Na: K Ratio of Cooked Brown Rice

| | Na | K | Na: K |
|---|---|---|---|
| U.S. rice | 374 mg | 28 mg | 1: 0.07 |
| Japanese rice | 2 mg | 27 mg | 1: 13.5 |

The most striking feature of the above data is the sharp increase in the sodium content of U.S. rice when the rice is cooked.

At first, I had intended to simply compare the composition of U.S. rice with that of Japanese rice. When raw, little difference is apparent in the values for either brown rice or white rice. For the most part, the figures fall within a reasonable range. However, the sodium values for cooked rice in the U.S. are clearly anomalous. These high sodium levels cannot be disregarded if the object of eating rice is to improve one's health or to treat illness.

As I have already indicated, the Na: K ratio in healthy blood is said to be 1: 5. For this reason, a life style in which the Na: K ratio in one's daily meals is brought as close as possible to 1: 5 is ideal. Moreover, it is desirable that the Na: K ratio in the staple food also be 1: 5. One of the most important reasons why a brown rice diet is good for the body is that the Na: K ratio in brown rice is close to that in the blood.

No data for rows (I) and (J) was found in the U.S. Food Composition Chart, so only Japanese data is presented here.

The Na: K ratio for diluted rice gruel prepared from half-milled rice was 1: 5, the Na: K ratio for rice gruel soup prepared from half-milled rice was 1: 4, and the Na: K ratio for rice gruel soup prepared from three-quarter-milled rice was 1: 3.5. Thus, diluted rice gruel and rice gruel soup prepared with brown rice, half-milled rice, and three-quarter-milled rice is highly ideal food.

Let us return now to the main subject at hand. We know from the composition table above that when rice is cooked in the U.S., the sodium level increases abnormally.

Because people in the United States already consume large quantities of animal-based foods, they should avoid ways of preparing rice that increase its sodium content. Taking in an excess of sodium in meat and other animal-based foods and also in rice produces a craving for the potassium available from sweetened foods, fruit, nonalcoholic cold beverages (soda, fruit juices, iced tea and coffee, etc.), ice cream, and other refrigerated sweets. Overindulgence in foods such as these create what we refer to generically as the degenerative diseases associated with modern civilization, such as cancer, heart disease, high blood pressure, diabetes, neuralgia, an allergy-prone physical constitution, and obesity.

I believe that the analytic values for rice in the U.S. Food Composition Chart are the results of the use of a certain type of cooked rice. I asked my wife, who is also an experienced cook, about this.

"When rice in America is cooked, the level of sodium in the rice increases. What do you make of that?"

"If you ask me," she answered, "I suspect, first of all, that people are adding salt to the rice when they cook it. A second reason might have to do with the type of water used for cooking in America. A third possibility is that an atomic transformation takes place within certain components of rice and water due to the effect of fire and pressure, causing these to turn to sodium."

Since the only possibility I had considered was that sodium is added during cooking, my wife's comments were a great help. As she suggests, it is important also to have a proper understanding of the differences in the water in localities with varying soils. One reason that meat-eating developed in the West and a more vegetarian diet developed in the East may be that soil in the West is alkaline, and so the weather and physiography in this part of the world more readily neutralizes the effects of meat-eating, which is an acidic diet. Because soil in the Orient is very often acidic, the claim is made that the climate and terrain of the Orient are better suited for an alkaline, plant-based diet. It is important that such considerations of soil, water, and air quality not be overlooked.

Due to lack of space, I am unable to pursue further here the reasons for the increase in sodium levels in rice cooked in the U.S. Perhaps you or those affiliated with macrobiotic organizations in America, such as the George Ohsawa Macrobiotic Foundation, will delve into this question and come up with an answer.

Once you have mastered the Universal Principle, you will be able to respond to all changes, and so regardless of what the composition tables say, you will have no reason for concern. However, should you have doubts because, although you are observing a macrobiotic brown rice diet, the results you had hoped for are not materializing, it might be wise to consult these tables for possible hints. If the values shown in the table hold for cooked rice throughout America, then the cuisine and menu for one's entire diet must be reconsidered. The primary cause of severe obesity is gluttony, but the hidden cause that gives rise to gluttony is an excess intake of salt. Checking the source of sodium present in cooked rice is essential also for measuring the salt content in one's overall diet.

Keeping this in mind, let us list here the points essential for assuring that your brown rice diet is a success.

(1)  About how much animal-based food, chemical additives, and chemical seasonings have you taken in thus far in your diet?
        (A)  a very large amount      (B)  a large amount
        (C)  a normal amount       (D)  I have not taken in very much
        (E)  I have taken in none at all.
Which of these applies to you?

(2)  If you answered (A), (B), or (C), try the appropriate use of diluted rice gruel or rice gruel soup prepared from brown rice, half-milled rice, or three-quarter-milled rice, and observe the resulting changes in your physical condition and appetite.

(3)  If you answered (D) or (E), observe the changes in your physical condition and appetite when you make ordinary pressure-cooked rice your dietary mainstay and occasionally eat diluted rice gruel or rice gruel soup.

(4)  If the increase in sodium is due to the addition of salt or the like during cooking, try using the macrobiotic method of cooking rice.

(5)  If cooking American rice always results in sodium levels like those in the table above, then try adopting the salt-reducing brown rice diet that I describe later on in this chapter. As for the question of how much to lower the level of salt, each person should set a target for him/herself (this target being approached in stages, such as 1/5, 1/4, 1/3, 1/2, etc.); one should make appropriate adjustments in the level of salt while observing the changes that take place in one's physical condition and appetite.

*Addendum:*  Even after writing the above, the increase in the level of sodium in rice cooked in America continued to weigh on my mind. I then took another, closer look at the U.S. Food Composition Chart, whereupon I found, in an explanatory note following the table, that salt is added when rice is cooked.

In Japan, we too add a small amount of salt when cooking rice to augment the flavor of the brown rice. I indicate what I mean by a small amount later on in this chapter when I describe how to cook brown rice. This salt is added only to augment the flavor of the rice; the purpose is not to add sodium. If adding salt is customary when cooking rice in America, then a comprehensive look must be taken at how rice is eaten in the U.S. New research should be done to determine the purpose for cooking rice in this way and the reason why salt is added. As I have already indicated, in order to correctly observe a brown rice diet, one must do everything from cooking to preparation by oneself. When one buys pre-cooked rice, there is no way of knowing whether the rice one is eating has the composition shown in the food composition charts.

# At What Stage Should One Begin a Brown Rice Diet?

It is true not only with rice but with all crops that the quality and taste varies significantly depending on where the crops are grown, the method of cultivation, the harvesting method, and the method of storage. There is no cause for anxiety when using crops grown by natural farming or organic gardening, but in order for these to be tastily and effectively eaten, it is necessary that one acquire correct cooking skills.

I learned that American rice too is of excellent quality. I found that there are at least seven grades of commercial rice, depending on the degree of polishing.

Perhaps you're wondering what grade of rice you should be eating. You should begin by eating just-hulled brown rice or regular brown rice. After eating brown rice for a full three years, one may try eating other rice polished to various degrees depending upon one's physical state.

If illness, unhappiness, and all other problems could be resolved merely by eating brown rice, then nothing would be easier and more welcome. That brown rice has an amazing power to cure disease and turn misfortune and unhappiness into good fortune and happiness is clear and undeniable. But one must observe the macrobiotic principles that make this amazing power one's own. In order to master brown rice macrobiotics, one must begin by acquiring a solid understanding of the fundamentals of a brown rice diet. At the same time, in order to acquire the power of Yin-Yang judgment, it is absolutely essential that one carefully study the Universal Principle.

Why is the Universal Principle necessary?

Because in this world there is only one you; you are unique to this world, and for you there is only your own way of life. True, many other people bear a close resemblance to you; many even share some of the features and characteristics—sex, age, personality, temperament, physical constitution, and even likes and interests. But these people only resemble you; they are not exactly the same as you. You must judge things for yourself, and for this the Universal Principle is essential.

**Table 6.2   Diet classification by George Ohsawa.**

| Regimen | Cereal grains | Vegetables (cooked or raw) | Soup | Animal-based food | Salad, fruit | Dessert | Beverages |
|---|---|---|---|---|---|---|---|
| 7 | 100% | — | — | — | — | — | |
| 6 | 90% | 10% | — | — | — | — | |
| 5 | 80% | 20% | — | — | — | — | |
| 4 | 70% | 20% | 10% | — | — | — | Take as |
| 3 | 60% | 30% | 10% | — | — | — | little as |
| 2 | 50% | 30% | 10% | 10% | — | — | possible, |
| 1 | 40% | 30% | 10% | 20% | — | — | but enough |
| −1 | 30% | 30% | 10% | 20% | 10% | — | to enjoy |
| −2 | 20% | 30% | 10% | 25% | 10% | 5% | |
| −3 | 10% | 30% | 10% | 30% | 15% | 5% | |

George Ohsawa classifies diet into the following broadly defined regimens, leaving the practice of these up to each individual's personal judgment.

Unless we have learned how to think and see things in terms of the Universal Principle, we have no idea how to properly apply this table; nor are we able to respond appropriately to physical changes within us. Consequently, despite the brown rice that we eat and the natural diet that we follow, we are unable to obtain fully satisfactory effects.

I too was like this, but if one were to first get a firm grasp of the Universal Principle and only then begin a brown rice diet, effecting the desired changes might take forever. Even if it means delaying our studies of the Universal Principle a little, the best thing to do is to go ahead and begin a brown rice diet. One can study the Universal Principle while continuing to eat brown rice.

As I have already noted, since I was yin in almost every respect—in my lineage, my physical constitution, and my diet after birth—the yangness of a brown rice diet suited my body perfectly, and so I was able to begin this with great ease. The same will not necessary work well for everyone. No one has exactly the same dietary history and physical makeup as anyone else; each of us has led a life that is unique and unlike that of any other person. That is why the brown rice diet and technique for becoming and staying healthy that works for me will not work in exactly the same way in anyone. In order to gain a broad understanding of what does work, a method for judging Yin and Yang is both essential and effective.

Allow me now to turn to the topic of your brown rice diet by asking you a couple of questions.

(1)  "Do you feel that you are basically yin or basically yang in terms of your own outward physical constitution and personality?" This question may be summarized as follows: "Do you think of yourself as more yin or more yang?"

There are two possible answers to this question. If you think of yourself as a yang type, then you ought to begin with Regimen No. 1 or 2 in the above table. If, on the other hand, you consider yourself to be more yin, then you ought to begin with Regimen No. 3 or 4.

If you are ill and are planning to start a brown rice diet in order to cure your illness, then, even if you are a yang-type person, you should begin with Regimen No. 3 or 4.

(2)  "Which do you prefer and which have you eaten more of: animal-based foods (meat, eggs, milk and milk products) or plant-based foods (grains, vegetables, beans, fruit)?"

If you like animal-based foods and have eaten more of these, then you should begin with Regimen No. 3. If, on the other hand, you prefer plant-based foods and are accustomed to eating these, then you ought to begin with Regimen No. 3 or 4.

For those people who are yang and both like and have eaten much animal-based food, I would recommend a diet that includes about 10% animal-based food. This is to avoid withdrawal symptoms in your body, which has built up an animal-based constitution. If, however, you are able to get by without taking animal-based foods, then there is no reason for deliberately taking any.

Stick to the above diet for three months initially (about 100 days).

The purpose of this three-month period is to prepare the environment in your stomach and bowels. Depending on the degree of destruction within this internal environment, various reactions appear in the form of pathological symptoms. Since the reactions during this period are necessary for improvement within the body, please regard such reactions as part of the process whereby the pathological state or diseased area disappears.

I have limited the discussion here to just the dietary stage or regimen at which one should begin a brown rice diet.

## How to Obtain, Cook, and Eat Genmai

Assuming that you now have an idea of what stage of a brown rice diet from which to begin, you must learn how to obtain, cook, and eat genmai.

*Obtaining Genmai and Telling Rices Apart:*   When I began eating brown rice in the early 1960s, it was hard to come by in Japan. Not only Japan, but the entire industrialized world was in a stage of rapid economic growth during which life styles became increasingly extravagant. This was a golden period in which advocates of modern nutritional science promoted the popularization in Japan of a diet that included the increased intake of animal-based foods, and primarily meat. That's why when one tried to come by brown rice, people looked at you in a strange way; it was, in fact, not easy to get brown rice at the time.

Today, this no longer is true. People devoted to the macrobiotics movement now live throughout the world, and are always happy to show others how to procure brown rice. Supermarkets and shops that sell natural foods are all able to supply brown rice.

But there are several things that one should pay attention to when buying brown rice. I list some of these here.

(1)   Make sure to ask for rice grown organically or by natural farming techniques. Wherever possible, it is best to be able to check where the rice was grown and by whom.
(2)   Ask for unhulled rice and hull it yourself or have it hulled just before you eat it.
(3)   Make sure the rice contains no empty hulls, grass seed, soil, or stones.
(4)   The rice should not contain "white-belly" rice, green kernels, red kernels, or other unusual kernels.
(5)   Make sure it is not hybrid rice.
(6)   The grains of rice should all be of uniform size, not irregular and nonuniform.
(7)   The grains of rice should be oval, of a translucent, amber color, and should have a luster.
(8)   The rice should be hard, heavy, and fully dry (but not bone dry).
(9)   The surface lines on the grains of rice should be shallow and the grain should be tacky enough to stick to the teeth when bitten.

I shall now briefly explain each of the above.

With regard to (1), in rice that is produced with the use of large amounts of chemical pesticides and fertilizers, economics (read "profits") is stressed over the life and vitality of the rice at every step of the way, including harvesting, storage, and distribution. There is an enormous difference in vitality and flavor between rice grown by organic or natural farming methods and rice grown with chemical pesticides and heavy machinery. The difference in flavor is readily apparent upon cooking and comparing the taste, while the difference in vitality is clearly manifested through the ability of the diet to cure illness.

The reason for eating just-hulled rice, as mentioned in (2) above, is to eat rice having the highest possible vitality and flavor. Every family should have its own rice huller.

In (3), the absence of extraneous matter such as empty hulls, grass seed, and dirt or stones is an indication that the genmai is choice rice that has been carefully cleaned and sorted.

In (4), "white-belly" rice is defective, low-grade rice that has not fully matured or in which maturation was hampered by pests. The presence of green kernels results from the mixture of different varieties having differing periods of maturation in a single rice field or is the result of harvesting immature grain. The presence of red kernels results either from changes in the rice that may be due to fermentation on account of insufficient drying during storage and preservation or from the admixture of old rice.

In item (5) above, hybrid rice is attractive to the eye, having a good grain shape, weight, and uniformity, but the problem with this is its vitality. I would suggest that a crop produced from hybrid seed is not God-given food, but should be regarded instead as a kind of food additive—call it a *food extender* if you will. One future topic of study for man should be an examination of the grave dangers of relying on this alone as one's staple food.

As for item (6), in rice grown by natural or organic farming, the uniformity and regularity of the size and shape of the grains is proof that each grain is fully mature and complete. A lack of uniformity in the shape of the grains can be regarded as an indication that the rice is not fully mature and is of less than complete quality.

In (7), although the color varies somewhat with the type of rice, a translucent amber color and good luster are indications that the rice is fully nourishing and has been properly stored and dried.

In (8), when the rice is hard, heavy, and gentle to the touch, this generally indicates that the rice is rich in quality and has been properly dried. The extent to which the rice has been properly dried is extremely important. Properly dried rice can withstand extended preservation with very little change in quality and is especially advantageous because it expands when cooked.

In (9), the shallow surface lines demonstrate that the grain has filled and matured well. The hardness and tackiness of the grains indicates that the rice is fully dried and contains a large amount of the starch that is a determinant of quality.

The above should give some idea of how to get hold of and judge brown rice.

*How to Cook Brown Rice:* The way in which brown rice is cooked varies subtly with such factors as the cooking utensils, the quality of the rice, the weather and outside temperature, the quality and temperature of the water, and the fuel or heat source used in cooking.

Rice cooking utensils include non-pressurizing pots and pans, these being made of enamel, ceramic, iron, aluminum, or other materials. As for pressure cookers, these include models that are heated with gas, electricity, charcoal, and so forth.

Because the utensils and appliances as well as the cuisine and methods of cooking that people use vary depending on whether they live in urban or rural areas, it is impossible to state categorically which method is the best.

The true secret to cooking delicious brown rice is love and enthusiasm. Regardless of the conditions under which rice is cooked, what determines how good the brown rice is when cooked is the love and enthusiasm of the cook. The first few times generally end in failure. Failure shows us the way to success; if you cook your rice with love and enthusiasm, then you will soon learn how to cook delicious brown rice.

George Ohsawa said that one can measure the love of the cook by the deliciousness of the rice that he or she prepares. I believe that he was right.

What is of first importance, though, is learning how to cook rice that tastes good to yourself and your family. Even when a family sits down to the same meal, the conditions at mealtime for each person differ, so fully satisfying everyone's sense of taste and appetite at once is an impossibility. Because the taste, appetite, eating habits, and physical constitution of each member of the family differ, you should learn first how to cook in such a way that you and your family can eat brown rice enjoyably. When cooking for guests, of course, you will have to make certain adjustments.

People's sense of taste differs widely from country to country, even with respect to any one food. The gustatory senses of your ancestors and family manifest themselves in their pattern of eating or diet over the years, and also in the physical constitution of the members of your family. These physical differences then emerge once again in the food preferences and gustatory senses of your descendants. So you should discover that way of cooking which you and your family feels is most delicious. Everything depends on the degree of love and enthusiasm that you as the cook bring to the task.

*Important Things to Watch for When Cooking Brown Rice:* If you are physically more yin ($\nabla$), try cooking your rice on the hard side ($\triangle$) with more pressure ($\triangle$), heat ($\triangle$), and natural salt ($\triangle$).

If, on the other hand, you tend to be physically more yang ($\triangle$), try cooking your rice on the soft side ($\nabla$) by applying less pressure ($\nabla$) and not adding salt ($\nabla$).

Try varying the yin and yang conditions in different ways such as to find the method of cooking that produces the most delicious results for you.

For the sake of reference, here is how we normally cook genmai at home. This method presupposes the use of a pressure cooker, town gas, and city water.
*Ingredients:*
   –5 cups of genmai (wash thoroughly and drain water)
   –6 cups of water (about 20% more water than genmai)
   –about 1/3 to 1/4 teaspoon of natural salt

1. Place all of the above in the pressure cooker and turn on the burner. Heat under a low flame for 10 minutes.
2. Next, heat under a high flame until the rice comes to a boil.
3. When the steam vent starts spinning rapidly, turn down the heat.
4. Heat under a low flame for 25 minutes, then turn off the fire and allow the rice to settle for about 5 minutes.
5. Remove the steam vent and allow the steam to escape.

**Fig. 6.3    How to cook brown rice.**

1. Place the water and brown rice in a bowl and let these sit for about one hour.

2. Wash the rice well.

3. Empty the rice into a bamboo strainer and drain off the water.

4. Place rice, water, and salt in a pressure cooker.

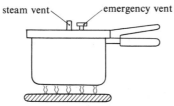

5. Turn up flame to "high" after cooking under low flame for 10 minutes.

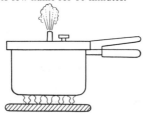

6. Cook under high flame until rice begins to boil.

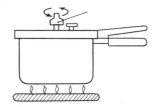

7. Reduce to low flame when vent begins to turn rapidly.

8. Cook under low flame for 25 minutes.

9. Shut off heat and allow rice to settle for about 5 minutes.

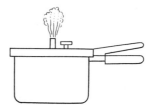

10. Release steam through steam vent.

*How to Eat Brown Rice:*

(a)   The Etiquette of the Meal:

"In Japanese, the word for food (*tabemono*) literally means 'that which is bestowed.' At each meal, one should take up one's chopsticks only after expressing gratitude for this gift from God and freely giving thanks for this food one is about to eat." That is how George Ohsawa puts it in his *A Practical Guide to Cooking and Eating Rice* (Japanese title: *Kome no chishiki to takikata, tabekata*).

Food is cosmic life in transmuted form, so it is without doubt bestowed upon us from the universe. Just as our lives have assumed human form after repeated differentiation and transformation from the great cosmic life, each single grain of rice in our food also is cosmic life that has undergone repeated differentiation and transformation. I have already symbolically described this in my Life Cycle Diagram (Fig. 5.1). Although I traced only human life in that diagram, my intention was to use man as an example; this same principle applies to all things in the universe. Another quote from Ohsawa will serve to clarify this further.

> It is only natural as humans that we give thanks at all times and at all places for this food which is bestowed upon us. Whether we eat our rice balls in the mountains or fields, open our lunch boxes at work, or break bread at a restaurant, it is only natural that we doff our hats and say grace before starting our meal.
>
> I hear that people in the West have the habit of conversing at mealtime, but in Japan the tradition has been to take one's meals in the utmost silence. The Japanese way here seems more rational also because of the need for proper mastication.

The Japanese custom to which Ohsawa avers above has almost vanished today. Japan is almost completely Westernized in this respect. At the same time, one finds that those in the West practicing a macrobiotic way of life and those who understand the ethos of the Orient have acquired and today observe those good table manners that were once so common in Japan.

The meal is a divine ritual. It is a precious and sacred act in which life that has differentiated from the universe and taken the form of food is granted as one's own life.

While having a meal with my children, I sometimes tell them: "Mealtime is a very blessed ceremony in which we receive the life of God, so we must quietly chew our food and eat it with care while thanking the Lord." However, the children pay more attention to the television than to what I am saying; they are more attentive to the show being aired than to eating itself. I have no idea how many times I have thought of bashing in the TV.

Today we live in an age in which the most important and basic awareness of what food and eating are all about is held to little account. It is very sad.

A macrobiotic brown rice diet is repentance (a change in diet) that people today absolutely must carry out for the resurrection of true man and in order to be reunited with the universe (God) and true life.

(b)   How to Take One's Meals:

I am often asked whether it is better to have two meals a day or three. The number of meals you normally take in a day and the time at which you take those meals have, through your life habits up until now, determined the biorhythms of your body. If you function better with two meals a day, then this is fine; the same can be said of three meals a day. Living as a member of society, one must accept various social constraints on one's habits. Choose the method that is most convenient for you and that is most appropriate for your physical and mental condition. The life style you follow will differ depending on whether you take two or three meals a day; you have no choice but to integrate this into your actual life.

I normally eat three meals a day. Brown rice is the staple in two of these meals, while a flour-based food such as buckwheat noodles, wheat noodles, or bread serves as the mainstay of the third meal. On vacations or holidays, I make it a rule to take only one or two meals a day. I am well aware of how doing so gives my alimentary tract and other internal organs a well-deserved rest. There is no need to be inflexible about the number of meals one takes per day. It is best to adapt to circumstances as they occur by eating in accordance with the situation that presents itself and one's physical condition at a particular day and hour. By so doing, the number of meals and the mealtime most appropriate to you will be determined naturally. The aim here is to maintain a hearty appetite and to always be able to eat enjoyably and deliciously. There are times when one does not feel like eating at mealtime. At such times, you might try skipping a meal. If your appetite fails to return in spite of this, then try fasting for a full day. Even though you have skipped a meal or fasted an entire day and feel terribly hungry, stay away from sweets, fruit, and cold, carbonated drinks. If your appetite returns, prepare your system first by drinking some miso soup, then take about half the amount of brown rice you are accustomed to eating with a small amount of secondary dishes and chew well.

Let us turn now to chewing. The importance of properly chewing the food that we eat is becoming increasingly clear recently. In fact, one could write an entire book on chewing alone. Here, however, I will simply enumerate the basic points.

Chewing one's food is the first and foremost condition for making full use of our digestive faculties. The ill and infirm who are able to chew their food should begin first by making the act of chewing their self-appointed duty. Rather than swallowing medication and receiving injections or infusions, they should chew their food with almost insane dedication. I understand the Japanese word for "chewing" (*kamu*) as a conjunction of the words for "God" (*kami*) and "joining together" or "uniting" (*musubareru, musubitsuku, musubu*). By chewing, we join our life with cosmic life. That is why the load on the stomach and bowels becomes large and the link with cosmic vitality weakens in the sick who cannot chew and in those people who do not chew by force of habit. As I have already pointed out, chewing serves to neutralize and detoxify the carcinogenic substances present in what we eat and drink.

In order to confirm for oneself the importance of chewing, one should try occasionally to eat without chewing. I think that once you have done this, you will be convinced that chewing is very important indeed.

Since the first object of mastication is to make full use of one's digestive faculties, at mealtime one should begin by sitting properly and giving a prayer of thanks for this blessing of food, either by saying grace or, as is done in Japan, by saying "*Itadakimasu*" ("I gratefully receive this food"). After a long journey, cosmic life has assumed the form of food and is about to became the vital force and energy for our own life. This is a great blessing.

The meal is begun by drinking some miso soup. This informs the tongue and the entire alimentary tract that the meal is about to begin. After drinking about five or six mouthfuls of soup, the stomach and bowels are primed and ready for action. It is at this point that one begins to eat genmai.

The amount of rice that you should place in your mouth is about the size of your thumb to the first joint. When too much food is taken into the mouth at one time, it gets passed down the stomach before it has been properly chewed. If a small amount of rice about the size of one's thumb is placed in the mouth and carefully chewed the necessary number of times, this will not inadvertently be swallowed before it is ready.

You should chew brown rice from 80 to 120 times or more per mouthful; do not bring your chopsticks (or spoon or fork, whichever may be the case) to your mouth until you are finished chewing. To avoid this, put down your chopsticks after each mouthful you take.

Regardless of whether you are healthy or sick, you should always eat in moderation. If you chew your food well, then you will find that this problem takes care of itself.

The amount of other foods that you eat along with genmai will depend on the regimen that you have chosen, but it is generally enjoyable to eat about one mouthful of a secondary food for every three mouthfuls of rice.

Until you have become accustomed to eating in this way, it may be difficult to chew as often as I have indicated above. The rice in one's mouth tends to disappear by the thirtieth or fortieth chew, but if you make an effort to chew often with every mouthful, then in time chewing properly will come quite naturally to you. With all this chewing, your jaw or temple may hurt at first for several days. I remember that my temple was sore for four to five days when I began eating genmai macro-biotically.

After finishing your miso soup, genmai, and side dishes, it is a good idea from the standpoint of nutrition, economics and, in Japan, even proper etiquette, to pour a little tea or water in your rice bowl and rinse out your mouth by drinking this down. After finishing one's meal, it is the custom in Japan to expresses one's gratitude for the meal by saying "*Gochisosama*." As long as such invocations at the beginning and end of the meal serve as an expression of thanks to the deity in which you and your family believes, then any such form of thanksgiving that you and your family is comfortable with will do fine here.

## How to Examine the Seven Stages of One's Dietary Past

Knowing nothing about your lineage, your grandparents, your parents, the dietary history and habits of your family, or even your own personal dietary past, I am unable to give you precise instructions or decide what sort of brown rice diet you should follow.

Your parents are in the best position to know your dietary past prior to your birth and during your infancy and early childhood, while you know best your own dietary past from your youth up until the present. Why don't you examine for yourself the Yin-Yang relationship between your dietary past and your physical constitution today; this exercise will have the added benefit of enhancing your own Universal Principle judgment. You might try writing this out in the following manner.

*Examining the Seven Stages in One's Dietary Past:*
1. The principal diet of your parents one year before you were conceived.
2. Your mother's diet while she was pregnant with you.
3. Your diet from birth until you were weaned.
4. Your diet from the time you were weaned until the age of six.
5. Your diet during childhood.
6. Your diet during adolescence.
7. Your diet since marriage.

The purpose of examining your dietary past in this way is, very simply, to know whether your body tends to be more yin or yang. This also helps you become better aware of your own physical constitution. For example, even if your basic foods up until now have been meat and fish, it helps a great deal to know whether this is beef, pork, chicken, or fish, and also whether that meat or fish has been fresh, frozen, canned, or what have you. Write down everything you can recall, including not just eggs, milk, butter, cheese, fruit, vegetables (whether these are leaf vegetables, root vegetables, potatoes, etc.), sugar, juice, soda, alcoholic beverages, but also nutriments and medications (even though these are not strictly foods). Mention also any illnesses and injuries that you have had in the respective periods of your life. By doing so, you will have some idea of what your body is primarily made up of. Putting this in more extreme terms, features distinctive of and contingent upon your diet—whether beef or pork or fish or chicken, whether cow's milk, rice or wheat, potatoes or beans, whether sugar or fruit, beer or whiskey, soda or drugs—will become clear. Once you have a general idea of what your cells are made of, then the way in which to improve your physical constitution will become clear. If you have an ailment, this exercise will be a great help in surmising the cause of this ailment and will make it possible to enhance the effects of therapy. Most important of all, the knowledge and understanding of one's physical constitution thus gained will serve as a guide for effectively carrying out a brown rice diet.

The following chart is an example of how one can go about examining the seven stages of one's dietary past. Why don't you study for yourself possible alternatives or modifications to this chart, and try designing a chart that better describes your own case?

Enter the results in the table as accurately as you can and in the greatest detail possible. It may be that you yourself will not be able to apply the results you enter to Yin-Yang judgment immediately. But if you bring this table to a macrobiotics teacher or a more experienced follower of macrobiotics than yourself, by referring to this chart and comparing the results with your current physical condition and state of health, he or she will be able to provide a more accurate diagnosis con-

**Table 6.3  Chart of dietary past.**

| | Meat | Fish | Eggs | Milk | Fruit | Vegetables | Seaweed | Grains | Sweets | Beverages | Medications |
|---|---|---|---|---|---|---|---|---|---|---|---|
| Average amount of intake | 1 steak or 1 hamburger per day | 1 whole or 1 piece per day | 1 egg per day | about 300 cc per day; cheese, butter, cream, etc. with each meal | 2–3 fruit per day | a plate of salad with each meal (1 tomato, eggplant, apple, banana, or orange) | about 40 g of *wakame* each day | 2 thick slices of bread or 1 cup of rice with each meal; if spaghetti is eaten, 1 plate of this | 1 cupcake or pastry or a cup of ice cream with each meal; chocolate candy | juice, soda, beer, whiskey, coffee (2 glasses of 2 or more of these each day) | occasional medication; nutriments or health tonic on a daily basis |

1  mother's diet before pregnancy
2  mother's diet while pregnant
3  mother's diet from birth until you were weaned
4  your diet from weaning to age of six
5  childhood
6  adolescence
7  after marriage

cerning your overall degree of Yin and Yang. Yin-Yang judgment is a compass for grasping the direction and inclination. The idea here is not to use this as justification in support of the prescription and preparation of very small amounts of synthetic drugs that is carried out in modern medical therapy. All that is necessary is that you be able to grasp, through a knowledge of the habits and inclinations of your own body, the direction that facilitates introduction of the cosmic life-force or vitality sought out by your body's own natural healing powers. Having grasped the degree of your body's yangness or yinness, you need only decide the appropriate way of cooking and preparing your food, and the manner and amount of consumption. It is not necessary to become finicky and particular. There is nothing dangerous about a macrobiotic brown rice diet. Even if one should err in its application, although the process may take time, by returning to the basics and starting over once again, you will invariably obtain good results. It is for this reason also that a flexible attitude and sound intentions are important. I myself am fond of the idea of being a "free spirit," and have continued to eat brown rice while constantly trying to approach this ideal state. The Universal Principle also serves as a way of acquiring this freedom of spirit.

## The Brown Rice Yin-Yang Diet for Your Physical Constitution

In the section entitled "At Which Stage Should One Begin a Brown Rice Diet?" I gave only very standard advice. I touched there upon the proportion of the food staple (brown rice) to the supplementary foods or side dishes, but you should be aware that the matter is more complicated than this; even with regard only to brown rice as the food staple, there exist the seven stages listed in the table below. Normally, so long as you adhere strictly to a general brown rice diet without becoming impatient or frantic and without giving up, then you will obtain convincing results. Depending on the inclinations of your physical constitution, however, unexpectedly severe reactions and symptoms can crop up. At such times, the need will arise for you to alter the degree of yinness or yangness of your brown rice diet in accordance with your overall degree of yinness or yangness as determined from your dietary past.

**Table 6.4**

| Yin ▽ | soft | wet | liquid | (1) | brown rice soup | |
|---|---|---|---|---|---|---|
| | | | | (2) | brown rice cream | |
| | | | | (3) | brown rice gruel | |
| | | moist | | (4) | soft cooked brown rice | large brown rice balls (*omusubi*) |
| | | | | (5) | normal cooked brown rice | small brown rice balls (*onigiri*) |
| | | | | (6) | hard cooked brown rice | brown rice sushi |
| Yang △ | hard | dry | solid | (7) | roasted brown rice | roasted brown rice balls |
| | | | | | | fried brown rice |
| | | | | | | brown rice balls fried in oil |
| | | | | | | dry brown rice biscuits |

The yin-yang character of one's physical constitution and body are not determined solely on the basis of one's dietary past. Although there is no question that the influence of what we eat is foremost, the amount of daily physical exercise or exertion, the weather and the outdoor temperature, and one's clothing and living environment all affect one's degree of yinness or yangness. Once we learn how to accurately perceive the degree of such changes and variations and become able to follow a brown rice diet that corresponds to these changes, it becomes possible to enhance the desirable effects on the body while enjoying the deliciousness of brown rice. Allow me to illustrate this here with one example.

In addition to the above, brown rice may also be eaten raw, but I will not describe this here as it is not a standard practice. More importantly, there exist a range of ways (from yin to yang) for eating brown rice cakes or *mochi*.

If your physical constitution and condition is always yang, then a diet that suitably incorporates (1), (2), (3), and (4) in the above table is desirable. On the other hand, people whose physical constitution and condition tend to be yang are better off with a skillful combination of (5), (6), (7), and rice balls applying these.

In the above table, the brown rice soup is classified as yin ($\triangledown$), but this is yin within the context of the brown rice diets in (1) through (7); compared to vegetable soups (such as onion, carrot, cabbage, squash, and consommés), vegetable and fruit soups, vegetable and meat soups, and the like, a brown rice soup is yang, so one should not have a fixed notion of brown rice soup as being yin. In fact, both brown rice soups and creams should be used with full awareness that these are the ultimate in yang foods for aiding hopelessly ill people. I refer here to brown rice soup for the sake of explanation, but even brown rice soup can be made yin or yang in widely varying degrees. For example, if brown rice *shiitake* soup is prepared by placing one-half to a full *shiitake* mushroom in brown rice soup, this is highly effective against headaches and sweating during colds. By the addition of a small amount of apple juice, orange juice, onion juice, grated *daikon*, soy sauce, or *umeboshi*, for example, it is possible to fully exploit the pharmacological effects of each of these and in the process obtain miraculous therapeutic results.

For the sake of explanation, I have divided a brown rice diet into seven stages above. Needless to say, each of these stages could in turn be yinnized or yangized into any number of smaller stages. Even in people whose bodies are made up of cells formed by eating meat, improvement in the physical constitution should be attainable without great difficulty through a brown rice diet that suitably combines brown rice diets (1) through (7). Unless one's physical constitution can be correctly improved, there is no hope for the proper treatment of illness. Dietary therapy is basic treatment, not tentative first-aid, so it is meaningless if it fails to fully improve one's physical constitution.

One of the biggest stumbling blocks in the conversion of people who are meat-eaters to a brown rice diet is the exchange of the new salt in a brown rice diet for the old salt in a meat-based diet. There are many instances in which people have experienced failure in the metabolism of old salt and new salt. The primary reason for this is that, although the old salt that has poisoned the body must first be eliminated, people hurry instead to take in nutrition from the new diet. As a result, they ingest new salt before having completely eliminated the old salt, resulting in a salt overload that upsets the body's metabolism. When you cling to one particular brown rice diet to the exclusion of other brown rice diets, this freezes the propensities of the body and prevents the full effects of the brown rice from emerging. In order to eliminate the old salt, this must be dissolved and removed. If you adopt a brown rice diet based on (1)–(4) above or a diet based on (5)–(7) as the staple diet, you must be flexible enough to allow for the use of vegetable soups, vegetable and fruit juices, and so forth in accordance with your physical condition.

A macrobiotic brown rice diet includes almost no animal-based foods. Foods that play an important role in place of animal-based foods include vegetable protein from soybeans and other plants, as well as seasonings such as salt, miso, and soy sauce. This is why there is often a tendency to take in an excess of salt. Care must be taken to avoid this from happening.

In addition to the above brown rice yin-yang diets, it is also possible to adjust the overall degree of yinness or yangness of the staple food by mixing and cooking together with the brown rice one or two foods such as Job's tears, millet, or other cereal grains; pulses such as adzuki beans, soybeans, green peas; seasonal wild herbs and cultivated vegetables; and sea vegetables such as *kombu* and *wakame*. This gives cooked brown rice various flavors and adds to the enjoyment of the meal. The judicious use of all these possibilities constitutes the practice of the Universal Principle.

## The Secret of Brown Rice Balls

In an age of abundant food and excess nourishment, people become fond of meals that are light and pleasing to the taste. Abundant food and excess nutrition is a yang ($\triangle$) phenomenon, which is why people favor light, pleasant, generally yin ($\triangledown$) foods. One consequence of this is an increase in obese ($\triangledown$) people.

In an age of food scarcity when people tend to be undernourished, luxuries such as light, tasty meals are not even mentioned. Any food that fills an empty stomach is eaten. An age in which food is scarce and people tend to be undernourished is a yin ($\triangledown$) age. For this reason, their diet is such that a small amount of food is made yang ($\triangle$) and packed as densely with energy as possible. Because people tend to be underfed and undernourished, obesity is nonexistent. Instead of becoming corpulent ($\triangledown$), people inevitably have small, compact bodies ($\triangle$).

The Yin-Yang causality in lands and periods of abundant food and in lands and periods of food scarcity are thus opposites. The same applies as well to individuals and families. In Japan, up until the time that scientific and industrial technology become firmly established following the Meiji Reformation, the common people constantly experienced food shortages. The fact of the matter is that for much of its history, humanity has lived almost constantly in a state of famine and want; an abundance of food has been the exception rather than the rule. In Japan, the long periods of famine and food scarcity gave rise to the innovation of the rice ball.

The rice ball is prepared by packing together rice with both hands. With the power of the left (yin; $\triangledown$) and right (yang; $\triangle$) hands, a ball of rice is united ($\triangle$) and densely packed ($\triangle$), resulting in a several-fold yangization of cooked rice. The degree of yangness in a rice ball also depends upon the yangness of the person making the rice balls. Rice balls made by a yin person have a low degree of yangness. The energy and vitality of a rice ball and the same amount of cooked rice differ considerably. A rice ball is an energy capsule. It is a life capsule that even in small amounts manifests a large energy.

**Fig. 6.4   How to make rice balls.**

1.  Measure out a suitable amount of rice with a container.

2.  Spread a little salt or *ume* vinegar in the palm of your hand.

3.  Take thr rice in the palm of your hand.

4.  Place an *umeboshi* plum, miso, or whatever you please at the center of the rice ball.

5.  Pack the rice ball with your hands. Shape it as you wish—round, triangular, or whatever.

6.  You may finish off the shaped rice ball as you like, with *nori*, miso, soy sauce, or sesame salt, for example.

Brown rice balls are often used in dietary therapy. These are effective primarily in sick people with yin physical constitutions and yin symptoms, being especially potent as a food staple in people with gastrointestinal disorders (esogastritis, gastric dilation, gastric ulcers, gastropsis, gastrospasms, etc.), gastric cancer, pleurisy, pulmonary diseases, pneumonia, cystitis, tonsillitis, sinusitis, colds, influenza, rheumatism, erysipelas, heart disease, kidney disease, neuralgia, and so forth.

Many different levels of yin and yang exist also in rice balls. Even when the same person forms rice balls of about the same size with about the same amount of strength, the degree of yinness and yangness varies with the degree of milling; i.e., depending on whether this is brown rice, quarter-milled rice, half-milled rice, three-quarter-milled rice, polished rice with attached germ, or white rice. This also varies with the amount of force with which the rice is packed and shaped into rice balls. Another factor is the salt, *umeboshi*, sesame salt, miso, soy sauce, *nori*, etc. that the rice balls are garnished with. If the rice balls are then roasted there is also the manner in which they are roasted: whether the rice balls are roasted normally, roasted after dipping them in soy sauce, roasted with miso on them, or cooked in oil. Each of these is effective for the treatment of different conditions.

In addition to the large *omusubi* rice balls prepared with two hands, there is also the *onigiri*, which is prepared with one hand. As a useful exercise, you might try determining how the *omusubi* differs from the *onigiri* in yin-yang terms and in vitality.

Aside from their use in dietary therapy for the sick, both the *omusubi* and the *onigiri* are commonly used in lunches and as emergency meals. Both are health foods. As a child, I lived in an age of want. That's why, whenever I went on a hike or an excursion, or took part in a school field day or assembly, my lunch always consisted of *omusubi* rice balls with *umeboshi* and *takuan* (pickled daikon).

My children had brown rice *onigiri* for their snacks. Brown rice *onigiri* is the best possible food for young children.

**Table 6.5   The Yin-Yang of *omusubi* and *onigiri*.**

| ▽ | Brown rice *onigiri* | made with left hand |
| | | made with right hand |
| | | made with *ume* vinegar |
| | | natural salt |
| | | *umeboshi*, soy sauce, miso, sesame salt |
| | Brown rice *omusubi* | roasted normally |
| | | roasted in sesame oil |
| | | garnished with miso or soy sauce and roasted |
| △ | | dipped in soy sauce and cooked in sesame oil |

In Japan, large *omusubi* rice balls containing an *umeboshi* plum and rolled in *nori* are still a very popular food. Some scholars (nutritional scientists and medical scholars) claim that these rice balls are nutritionally deficient as food. True, this is a reasonable concern for rice balls made from white rice. But such concerns are unnecessary in the case of brown rice *omusubi*. In fact, the brown rice *omusubi* contains an amazing and awesome power that cannot be measured. Although this power depends also upon the degree of health and yangness of the person making the rice balls, the vigor and energy imparted to the rice ball when it is made is augmented by a subtle mechanism that imparts an effect beyond that of just the nutrients.

Recently, machine-made *omusubi* rice balls have appeared on the market. These attractive looking *omusubi* all contain the same amount of rice and have the same shape. In fact, even the number of calories in them have been calculated.

But what an enormous difference in the effect on life there is between a rice ball fashioned in the hands of a healthy person and a rice ball shaped by a machine. Machines have no vigor or love. What gives the *omusubi* and the *onigiri* their amazing powers is the care and devotion with which they are made. You should try making the fullest possible use of rice balls prepared with care and devotion in your genmai diet.

## Miso Soup and Secondary Foods in a Brown Rice Diet

One particular traditional Japanese diet is known as the "one-soup-and-one-vegetable" diet. Today, it is regarded as fitting fare perhaps for ascetics or monks, but I believe that reviving this venerable diet is the only hope we have of salvation from our age of gluttony. And the only way to revive this diet in our day and age is a macrobiotic brown rice or other whole grain diet based strictly on the principle of the inseparability of the body from the land.

A basic notion in Western nutritional science is that one should obtain many nutrients from a large variety of foods. In a macrobiotic brown rice (or other whole-grain) diet, however, one receives nutrition (life) from the smallest possible amount of food.

One condition for receiving the required nutrition from the smallest amount of food is that all the food taken in be packed with nourishment and charged with the vitality of the heavens and earth. This vitality is not a force that can be created through scientific technology in the laboratory or the factory. The most important condition in making a one-soup-and-one-vegetable diet possible is that this consist of natural crops from the land and sea which have been fully nurtured with the vitality of the heavens and earth.

All the foods in the brown rice diet that I mention in this book should be wild or natural foods. Even in the case of processed foods, natural forces are of greatest importance; artificial forces should serve only to assist in the receipt and fullest possible use of natural forces. Even processed foods such as salt, miso, soy sauce, vinegar, *mirin*, and oils must be produced through the agency of natural forces.

*Miso Soup:*  Miso is a veritable treasure chest of nutrition, containing protein, minerals, enzymes, and the like not entirely available from brown rice. Miso soup is soup made with miso as the key ingredient.

There are different types of miso, depending on the raw materials from which it is made; rice miso, barley miso, and bean miso are typical of these. In macrobiotics, these three types suffice.

The degree of yinness and yangness differs in rice, barley, and beans; miso made from these likewise differs in its yinness and yangness. Other factors that determine the relative yinness or yangness of miso include the concentration of salt, the length of the fermentation period, the method of fermentation, and the climate and other physiographic features of the locale where the miso is produced. Since nature plays the leading role in the production of naturally fermented miso, variations in natural conditions have a subtle influence on fermentation; hence, miso of consistently identical quality cannot always be produced. This gives miso pastes a flavor characteristic of the area where they are produced.

The question of which miso to use in what way depends upon the yinness or yangness of your own physical constitution. When you have succeeded in preparing miso and miso soup that is most delicious for you and your family, then you may accept this as being best suited to your physical constitution.

It is a good idea to apply oneself diligently to the preparation of miso soup simply as a practical yin-yang problem. A yang miso should taste delicious to someone of a yin constitution; in such a case, a yang miso soup is effective both for curing illness and for restoring vigor.

When the same miso is to be taken also by someone with a yang constitution, the miso soup will taste better and be better for the body if the amount of miso paste is reduced somewhat to give a thinner soup with a lower salt level. Preparation of the miso soup in accordance with the season and the climate is also important. A more yang miso will taste better in a cold climate or a cold season, while people in a warmer land or season will prefer a more yin miso.

As an exercise in Yin and Yang, you might try studying for yourself which miso pastes are yin and which yang.

*The Ingredients in Miso Soup:*   These should consist of seasonal herbs, vegetables, and seaweed that can be gathered in the area where you live, such as daikon, carrot, burdock, lotus root, onion, scallion, cabbage, Chinese cabbage, taro, *kombu*, and *wakame*. Tofu and *aburage* (fried tofu)—both processed foods made from soybeans, as well as *seitan*, which serves as a meat substitute, may be used as appropriate in miso soup. Depending on one's physical condition, the weather, and other considerations, these ingredients may be sautéed in a little sesame oil and added to complete the miso soup. There is no need to sauté the ingredients in oil every day. Whether a mildly flavored miso soup or a strongly flavored miso soup prepared by sautéeing the ingredients is better depends on your degree of yinness or yangness and, if you are nursing an ailment, your symptoms.

Miso soup is more than a treasure-trove of nutrition; it also has the pharmacologic effect of conditioning the gastrointestinal system. There are cases where a single mouthful of miso soup prepared with loving care can even revive one who is critically ill and near death. Mealtimes are begun by drinking some miso soup. This prepares the alimentary tract, and also the entire body for digestion. After the stomach has been prepared with miso soup, we are ready to receive our rice.

*Side Dishes:*   Side dishes provide an accent to the meal and serve to supplement nutrition not available from the primary food alone. But, as the term "side dish" implies, since this is strictly supplementary food; a way of eating that disregards the primary food is undesirable. The ratio of the brown rice serving as the food staple to these secondary foods should be about one mouthful of the latter to every three to five mouthfuls of rice. This should give you a good idea of the approximate amount of secondary foods to be eaten.

Ever since learning about a brown rice macrobiotic diet, I have studied with fascination the diets and eating habits of many people. As a result, I have noticed that those who are ill or tend to become ill easily generally eat more secondary foods than food staples. Modern nutritional science has made meat the staple food and relegated grains and vegetables to the status of mere side dishes. This is a mistake. Whether in the East or the West, this organism we call man must take grains as his staple food; that much is clear from ecological, biological, physiological, biochemical, and other evidence. There are special circumstances, such as in very cold lands where grains are impossible to grow, where meat does become the food staple, but grains should in general be the primary source of food. If people must eat meat at all costs, then this should be consumed as a secondary food.

When one looks at the diet of healthy people, one can see that, without being conscious of it, they generally take one mouthful of secondary food per three to five mouthfuls of staple food. There is an order to the human body. Correct order in the diet guides the body to a correct order.

Well then, what kinds of secondary foods are there? Because these are so very numerous, it is impossible here to describe them all in detail. Since the variety of secondary food types and products exceeds the number of cooking methods, you should refer to specialized cook books on the various secondary foods. References include *Shokuyo ryoriho* by George and Lima Ohsawa, *Macrobiotic Cuisine* and *Lima Cooking* by Lima Ohsawa, and many other excellent books.

The "vegetable" in the Japanese "one-soup-and-one-vegetable" diet does not refer to one type of cooked secondary food; rather it refers to one kind of vegetable, wild herb, seaweed, or the like prepared as a preserved food by pickling.

Secondary foods must be eaten in a quality, amount, and way that enhance the effects of the staple food, add to the pleasure of the meal, and heighten one's daily health. Depending on how secondary food is consumed, it can make one ill or aggravate an existing ailment; on the other hand, it can speed recovery from illness.

From my own personal experiences, I am convinced that eating secondary foods in the smallest possible amount is good for one's physical condition. This is why the brown rice serving as one's staple food must be rice that has been grown by natural or organic farming and is charged with the highest possible level of nourishment; one must follow a diet that places one's life in the hands of rice. Even though secondary foods are taken in small amounts, this small amount must also be replete with the life and nourishment of the heavens and earth.

## The Three Sacred Treasures of a Brown Rice Diet

Food is the vessel of life. Because life is another name for God, food could be called "the vessel of God."*

I will now discuss three especially important treasures in a brown rice diet: *gomashio* (sesame salt), *takuan* (pickled daikon), and *umeboshi* (pickled plum). Because these three secondary foods are indispensable to a brown rice diet, I like to call these "the three sacred treasures of a brown rice diet."

---

* "Jingi," generally rendered in English as the "sacred treasures," is written 神器, which literally means "vessel of God."

Through learning, modern man distinguishes between what is nutritious and what is not using numerical values that indicate the nutritive value of foods and food products. He is swayed and persuaded by numerical values; numerical values set his mind at ease and satisfy him. Now, there is no question that numbers are useful for describing certain tendencies, states, and conditions. However, many things cannot be described in terms of numbers. For example, how could one begin to express "life" and "vitality" with numbers? It is no easy task to represent something having life in terms of formulas and numerical values. But it would foolish to state that what cannot be expressed in this way does not exist. While life and vitality both unmistakably exist, they clearly cannot be expressed with numbers.

I began a brown rice diet out of a desperate desire to save my daughter's life. I did not chose to adopt a brown rice diet because I knew the nutritive value and ingredients of brown rice and understood that this food would save her life. I took up a brown rice diet because, having been told that brown rice had a vitality that triggers miracles, I accepted this as an article of faith.

Nor did the relationship between a brown rice diet and the triad of *gomashio*, *takuan*, and *umeboshi* originally come about as a result of an analysis of their nutritive value and ingredients. At some point, these three foods became essential adjuncts of a brown rice diet as a result of an empirical rather than theoretical learning process; out of many secondary foods, these three were found to be especially compatible with brown rice and were recognized as promoting health and being effective in the treatment of disease. If each were submitted to nutritional analyses by modern scientific techniques, they would no doubt demonstrate theoretically desirable results. It is with this in mind that I describe each of the three below based on recent materials and data.

*Gomashio (with Black Sesame Seeds):*   An excellent book has been published recently in Japan on black sesame. For the sake of reference, the translated title is "Black Sesame was a Carcinostatic and Anti-Aging Substance."* I quote below from this source.

*          *          *          *

(1)   The morning edition of the May 16, 1985 *Mainichi Shimbun* (a leading daily newspaper in Japan) carried the following article, entitled "Chemical Structure of New Component in Sesame Revealed: Opens Up New Avenues in Carcinostatics and Food Processing."

A research group headed by Professor Michio Namiki of the Food Processing Department in Nagoya University's Faculty of Agriculture has succeeded in extracting from natural sesame seeds a lignin analog that suppresses the formation of peroxidized lipids (which are carcinogenic and cause aging), and has determined the chemical structure through x-ray analysis. Since antiquity, sesame has been reputed to have an invigorating effect, but

---

*   Japanese title: *Kurogoma wa seigan furo no busshitsu datta*, by Kazuhiro Yasuda, Professor and Doctor of Medicine at the Teikyo University Faculty of Medicine.

virtually no research has been done to elucidate the chemical structure of the active ingredients responsible for this effect. Specialists too regard this as highly significant research which will open up new avenues in food processing and the development of new pharmaceuticals.

(2)   The Sesame and Man: Throughout human history the sesame has left a legacy in both East and West as a health food par excellence and as a mysterious food having divine powers.

Sesame is said to have first been used 5,000 or 6,000 years ago. In the course of this time, the effects of the sesame has been most closely studied and analyzed by the Chinese. From the time that the sesame first entered China in the second century B.C., brown sesame in particular has been called "kunyaku" and has been revered as the best food for sustaining health.

The sesame is believed to have originated in India or in eastern Africa.

The first document to mention the efficacy of the sesame seed is the *Shen Nong Ben Cao Jing* [Divine Husbandman's Classic of the Materia Medica], a classical Chinese text on medicinal herbs. It lauded black sesame as the very source of life and attributed to this food the following effects:

1.   Cures weakening and injury of the internal organs;
2.   Invigorates the functions of the liver, heart, spleen, lungs, and kidneys, giving one physical vigor and strength;
3.   Stimulates brain activity.

Moreover, this also claimed that the long-term ingestion of black sesame not only lightens the movements of the body but also halts aging.

The *Ben Cao Gang Mu* [Grand Materia Medica], a large pharmacological tome published during the Ming dynasty in China goes into even further detail on the beneficial effects of eating sesame. In addition to the above, this states that sesame enhances muscle tone, improves the functioning of the five senses, gives one the strength to withstand hunger and thirst, suppresses epidemics, injury, pain of various types, and fever, and also prolongs life. This work also states that sesame is pharmacologically effective against rheumatism and colds, helps ensure an easy birth, cures swellings and tumors, hemorrhoids, toothaches, hypertension, arteriosclerosis, autonomic disorder, and other conditions. Moreover, sesame is also reputedly effective in diseases of the lower half of the body and has an invigorating effect on males. It was regarded as *the* nourishing tonic, the best of all medicines.

These effects of brown sesame are demonstrated even today, but they are explained as being due to the action of vitamin E and $B_1$, minerals such as calcium and iron, or essential amino acids.

(3)   The Secret of the Zen Monk's Physical and Mental Strength:

It is well known that the traditional *shojin-ryori*, a type of vegetarian cooking practiced by zen monks, uses a lot of sesame. Most of the sesame cooking that people eat in Japan today, such as sesame tofu, sesame miso, *gomashio*, and sesame dressings, reportedly emerged from *shojin-ryori*.

(4)   Why 25 Grams of Sesame Builds a Stronger Body than 200 Grams of Steak:

Let us compare the nutritional value of the sesame with that of other foods. For example, did you know that someone who eats just 25 grams of sesame seeds a day can maintain a much stronger body than someone who eats 200 grams of meat each day?

Twenty-five grams is about two tablespoons worth of unground seeds, or about one tablespoon worth of ground seeds. If you take this every day, your stamina will never lag behind that of the healthiest person. The fact is that 25 grams of black sesame seeds contains 13 grams of lipids, 5 grams of protein, 300 milligrams of calcium (equivalent to 2 glasses of milk), and 145 calories (about two-thirds the number of calories in a bowl of rice).

Twenty-five grams will not give you all the vitamins and minerals you need, but because the other foods that you eat every day contain vitamins and minerals, there is no need to worry. Of course, to benefit from this nutrition, one must continue taking 25 grams of sesame every day.

You can increase your daily intake of sesame by using also sesame-based products such as sesame oil in your cooking.

The moisture content of the sesame seed is only 4.7%, which is very low. This compares with 6.2% for peanuts and 57.4% for gingko nuts. Because the sesame seed has a hard ovarian wall, the moisture level is lower than that of other fruit. For this reason, the protein and lipids combined exceed 70%, giving a richer flavor. When roasted, ground, or kneaded, sesame gives off a distinctive flavor.

(5)   Things to Watch Out for When Buying Sesame Seeds:

A shopper will ordinarily compare two brands of brown sesame in the supermarket and, without further thought, place the less expensive package in his/her shopping cart. This person may be eating imitation black sesame. People tend to accept dark-colored sesame as black sesame and light-colored sesame as brown sesame, but some low-grade products are colored black or bleached and sold as black or brown sesame. Sesame is an extraordinary food that improves the health. But not just any sesame will do.

Please try to remember the following. The sesame that you buy should have well-filled seeds of uniform size. Always choose the freshest product possible. Avoid sesame that has a musty odor. Fresh, high-quality sesame and stale, low-grade sesame differ vastly not only in taste but also in their nutritional value.

If at all possible, buy *raw* sesame seeds. Toasting the seeds yourself before you use them allows you to enjoy sesame seeds at their most delicious and aromatic. It appears that much of the sesame sold in food stores is already toasted. Pre-toasted sesame may be convenient and timesaving, but the unsaturated fatty acids have oxidized, resulting in the formation of peroxidized lipids, the level of vitamin E has dropped, and the flavor is just not the same. When you shop for sesame seeds, make sure to do so at a grocery store or supermarket that has a rapid turnover of product; buy the amount that you need and use it up as quickly as you can.

Generally speaking, there is not that much difference nutritionally between the brown sesame and the black sesame. However, recent studies show that black sesame is preferable in a number of respects. First of all, the ingredients responsible for the color of the hull in black sesame are anthocyan and riboflavins. Riboflavins are vitamin B$_2$, which means that this layer is rich in vitamins. Moreover, the content of aromatic oils present on the inside of this layer is higher in black sesame than brown sesame. Also, it has been reported that black sesame is more resistant to oxidation.*

*    *    *    *

Let us look now at how black sesame salt (*gomashio*), one of the three treasures of a genmai diet, is prepared.

It is very important that you examine and reflect on how much animal-based food you and your family have eaten in the past. As I have already pointed out, the intake of animal-based foods results in a buildup of sodium in the body. Hence, unless people are careful about the *gomashio* they eat, they sometimes take in too much salt, resulting in health problems. This is something to watch out for.

Use 10 grams of salt per 100 grams of black sesame (this must not be sesame seeds that have been colored black). The ratio of black sesame to salt is normally 10: 1. Make sure to use natural salt. Vary the amount of salt according to your physical condition and the symptoms and nature of your illness (if you are sick).

The following instructions on preparing *gomashio* are taken from *Genmai seishoku ryoriho* [*Macrobiotic Brown Rice Cooking*] by Hisako Yamaguchi.

"First, warm the mortar (*suribachi*) and pestle with the fire. Begin by carefully roasting the salt. This lets off hydrochloric acid which emits an unpleasant odor, so don't bring your face too close. Once the odor has vanished and the salt is sufficiently parched, transfer this to the mortar and grind it vigorously to a fine powder. This should be fine enough to fly up with a breeze. If you work the pestle from the top to the bottom of the mortar, it will be easier to put your strength into the grinding. Next, warm a small, thin-walled pan with a tight-fitting lid in the center of the fire, place a small amount of sesame seeds (just enough to cover the bottom of the pan when spread out) and close the lid. Holding the pan by its handle, press down on the lid and listen carefully. When you hear a crackling sound and two or three sesame seeds popping, raise the pan straight up above the fire to the top of the flame and shake the seeds inside the pan up and down. After a short while, empty the toasted sesame seeds onto the salt. If no smoke emerges, then the sesame is still raw. If the smoke that emerges has a burnt smell to it, then the sesame is overtoasted. The sesame will burn unless the lid is opened and the sesame is rapidly transferred to the mortar, so make sure to place the mortar near the fire.

"Once all of the sesame has been toasted, if you stand squarely in front of the mortar with a straight back and hold the pestle vertically, you will be able to grind the sesame and salt without straining. Don't grind too hard as this will force out the oils and make the sesame salt tacky and poor-tasting; the resulting *gomashio* will also spoil faster. You will not have to put that much

---

* Let us make a Yin-Yang judgment of black and brown sesame. Neither is better or worse than the other. What is important is to determine the level of yin or yang of each and use them in a fitting manner.

effort into it if you work the pestle from the bottom of the mortar to the top—the opposite of when grinding the salt. Generally you continue grinding until about 70% of the sesame seeds have broken open and about 30% are intact, but if you prefer you may continue grinding until all the seeds have been crushed. Take as much care with this as you would when handling a little baby—each tiny grain of salt should be enveloped with sesame. By so doing, the result will be delicious and good for the body as well. Not just sesame salt, but all macrobiotic cooking is carried out in this manner—with Yang placed at the center and this wrapped on the outside with Yin.

"*Gomashio* can be kept for a while, but the oil eventually breaks down so it is best not to make too much at once. Prepare a small amount and keep it in the refrigerator in a glass jar, for example, so that you always have some on hand to sprinkle over your rice when you want."

*How to Prepare Black Gomashio:*  It is best to begin by limiting the amount of *gomashio* taken in a single meal to about half a teaspoon's worth. I am always amazed at how many people are in such a hurry to improve their symptoms and state of health that they eat large amounts of black *gomashio* at one meal. Although this may have satisfactory effects at first, over the long run it tends to upset the Yin-Yang balance. It is far better to gradually become accustomed to *gomashio* by using a little at a time while carefully observing ensuing changes in one's physical condition. After experimenting with various amounts myself, I sensed that continuing to take about a half-teaspoonful each day was best for me. There will be times when you won't want or won't be able to take even such a small amount as this. You need not force yourself to take some when you don't care to. The idea is to eat *gomashio* when you feel you want some or when it tastes good to you.

*Takuan:*  *Takuan* is pickled daikon prepared with rice bran and salt. Pickled foods of many different kinds have emerged from the varied climates and terrains of the world, each of these foods bearing the distinctive mark of the local people. Of these, *takuan* is surely one of the pickled foods best suited to rice-eating. *Takuan* is an invaluable food in a brown rice diet. But to people other than the Japanese, it does take some getting used to. When the Japanese first tried tasting the cheeses of the West, the odor was so repugnant to them that they were unable to eat any. *Takuan* is the same; although the Japanese readily accept and enjoy *takuan*, people of other cultures seem to have a bit of trouble with it at first. In fact, in some quarters, it is even claimed that the Japanese have a body odor like that of *takuan*, so perhaps those not accustomed to this food must feel that it gives off a powerful and offensive odor.

But it is in part from this distinctive odor that *takuan* derives its worth. *Takuan* is a precious and invaluable secondary food for rebuilding one's body and mind and improving one's physical constitution with a brown rice diet. In the same way that cheese promotes the proper functioning of the intestines in meat eaters, *takuan* promotes the healthy functioning of the stomach and intestines in rice-eating vegetarians. Far more than just a secondary food, this simple food displays a variety of incredible pharmacological effects.

Until I learned about a brown rice diet, I was ignorant of the true worth of *takuan*. When I was a child during the war, the Japanese lived in a constant state of material need; each and every household prepared its own *takuan* and *umeboshi*. In our home as well, my mother prepared *takuan* every year in the late fall. If you had *takuan*, then you could save on other secondary foods. But we never were grateful for this *takuan* and craved other, richer foods.

I suspect that many people today in Japan think of *takuan* and rice as a poor man's meal. Our recollections of poverty during the war years are still very strong, which is perhaps why we so recklessly pursue our desires for wealth and sumptuary extravagance. Oblivious to the important role played by *takuan* in a rice-based diet, we cherish instead foods that merely titillate our palate. The lack of a new education in diet and of a correct way to look at the food that we eat is surely one of the reasons why *takuan* is now so underrated.

As people eat an increasing amount of delicacies and rich foods, they catch more and more diseases and die. Seeing this has at last made me pause and reflect awhile on food. It was not until I started a brown rice diet that I learned the true worth of *takuan*.

At the beginning of this section, I stated that *takuan* is pickled daikon prepared using rice bran and salt. But this is not entirely correct. *Takuan* is in fact pickled daikon prepared with rice bran, natural salt, a heavy stone, air, the microbes in air, a pickling vat, spices for flavoring, and time.

I have already noted elsewhere in this book that a healthy gastrointestinal system is the foundation for a healthy body. *Takuan* has an amazing pharmacological efficacy for rendering the gastrointestinal system healthy. While it is regrettable that this efficacy of *takuan* has yet to be scientifically explained, living a life style based on a brown rice diet and *takuan* provides the best proof possible. It is clear that eating a little brown rice and *takuan* is far more pharmacologically effective than ingesting a lot of gastrointestinal medications.

*Takuan* is an ideal material for studying the Universal Principle of Yin and Yang. Let us examine the Yin and Yang of *takuan* to determine how many slices are good for the body and whether this has the effect of keeping the stomach and intestines healthy.

In my definition of *takuan* above, I mentioned the following:

    (1)   rice bran
    (2)   natural salt
    (3)   heavy stone
    (4)   air and microbes
    (5)   the vessel (a pickling vat)
    (6)   spices
    (7)   time
    (8)   daikon

These are the elements we will need to consider the Yin and Yang of *takuan*. Because *takuan* is pickled daikon, the daikon is of central importance.

Let's begin by asking why raw daikon is pickled in the first place. Not only daikon but many other vegetables as well as fruits are pickled. Just why do people prepare pickles with salt anyway? This should become apparent if we consider for a moment the effect of salt. I imagine that it is already clear by now whether *takuan* is the product of yangizing or yinnizing raw daikon, but before getting into this let me describe the process of pickling daikon to form *takuan*.

*How Takuan is Prepared:*

(1)  *Materials:*  A wooden keg or bucket or a ceramic crock that holds about 18 liters, a heavy stone (weighing about 30 kg), 500 g of rice bran, 900 g of natural salt, a push-down lid for the crock, 8–10 cloves of garlic, and 20–25 dried daikons.

(2)  *Directions:*

1.  Mix together the rice bran and salt.
2.  Peel the garlic and slice thinly.
3.  The daikon should consist of good daikon roots that have been dried in the shade until they are pliable enough to fold over in two.
4.  Spread a little of the bran and salt mixture on the bottom of the crock, spread half of the garlic on top of this, then tightly arrange a layer of daikon on top of this. Follow with alternating layers of bran and dried daikon, then scatter the remaining garlic throughout the crock and cover the daikon with dried daikon leaves. After this is done, place the lid on top of the contents and perch the heavy stone on top of the lid.
5.  Dried persimmon skin, orange rind, apple skin, or *kombu* may also be used in place of the garlic.
6.  *Takuan* pickled in this fashion at the end of the year is ready to eat the following May or June. Those who want to eat their *takuan* even earlier should increase the amount of rice bran and decrease the salt.

    The bran and the salt are roasted separately. This gives the *takuan* a mellower taste. The use of garlic prevents the *takuan* from spoiling and improves the flavor.

In the above method of pickling *takuan*, the drying of raw daikon in the shade, along with the use of rice bran, salt, a heavy stone, and about six months of time transforms the daikon into an extremely yang fermented food. Nor does this merely become a yang pickled food; it absorbs the plethora of vitamins and minerals in the rice bran as well as the minerals in the natural salt. In addition, beneficial microbes in the air act upon daikon, forming digestive enzymes. This series of synergetic effects results in the creation of a mysterious secondary food. In fact, in *takuan*, we have a prime example of the application of the most highly advanced biotechnology to foods. Because a brown rice diet is catching on also in the United States and Europe as a way to health and beauty, I would encourage the full production and use of *takuan* in all parts of the world. But first, why don't you start by trying to make this at home?

In modern Japan, people no longer pickle *takuan* at home. Home-made *takuan* is a real treasure that makes the gastrointestinal system robust and healthy. But the Japanese have abandoned this and instead buy *takuan* that is produced in factories and contains coloring agents, artificial sweeteners, and chemical seasonings. Instead of making *takuan* at home, it is cheaper and easier to buy it ready-made in a store. But the dietary and medicinal effects of the two differ completely. Home-made *takuan* contains various beneficial microbes that promote health, while factory-made *takuan* is a harmful food product containing many injurious additives that destroy beneficial intestinal flora. So, even though it may involve a lot more bother, time, and money, do try pickling your own *takuan* at home.

*Umeboshi:*   Like *takuan*, *umeboshi* is a food with which the normal meat-eater has little familiarity. *Umeboshi* forms a highly compatible combination with a rice diet, but the truth of the matter is that *umeboshi* is nowhere more necessary than to the meat eater. Since my intention in this book is to promote a rice-based diet over a meat-based diet, and a diet based on genmai rather than white rice—that is, a macrobiotic brown rice diet—I will leave it to others to explain the benefits of eating *umeboshi* in a meat-based diet. Here I will discuss only *umeboshi* in a rice diet.

As a child I had a weak gastrointestinal system. I often had diarrhea, my tonsils would swell up, and before I knew it I would have caught a cold and be sporting a high fever. It didn't take much to put me in bed with a cold or other malady. When I was a child, if you were sick in bed the only thing you were fed was a rice gruel with *umeboshi* or salt. I remember that my first encounters with *umeboshi* were in those meals I had when I was sick. The rice gruel I ate at the time was made from white rice, yet astounding as it may seem, even such a simple meal as this cured me of my illness. Had this gruel been prepared with brown rice, the effects would surely have been much stronger, but at the time I knew nothing yet of brown rice diets. Today, I would recommend a brown rice cream or brown rice gruel with *umeboshi* in it as the ideal meal for treating sick people. I firmly believe that this is the best food and best therapeutic diet available to man.

I began this discussion of the *umeboshi* by writing of its connection with rice gruel, but the Japanese have a very intimate association with *umeboshi* throughout all aspects of life. One could easily write an entire book on this. In fact, an excellent work has been written on the subject by Dr. Moriyasu Ushio, a student of George Ohsawa's and a veteran of the macrobiotic movement in Japan. Below, I quote one particularly pertinent passage from his book, which is entitled *Umeboshi no shinpi* [The Mysteries of the Umeboshi].

\*     \*     \*     \*

*The Umeboshi and the Krebs Cycle*: How the Citric Acid in *Umeboshi* Plays a Pivotal Role within the Krebs Cycle—

The *umeboshi* is not good for the body simply because it is an alkaline food. The fact is that this food plays an extremely important role in the body.

In modern nutritional science, five groups of substances are cited as nutrients essential to the human body: carbohydrates, protein, fats, vitamins, and minerals. The calories represented by these components (other than vitamins and  minerals) are computed, based upon which food nutrition charts are drawn up and energy replenished by a combination of foods. Whether or not one or two *umeboshi* are eaten each day makes little quantitative difference in terms of  nutritional value calculated in this manner. But this is a great mistake, which I shall now explain.

The nutrients in food don't become energy directly. In the body, they undergo many different changes, releasing energy in the course of these changes. It was Dr. H.A. Krebs who, noting the remarkable action of the Japanese *umeboshi*, threw light on the overall mechanism of nutrition. The theory of this mechanism of nutrition is known variously as the "citric acid cycle," the "TCA cycle," and the "Krebs cycle." In 1953, Krebs was awarded the Nobel prize for his research on the cellular metabolism of substances.

Nutrients such as carbohydrates, protein, and fats are oxidized and broken down within the body into carbon dioxide and water. Energy is released during this process and is utilized in biological activity. Even this much was mentioned in the old science textbooks. But the overall picture of what sort of metabolic processes these nutrients pass through to result in the release of energy was not yet well understood.

In 1943, Krebs published a theory explaining just this. His theory clarified in detail the process by which carbohydrates—including starches, glycogens, and glucose—are oxidized and decomposed. The importance of Kreb's theory became increasingly apparent as time passed. The fact that citric acid and oxaloacetic acid play pivotal roles in this nutrient cycle process explains why the *umeboshi*, which contains a large amount of natural, high-grade citric acid, attracted such sudden attention.

*The Citric Acid Cycle:*   First, glycogen is broken down, turning glucose into pyruvic acid. Part of this then becomes lactic acid, and half of the lactic acid passes over a different pathway, returning to glycogen. A very small portion of this lactic acid is excreted outside of the body in the urine.

In addition, some of the pyruvic acid returns back to glucose by the same pathway, and some of the lactic acid returns to pyruvic acid. However, what happens to the majority of the pyruvic acid which is not converted back into glucose and does not become lactic acid? This enters the Krebs cycle.

When pyruvic acid enters the Krebs cycle, this is subjected first to oxidative decomposition; reaction follows upon reaction until the pyruvic acid is broken down completely to carbon dioxide and water. This process releases a large amount of energy. Thus, pyruvic acid is a key substance in the Krebs cycle; it plays a major role in energy transformation within the body.

Pyruvic acid reacts in this way with one after another of the many enzymes in the tissues of the human body, changing form and, in the course of the Krebs cycle, emerging again as new pyruvic acid.

Let us take a closer look at a single pass through this pyruvic acid cycle. First, the pyruvic acid reacts with oxaloacetic acid within human tissue to become citric acid; this citric acid then leads to a series of reactions giving the following substances: aconitic acid → isocitric acid → α-ketoglutaric acid → succinic acid → fumaric acid → malic acid. This malic acid loses a hydrogen, thereby returning to the original oxaloacetic acid. This oxaloacetic acid reacts with the pyruvic acid, leading to another circuit of the Krebs cycle.

If pyruvic acid remained in this form within the body, it would be a harmful acidic substance, but by reacting with oxaloacetic acid it is drawn into the cycle and continues to react in a stepwise fashion while releasing energy, ultimately breaking down completely into carbon dioxide and water.

*Oxidative Decomposition within the Krebs Cycle Multiplies the Energy Twenty-fold:*
What is interesting here is that 36 calories of energy are released during the decomposition of a single molecule of glucose to pyruvic acid, whereas 650 calories of energy are released in the process of oxidative decomposition within the Krebs cycle. In other words, 95% of the energy released by glucose is released within the Krebs cycle.

Most of the rice serving as the food staple of the Japanese, and the wheat constituting the raw material in bread and *udon* (wheat noodle) flour consists of carbohydrates. This is converted into glucose within the body, becoming a valuable energy source. From what we have seen above, it should be clear by now that this energy is not released all at once, but rather is gradually converted to energy over a number of steps. When this carbohydrate is decomposed, if organic acids such as the citric acid in *umeboshi* are available, this allows the oxidative decomposition process to proceed smoothly, enabling the release of large amounts of energy and thereby promoting activity. That one *umeboshi* in the morning is far more than just a unit of nutrition. It serves the role of a catalyst in activating the body's functions.

Not just carbohydrates, but all carbon compounds (all organic nutrients), including of course proteins and fats, are oxidatively decomposed in this cycle. A portion of the protein is converted from alanine to pyruvic acid, at which point it enters the Krebs cycle; aspartic acid is similarly converted to oxaloacetic acid, while glutamic acid becomes $\alpha$-ketoglutaric acid. In fats, the glycerin becomes pyruvic acid via glycerophosphoric acid, while the fatty acids become oxalo acids.

The source of the kinetic energy when we move or lift objects is stored in the form of adenosine triphosphate (ATP) and released when needed. Therefore, unless the cycle works properly, there is a danger of this reservoir of energy becoming depleted; the Krebs cycle is the core of the body's activity. When this fails to work properly, pyruvic acid builds up in the body, forming lactic acid. Pyruvic acid and lactic acid are acidic substances which are harmful to the body.

The structural formula for lactic acid is the same as that of pyruvic acid, except for the presence of two additional hydrogens ($CH_3CHOHCOOH$). Pyruvic acid that fails to enter the Krebs cycle becomes lactic acid; the gradual accumulation of lactic acid in the body causes illness. This lactic acid is the cause of sore muscles after exercising and of stiff neck and shoulders in the elderly. When lactic acid bonds with protein, it forms complexes that cause arteriosclerosis and cell aging.

*Umeboshi Helps the Krebs Cycle Work Smoothly:*  What then should be done to enable the Krebs cycle to function properly?

First of all, vitamin $B_1$ is necessary in order to introduce pyruvic acid into the Krebs cycle. Pyruvic acid is converted into activated acetic acid (coenzyme A) in the step prior to becoming citric acid; the vitamin $B_2$ group, and especially pantothenic acid, takes part at this stage. All the enzymes, as well as vitamins $B_1$, $B_2$, phosphoric acid, and other substances involved in this process are present in rice bran. In other words, eating unpolished brown rice allows the Krebs cycle to proceed smoothly. When one's staple food is white rice, however, these enzymes and vitamins are absent from the rice. Moreover, instead of entering the Krebs cycle, the pyruvic acid formed from the starch in white rice accumulates to high levels in the blood, resulting in the formation of lactic acid. This makes the body tire easily, causing chronic fatigue and all the diseases associated with this.

Another essential substance is oxaloacetic acid. This is an organic acid produced from *umeboshi*, vinegared dishes, *natsumikan* (Japanese summer oranges), and other similar foods. When too much white rice and bread is eaten and lactic acid accumulates in the body, one should take in organic acids such as citric acid. Citric acid causes the production of oxaloacetic acid within the body, which in turn holds lactic acid in check and decomposes it to carbon dioxide and water, then eliminates it from the body. When rice serves as the primary food, foods containing citric acid should be taken. The food product containing the highest level of natural, high-grade citric acid is none other than the *umeboshi*. Whether in terms of economics or from the standpoint of a preservable food that is readily available around the year, nothing beats taking one *umeboshi* with breakfast each morning.

The chief role of the *umeboshi* is to assist the smooth operation of the Krebs cycle. The Japanese of the past who ate *umeboshi* with their unpolished brown rice had greater stamina than people today and enjoyed a truly sensible and superb diet.

*The Five Major Effects of the Umeboshi:*
1. Prevents aging;
2. Purifies the blood;
3. Promotes vigor;
4. Conditions the intestines; has bactericidal effects
5. Assists in recovery from fatigue.

This is a superb food that, when eaten, is effective in curing disease, including ekiri, dysentery, colds and the flu, anemia, low blood pressure, gastrointestinal ailments, heart disease, and liver disorders. It is also highly effective as an external application in the treatment of such conditions as toothache, headache, and neuralgia.

*How to Prepare Umeboshi:*
*Materials:* 10 kg of green, unripened *ume* plums. 2–3 kg of coarse salt (natural salt); this should be prepared for use by roasting.
*Directions:* Soak meaty *ume* plums overnight in cold water, then drain water. Place a little salt in a crock and arrange a layer of the plums over the salt. Alternate with layers of salt and plums, then place a light pushdown lid on top of this and leave the plums to stand for one month. After a month, take the plums out of the crock in the morning and dry them all day; in the evening return the plums to the *umezu* (*ume* plum vinegar) that has formed in the crock. After repeating this daily drying process for seven days, the *umeboshi* are ready to store and eat.

# Sea Vegetables, Vegetable Oils, and Sweeteners

In this section, I will briefly discuss other foods essential to a brown rice macro-biotic diet.

*Sea Vegetables:* The first of these are the seaweeds, or "sea vegetables," as they are often called today. Both land vegetables and sea vegetables are very important. Sea vegetables include *kombu, wakame, hijiki,* and *nori;* these are richer in different nutrients than land vegetables, including minerals, vitamins, and calcium. You should make an effort to eat a small amount of some sea vegetable each day.

The *kombu,* of which many different types exist, are brown algae. In addition to calcium and iron, these contain iodine and vitamin A. Aside from having an invigorating effect on the body and mind, it prevents rickets, has a beneficial effect on the hair, and enhances the digestion of starch and beans. Because *kombu* improves the flavor of miso soup, make sure to include about five square pieces (each measuring about an inch to a side) in the soup. When fried without batter, this makes a great snack for the kids, a treat to go along with beer or whiskey, and an easy-to-prepare side dish. Another excellent side dish that can be prepared from *kombu* is obtained by boiling this down together with soybeans or root vegetables, and flavoring with soy sauce. When I was a kid, candies and other sweets were not as easy to come by as they are today. Instead, we would chew hard, dried *kombu* just like kids chew gum today. In today's affluent world, we are better able to appreciate how this served as a rich, natural treat in an age of poverty. Today's stores are filled with sweets and other treats, but these are made of very poor ingredients. It makes one wonder which age was really richer and better for children.

In addition to the above, there are many other ways of eating and using *kombu.* Why don't you try experimenting with new ways of preparing this excellent food yourself?

*Wakame* is easy to eat because it is softer and more pliable than *kombu. Wakame* contains the sugar mannitol and a high level of iodine; it is effective against heart disease and diabetes, and lowers the blood pressure. It can be used in miso soup or in dishes dressed with sauce, and can even be eaten raw.

*Hijiki* contains the highest calcium level of all sea vegetables. In addition to its outstanding efficacy against heart disease, diabetes, neuralgia, constipation, chronic ailments, and intestinal diseases, it has recently been found to be extraordinarily effective in preventing cancer and in the treatment of disorders resulting from radiation exposure.

Like sesame seeds, these sea vegetables are outstanding sources of minerals; eating a little each day is important. There is no need to take a lot at one time. Even one or two mouthfuls is quite enough.

*Vegetables Oils:* Unlike animal-based fats, vegetables oils such as sesame oil, soybean oil, rapeseed oil, and camellia oil have the ability to invigorate those who are feeble or sick. They contain no cholesterol and do not cause illnesses such as arteriosclerosis, hypertension, and obesity. Because these are rich in unsaturated oils and linolic acid, they play a vital role as "lubricants" in the body's physiological activity.

People stricken with neuralgia, rheumatism, skin diseases, and chronic ailments should make full use of cooking that employs sesame oil with leaf vegetables, root vegetables, and sea vegetables in treating their condition. With these, one can prepare much delicious food, including tempura dishes of leaf and root vegetables and also wild herbs.

By heating a tablespoon of sesame oil over a low flame to a simmer in two tablespoons of grated *daikon*, then pouring this onto unheated grated *daikon* and sprinkling a suitable amount of naturally fermented soy sauce over this, one can obtain a concoction that is outstandingly effective against neuralgia when taken with one's breakfast and supper. Anyone suffering from neuralgia should by all means try this.

It is also an excellent idea to thoroughly sauté leafy and root vegetables that are in season and add these to miso soup. This is known to be effective in treating high blood pressure, heart disease, chapped skin, irregular menses, neurosis, and disorders of the eyes. Vegetable oils should be used only in small amounts; in large amounts, these have adverse effects.

*Sweeteners:*   Virtually all people who consistently eat animal-based foods, and primarily meat, also use large amounts of white sugar. I have already stated that eating large amounts of meat and white sugar are the greatest villains in making the body cancer-prone. Although I am certain that the evils of overconsuming meat are already clear, using refined white sugar also has many adverse effects on the human body. While the occasional use of highly refined seasonings and processed foods is acceptable for medicinal purposes, their habitual use is extremely dangerous.

Sugar is unnecessary in a brown rice diet. Some say that a small amount may be used to flavor one's cooking or beverages, but I believe that sugar is simply unnecessary. There is clearly no need to ingest any white sugar, but I believe that we need not deliberately take in even natural sweeteners such as turbinato sugar or honey. As long as you quietly and meticulously chew the brown rice that you eat, your body will not need any sugar.

Well then, what about sweeteners required for cooking? You should make an effort to learn how to cook in such a way as to skillfully draw out the natural sweetness of vegetables such as carrots, onions, squash, cabbage, taros, and so forth. Another good idea is to make use of the sweetness of fruits. Naturally, the use of artificial chemical sweeteners should not even be considered.

## The Mechanism of Heart Disease as Seen through Macrobiotics

*The Yin and Yang of Vegetable and Animal Oils:*   When I was a kid, I used to enjoy watching American Westerns. Those Westerns featuring such stars as John Wayne, Gary Cooper, and Burt Lancaster were fun to watch and inspired in us a pioneering spirit. I remember especially the barroom scenes. Somebody would come riding in on a horse and enter the bar, where the first thing he did was to swallow a shot of whiskey. That's straight whiskey. I don't recall ever seeing a scene in which someone drinks whiskey-and-water like people do today. When people in Japan or in the East talk of getting a drink they usually mean tea. Even those who prefer alcohol over tea drink *saké,* which has far less alcohol in it than whiskey. True, some people in Japan prefer drinking stronger spirits, but even these are generally less potent than straight whiskey.

I had a weak gastrointestinal system, so I just couldn't get that picture of those guys downing a shot or two of whiskey out of my mind. I worried whether it didn't upset their stomachs—drinking whiskey straight like that without having eaten anything. I wondered if that liquor didn't scorch their intestinal walls and was certain that if I ever tried doing the same thing I would soon develop gastric ulcers and other stomach troubles. For the longest time, I was puzzled as to why Westerners liked whiskey so much and was more than a little amazed as to why they could drink like that.

It was only when I began studying the Unifying Principle of Yin and Yang that I began resolving these questions one by one in my mind. When I weighed the Yin and Yang of animal fats and vegetable oils, the physiological mechanism that craves whiskey became clear to me. Why don't you try learning about Yin and Yang here with me using fats and oils as our example?

According to the dictionary I have before me, vegetable and animal oils are distinguished from each other as follows:

*Vegetable Oils:*   Flammable liquids extracted from the seeds or other parts of plants.
*Animals Oils:*   Fat attached to animal flesh.

Thus vegetable oils are regarded as "oil," while animals oils are regarded as "fat." This alone is enough to show which is yang and which is yin. Hence, the Yin and Yang of animal and vegetable oil is not complicated at all, and can in fact be easily understood by anyone. Let us then examine the action of each of these on the human body.

The animal fat typically used in everyday cooking is lard, while the vegetable oils used are normally corn oil, rice oil, soybean oil, sesame oil, rapeseed oil, coconut oil, and the like.

Let us compare lard and sesame oil.

At normal temperatures, lard is a solid that does not require cooling or warming, while sesame oil is a liquid. Lard is already a solid at normal temperatures, but sesame oil remains a liquid. This alone is enough to indicate which is more yin and which more yang. What do you think?

Because the staple food of people in the West is generally meat, their intake of animal-based fats and oils such as lard and butter also tends to be quite high. Since these are oils that solidify at normal temperatures, in the human body they either take on a liquid form that readily solidifies or they are incorporated as solid fat within the body. This animal-based fat tends to become subcutaneous fat located on the surface of the body near the exterior.

When subcutaneous fat spreads throughout the body, this gradually solidifies starting in those parts of the body where the temperature is the lowest; it then invades the organs at the interior of the body and adheres to these, eventually forming deposits even in the blood vessels and heart, which results ultimately in "seizure" of the heart's action. This is the most common mechanism for heart disease associated with obesity. Obese people have a cool body incapable of completely burning fat. They eat yang food such as meat, but because their eating habits are all wrong, they develop yin bodies that are prone to chills and oversensitive to the cold, and even acquire yin temperaments.

After the Second World War, the diet of the Japanese became Westernized; the consumption of animal-based foods, and especially meat, eggs, and milk and dairy products, was widely promoted. This was a massive attempt to convert the Japanese to a diet based on meat and dairy products. As a result, the diet of the Japanese underwent a great change and the consumption of items such as sugar, fruit juices, soda, coffee, beer, and whiskey also rose dramatically. These foods all have a physiological relationship with meat-eating. Meat and meat-based cuisine contains large amounts of animal fat. This animal fat creates a desire for whiskey and other strongly alcoholic beverages. The physiological instinct that urges the body to burn the fat adhering to the tissues and organs is what creates a thirst for whiskey. Whiskey could be regarded as an altered form of fire or perhaps as an ignition fluid. But such artificially induced physiological activity cannot be maintained for very long. When such a practice is habitual, this eventually gives rise to abnormalities in the intrinsic physiological activities of the human body. If a lot of meat is eaten, then the ingestion of animal fat naturally increases; this in turn creates a craving for whiskey. The reverse is equally possible; the habitual intake of alcoholic beverages excites a desire for meat and other animal-based foods, establishing a mechanism in which a negative cycle feeds on itself. This has made heart disease the leading cause of mortality in the United States.

People are turning more to meats lower in fat because they hear that fat is bad for the heart. They opt now for leaner beef, chicken, or fish. It may well be that reducing the intake of fats has a good effect on heart disease, but people have not reduced the amount of meat or fish they eat. In fact, while the fat intake has decreased, the intake of high-protein meat may have increased. When this happens, the desire for an agent to promote the digestion and absorption of the increased amount of protein grows. This desire manifests itself as an increased consumption of sweets, fruit juices, soda, ice cream, and fruit. White sugar is a key ingredient in all of these foods. The excessive intake of meat and white sugar has given birth to a virtual epidemic of cancer. Today, cancer is a leading cause of death in Japan, but this is merely an inevitable physiological mechanism for processing the evils of eating meat. Meat-eating unleashes a mechanism that promotes the degradation of the human body and mind, while a macrobiotic diet consisting of genmai (or other whole grains), vegetables, and sea vegetables has the opposite effect. We must become aware of the fact that different foods have very different effects on the physiological mechanisms of the human body. As long as improvements in diet founded on this awareness are not made, we cannot overcome the degenerative diseases that plague us today.

What then becomes of your body and your way of life when you use vegetable oils such as sesame oil?

Sesame seeds are very small, as is true of most vegetable seeds. These small seeds have a vitality such that when sown on the ground they send up shoots, grow into mature plants, and eventually bear many seed. Sesame oil is extracted from each one of these sesame seeds. A single spoonful of sesame oil contains the oil of many complete sesame seeds. How does this compare with a spoonful of lard? A spoonful of lard is subcutaneous fat, which represents only a very tiny fraction of the body of an animal. Although an animal is a single, complete organism, a small bit of meat or fat can hardly correspond to the entire life of that animal. By merely comparing a spoonful of sesame oil with a spoonful of lard, one can see the enormous gap that exists between their respective vitalities. The vitality and life-force of thousands and perhaps tens of thousands of seeds are contained in that spoonful of sesame oil, whereas a spoonful of lard corresponds to only one part in several thousand or several ten thousand of the vitality of one organism.

Because the fats that Westerners eat are generally contained in meat, cooking in oil appears to be rare. However, in the East, the rarity of meat-eating until recently has enabled a cuisine based on the use of vegetable oils to flourish. This is because, rather than using the oil alone, fire is used to induce its assimilation into the food, in which form it is later ingested. Compared with carbohydrates and protein, fats and oils are basically yin, so eating these after first yangizing them with fire makes a lot of sense. It is because of such cooking that the ratio of this oil which adheres to, settles on, and accumulates as fat in the internal body tissue and organs is very small. Moreover, the number of instances in which people develop vascular disorders and heart disease due to cholesterol ingested in this way is small. In the days before meat-eating became common in Japan, heart disease was rare. But as meat-eating has become more popular, heart disease has become second only to hypertension as a cause of death in Japan. Lard is an animal-based substance, while sesame oil is a plant-based substance. Since animals are yang and plants are yin, clearly lard is more yang than sesame oil. At normal temperatures, lard is a solid and sesame oil is a liquid. Solidification, as represented by the freezing of water to ice, represents yinnization; thus, at normal temperatures, lard is yin and sesame oil is yang. This sesame oil is almost never used raw, however; it is subjected to the extremely yang agent known as fire and made a notch more yang before being furnished for consumption. This is where the degree of yin and yang in lard and sesame oil differ greatly. The reason that heart disease and vascular disorders are uncommon among Orientals is due to their cuisine, which yangizes oils and fats before ingestion.

While we are comparing animal-based oils and fats with vegetable oils, it might be instructive to take a look also at butter prepared from milk and sesame butter.

Dairy butter is a solid at normal temperatures and below, but when heated slightly it turns into a liquid. This consists of fats and oils produced by animals, which are strongly yang ($\triangle$) components. Despite the presence of yang components, butter is dominated by the yin nature that is characteristic of fat. Although a great deal of dairy butter is used in cooking, even more is employed in the production of sweets and baked goods. The reason that milk and dairy butter go well with sugar ($\triangledown$) is that the yang components in these animal-derived products complement the yinness of sugar. In fact, the yang components are neutralized by the sugar so that most such cakes and sweets are yin foods dominated by the yinness of sugar. When people eat meat ($\blacktriangle$), the reason that they desire alcoholic beverages such as whiskey and also crave sweet ($\triangledown$) and cold ($\triangledown$) after-dinner treats such as cake and ice cream is that they need these to neutralize the extreme yangness ($\blacktriangle$)

of meat and to promote its digestion and assimilation. It is through eating habits such as these where fat ($\nabla$), sugar ($\nabla$), cold treats ($\nabla$), and fruit ($\nabla$) are customarily eaten together with meat that people take in an excess of fat and become obese ($\nabla$), which is a yin physical constitution. This starts them on the road toward physical debility through the development of yin tissues that harden and tighten the blood vessels and heart.

Instead of dairy butter, I use sesame butter. This is a liquid at normal temperatures, but thickens and solidifies when heated ($\triangle$), which makes it vastly different from dairy butter. Because it is an oil derived from plants, it quite naturally has the yin ($\nabla$) character of plants. While the components are yin, the sesame butter itself is surprisingly yang. That is why, unlike dairy butter, it does not harmonize at once when heated ($\triangle$). Sesame butter must find a compatible substance other than heat which has a yin character to it.

For example, when my wife teaches sesame butter cuisine at a macrobiotic cooking class, she uses several drops of *saké* to break down the butter. The alcohol ($\nabla$) present in *saké* corresponds well to the degree of yangness of the sesame butter, rendering the butter into a liquid, which is easier to work with in cooking. The reason that alcohol ($\nabla$) works better with sesame butter than the heat ($\triangle$) of a fire ($\blacktriangle$) is that the butter has a considerable degree of yangness. This principle also helps to explain why meat eaters like their whiskey so much. Alcohol ($\nabla$) has a temporary but specific effect of rapidly thinning blood that has become too thick and yangized ($\triangle$) through eating meat.

Although both are regarded as being in the same family of substances (oils and fats), animal-based fats and vegetable oils differ vastly from one another. These have completely opposite effects and influences on the body and mind. True health and happiness cannot be attained without learning and mastering this principle.

# 7

## Truths and Reflections

There are many different kinds of journeys. Although they may appear alike, each is different. No two journeys are exactly the same. It is because each journey is unique and special that people enjoy traveling. Isn't a journey a personification of the body? No, it is surely the other way around: our bodies are incarnations of the journeys we take.

Voyages of many kinds are taken toward the universe and toward cosmic life. Various trips toward the universe and cosmic life are in the process of beginning just now. Today, space rockets are blasting off and artificial satellites orbit the Earth.

Instead of making a rocket of my body, I made a rocket of my mind and ventured on a journey to cosmic life. This journey to cosmic life is my present body and flesh.

Because my journey was unconventional, I suppose that I am myself eccentric.

The fact that such a "wacky" journey is possible serves as proof that the mind is free. I wish that the body could become as free as this, but the freedom of the body and mind appear to be inversely proportional to each other.

What this may mean is that the freedom of mind I gained to travel on a journey to cosmic life may be supported by a lack of bodily freedom.

Or perhaps the reverse is true. It may have been because I was able by some good fortune to withstand the limits of the body that I was blessed with the freedom to travel to cosmic life.

The journey to cosmic life was a trip in which I studied Yin and Yang. I would like to consider here whether or not this was in fact the case, whether this began and ended merely as an eccentric experience; I would like to compare this with the real truth and determine whether this journey has become incorporated within myself, whether it has become me.

## Two Things that Mankind Must Do at Once

Man must do two things at once. One is to make unrefined, unbleached grains (brown rice, wheat, barley, buckwheat, millet, etc.) his food staple. The other is to abandon nuclear weapons and nuclear power.

I turned to brown rice and became healthy at long last. But I wonder now, is it enough to have become healthy? I am profoundly grateful that I have finally come to know health and that my family too is free of illness. But even so, what then?

It is only natural that people be healthy and that a family be free of illness. What special significance could such a natural outcome obtained from doing what is perfectly natural have?

Because I am a foolish person, through myself and my family I was able at last to see things on another plane.

I thought of nuclear arms and nuclear power as things that exist far away. Never in my wildest dreams had it occurred to me that nuclear weapons and nuclear power are out there poised right over my head, are in the air that I breathe and in the water and food that my children drink and eat.

Hiroshima and Nagasaki were becoming to me events dimmed by time and distance. Yet, in spite of being the wretch that I am, it occurred to me that if people learn how to become healthy and stay that way, this makes them, their families, the people of their country, and all the races of this world happier.

The earth is enshrouded by a cloud of nuclear weapons, nuclear power, and radioactivity.

There was a time when, possessing sophisticated weapons and tools, we prided ourselves on the victories gained through our knowledge and skills. Why, we even celebrated nuclear weapons and nuclear energy as agents that brought a world war to an early close, established a state of peace and equilibrium in the world, and provided salvation from depletion of the earth's resources. But this was a very grievous error indeed.

As Hiroshima and Nagasaki demonstrated, the bomb is none other than an executioner which demolishes everyone and everything indiscriminately. This executioner hangs over our world, spreading death to all things.

We tend to think that because we are alive today, we will be able to survive tomorrow. We feel that if we can only survive this day, we will survive the next day as well. This lends an urgency to surviving the present.

The reason the atomic bomb was built was also to win and survive. And the reason those who dropped the bombs did so was to survive. Were they alive today, all the people killed by those bombs would also believe in a tomorrow.

The same logic explains why countless nuclear missiles are deployed and why nuclear reactors have been built all over the world in order that we may live in peace. And here we are, all of us, alive and well, so surely we will be alive tomorrow, even with all of that—that is what we want to believe. Because I myself am healthy and strong today, then I believe that there will surely be a tomorrow and a day after tomorrow.

My journey to cosmic life showed me that man has introduced into the terrestrial ecosystem something that does not belong there. I learned that nuclear weapons and nuclear power create phenomena and substances which have no place in the terrestrial ecosystem.

Strange and anomalous phenomena which should not arise on the earth are today emerging in various fields of endeavor. Phenomena connected with the destruction of the earth and the organisms it nurtures are rearing their heads *this very moment*. This is not a vague threat relegated to the distant future, but something that faces us *now*.

Until recently, I believed that if we are alive today, then we will surely be alive tomorrow as well. But this "now" has become filled with the phenomenon of death; in a sense, it has become a present that exists for death.

I believe that we can with greater assurance say that tomorrow we will be dead, not alive.

We must get rid of that which we should not possess, and we must firmly grasp that which it is our duty to possess.

These two tasks that man must undertake at once—the elimination of nuclear arms and power and the conversion to whole grains as his food staple—is the very least we must do in order for humanity to survive in cosmic life.

# God Dwells in a Single Grain of Rice

In a single grain of brown rice, there lies a universe;
    an infinite universe, compressed and reposing.
God sleeps in that grain of rice.

If your eyes were millions and billions of times stronger,
    then you would see, in a single grain of brown rice
    green meadows and gods relaxing in a peaceful paradise.
The gods rest before setting off on their next pleasant journey,
    dreaming of their next stopping place.

Polishing and milling the rice has destroyed the sanctuary of the gods.
It has turned those green meadows and that peaceful paradise
    into a white city and white sugar.
No longer is this a paradise where the gods can enjoy a tranquil sleep.

Polishing rice destroys the universe of the rice;
    it destroys the nature within the rice.

Because white rice is barren of divine life, natural life, and cosmic life, one cannot partake of divine life by eating white rice. Nor does eating white rice help to nurture the mind or instill devotion to God.

The famous Ise Shrine in Japan is a sanctuary that has various aims and effects, but I have learned that it is also a shrine for illuminating a way of life based on rice and salt, and the order of that way of life.

People today use visits to the Ise Shrine as a false excuse for justifying themselves. Although they drive out the gods by refining rice and salt in the same way that drugs and chemicals are made, they believe that by following the religious observances and offering up pious utterances in honor of these departed gods, everything will be taken care of. To such people, visiting the shrine serves as nothing more than a tranquilizer.

Because the culture and civilization of polishing destroys the resting place of the gods, breaks up the road over which they travel, and dilutes the life in food, this has weakened our body and mind. The hospitals have become white shrines for rectifying this situation, and people today praise and revere hospitals as if they were the true sanctuaries.

We think up diverse expedients for driving out the gods. But eventually the gods will exact sacrifices from man; they will exact sacrifices that cannot be paid merely by pious visits to the shrines.

Because we do not protect the universe within a grain of brown rice, because we do not respect and revere that life in our food, we must bear the burden of building all those many different shrines.

Cancer wards and children's hospitals are no longer enough. Nor are neurological clinics, psychiatric treatment centers, psychiatric wards, or human organ banks. All of these are white shrines where refining priests serve. The Japanese are dependable worshipers.

If you truly respect and revere the gods, then shouldn't the first thing you do be to build a shrine within your own body? Isn't building a shrine within your own stomach the first act of reverence?

God dwells in a single grain of rice. God dwells in proper food. Greet in your belly the gods who have come to you from the universe in the form of food, and let them rest here quietly for as long as they please.

I believe that this is the most elementary and basic duty we have as people.

## Nuclear Development Has No Place in the Terrestrial Ecosystem

Please take a long, close look at my Life Cycle Diagram (Fig. 5.1).

Waste or failure do not occur in the atomic transformations carried out by God. These transformations—in our bodies, in objects, the atmosphere, outer space—all take place according to God's will (the Order of the Universe).

The atomic reactors that turn atoms into energy have their places within the respective universes.

The atomic reactor for the solar system has its place in that solar system, and the atomic reactor for the Milky Way has its place within that Milky Way. Similarly, in cosmic space far, far away, there is a place where energy is transformed into elementary particles, and a last reactor where elementary particles are transformed into energy.

In energy transformation within the universal order, means are provided for fully processing pollutants. What God does is without waste or violation. Energy is born at the source of this order so that all things may live and enable each other to live. It is by virtue of this energy that organisms are born.

The very word "development" has a paralyzing effect on our thinking.

When we talk of "development," it appears as if we are announcing that the universal order is to be violated. For example, the development represented by the unrestrained toying with the atom in the terrestrial ecosystem has been a declaration of war on God.

Small local development has led to the development of nuclear arms and atomic power. And, at some point, this has become sanctioned as "development." The very word "development" has a magical quality about it that justifies all sorts of things.

"Nuclear development" has become atomic weapons, hydrogen weapons, and neutron weapons. "Atomic power development" has become atomic power plants and the atomic energy industry.

And, when we use atomic or nuclear energy, what in the world happens to the nuclear wastes after the energy has been extracted?

The reason nuclear energy has so much influence on this earth is that it is energy which does not belong on this earth. Nor do the nuclear wastes cast off as the dregs of this nuclear energy belong here. Such wastes have no place on this earth.

The natural terrestrial ecosystem is an ecosystem that determines itself. It is not something that should be or should have been forcibly determined.

Because nuclear energy and nuclear wastes are both phenomena forcibly introduced by man, forcible effects or actions upon the terrestrial and biological ecosystem must be taken in order for these to return to their proper place. After all, nuclear energy itself only seeks restoration to its original self.

I do not know whether it is correct to speak of the "ecosystem" of energy and the "ecosystem" of elementary particles, but it must be appreciated that the universe has natural ecosystems for each of these.

In order to introduce ecosystems from other dimensions into the terrestrial ecosystem and to reproduce the phenomena of those ecosystems within the terrestrial ecosystem, one must begin by creating an environment for such ecosystems. But doing so is incompatible with the terrestrial ecosystem.

Nuclear and atomic development require enormous outlays of money, However, it is clear that such investment will end as extravagance. The expenses that can be borne by the terrestrial ecosystem are limited. Even if the entire earth were poured into the bargain, it would still be impossible to bring forth an environment of a different dimension onto the earth; in fact, even such an investment would amount to no more than a single drop in a large sea. Yet, in spite of this, the impresarios seeking a profit from the performance continue to push forward such development, while the audience merely holds the futile hope of seeing a single vision as a farewell gift in their journey to the great beyond.

No matter how one looks at it, it is impossible to find even the smallest sliver of ethics or morality in the promotion of nuclear and atomic development. After all, it is a transgression of the Universal Order.

The natural ecosystem on earth is not a fitting place for nuclear development.

## God's Greetings

What sort of greeting does God give to the strong and the weak?

The strong are yang and the weak are yin. Please try to remember this (even allowing for the existence of exceptions to this rule).

One other point: all substances exist as a harmony of Yin and Yang. Nothing is purely yin and nothing is purely yang. Please try to keep this in mind as well.

In the natural world of this terrestrial ecosystem, if "ultra-yang" high energy is obtained from the atomic nucleus, one would expect "ultra-yin" radioactive wastes and fallout to be left behind in its wake.

The moment that it is released, ultra-yang high energy seeks ultra-yin with such an intensity that it sears things in this world; having found its ultra-yin partner, it finally becomes neutralized.

And where do the ultra-yin radioactive wastes and fallout go on the earth? Although these move slowly, they most likely search for a yang or ultra-yang partner, marry as fitting and, becoming neutralized, settle down.

The most yang worlds in the natural terrestrial ecosystem are the sea of fire deep in the earth's interior; the strata of yang elements; and those places on the earth's surface where solar energy is most abundant and ubiquitous. In organisms, the most yang world is that of meat-eating peoples who eat animals, which are themselves yang. These are some of the more strongly yang worlds on our earth.

Because the ultra-yin radioactive fallout seeks a yangness like that of the "husband" which up until a moment before had embraced it tightly, most of the fallout probably attempts to approach the sea of fire within the earth.

But, because of the sadness of yin, the fallout loses the strength to reach the sea of fire and instead takes as its tentative mate the yang elements that it finds in the earth on its way down and takes up residence here.

It enters the bodies of fish and shellfish from the sea, and through the medium of fish and shellfish as food, enters the human body. At the same time, it enters plants from the soil, and from plants makes its way into the food chain in the form of food.

Other fallout components which lack even the vigor to burrow into the earth disperse in the air and water and, while floating about as such, find in the human body a suitable degree of yangness.

Among people too, there are those who are yang and those who are yin. Because the radioactive fallout is itself yin, it seeks out and is attracted to those people who are more yang.

Of the strong and the weak, radioactive fallout is attracted most to the strong. The reason why the "strong" are readily afflicted with cancer and, once afflicted, succumb rapidly and are soon on their way to the other world is most likely due to the attraction of fallout to the yang nature of the strong.

Listen well, you the strong! For the pranks you play with the atom that has no place in this terrestrial world of ours, the gods greet you with the law: "as a man sows, so shall he reap."

The yin of radioactive fallout seeks in the yang of the strong a permanent abode and mate.

Nor is it only the yin of radioactive fallout that is fond of the yang of the strong. Cancer factors and carcinogenic substances too are all yin, and while they are not as intensely yin as radioactive fallout, they too fancy the perverted yangness of the strong.

The eccentric yin that does not care for the strong will search after the deviant yang of the weak, and it is there that cancer will make itself at home.

Is not this the greeting that God will make to the strong and the weak?

God will respond appropriately to both the strong and the weak in proportion to the extent of that arrogance which drives humanity to commit acts which have no place in this world.

## What Rice Is to Americans and to Mankind

The United States is trying hard today to sell American rice to Japan. Let me point out several of the problems that must carefully be considered here.

(1)   The reason why the U.S. began producing rice was exactly the same as with the other agricultural products it makes; the idea was to make rice into a commercial product. Rice growing was begun with the intent of developing rice into a major agricultural product—in the same manner as wheat, corn, oranges, and beef—and selling this to Japan and other rice-eating countries. Japan was no doubt viewed as an especially promising market and so, foreseeing that the U.S. could easily prevail competitively in terms of price, large-scale rice cultivation was promoted.

 Because rice is such an outstanding and valuable food for man, I believe that it is acceptable even if rice production is started as a tool for profit. I would not have much regard for the increased production and high-pressure sales of meat, eggs, and dairy products as I could not see this as being in the interest of man; however, as long as we are talking of producing direct food for man and increasing the rice-eating population of the world, even if profit is the original motive, this cannot possibly be to the detriment of man's future.

But in order to increase the rice-eating population, it is of overriding importance that rice-producing countries become the largest consumers of their own rice. In other words, Americans must themselves eat far more of the rice grown in America. I cannot overstress the importance of this. It is the most proper relationship of Americans to rice for it is consistent with the notion of the unity of the body with the land. The idea is not to merely sell rice as a commodity to other countries, but to eat the rice in one's own country and, more to the point, to eat the rice with the express purpose of improving one's diet such that this rice becomes one's food staple. By so doing, this no longer constitutes merely monetary profit, but by serving to improve and benefit health in the U.S. as a whole, becomes instead "life profit." Such a step will help rid the U.S. of the degenerative diseases of modern civilization that are rampant there.

(2)  Eating meat will destroy humanity. This hardly bears repeating; the evidence is all around us. For an explanation of why eating meat will destroy mankind, please read and consider Ohsawa's reasoning in *The Order of the Universe*. This important work also casts light on the basic cause of modern diseases. The more meat people eat, the greater the regression that results. This tendency will remain the same in the future. Hence, before the U.S. seeks markets in rice-eating nations for the excess rice that it produces, it would be wiser and more proper for it to develop entirely new markets by encouraging improvements in the diets of meat-eating countries and peoples. Eating habits and customs whereby meat serves as the staple food must be corrected by man. Given its leadership status in the community of nations, America is duty-bound to conduct a peace movement that guides humanity to dietary habits in which grains serve as the staple food while meat, vegetables, fish, and seaweeds serve as supplementary foods.

(3)  Man must adopt grains as his staple food. Unless a campaign is launched to encourage all of humanity to eat grains as the food staple, it will be impossible to achieve a world that is everywhere at peace.

I believe that the peace of humanity is proportional to the percentage of mankind that eats grains as its staple.

If the purpose of rice production in the United States is not merely to lay hold of the world's money, but also to furnish rice to meat-eating lands, to countries of food scarcity where people do not know from day to day where their next meal will come from, and to starving peoples everywhere, then this will raise to even greater heights the respect and dignity accorded to America as a great savior nation and to American rice agriculture as a savior of humanity.

(4)  The U.S. must do the above in order to justify rice agriculture. Also, the market liberalization of grain crops on a global scale is necessary for the normalization of grain trade between nations. Not just rice, but all grain transactions should

be freed of controls. This is essential in order that all humanity and all organisms achieve freedom and peace. In order to enable grains to reach all people equally, it is necessary that meat-eating be discontinued and, at the same time, that the distribution of grains be globally liberated; this means that a system of free, unhampered distribution is needed that does not permit commodity price manipulation due to monopolization by large capital. In order to ensure that grains be inexpensive, readily available, and eaten as a food staple everywhere and by everyone on the earth, it is, necessary that high-grade (having vitality), low-cost rice be produced and sold in large quantities. Once this spirit is adhered to, then Japan will be obliged to open its rice markets not only to the United States but also to the entire world.

(5)   If I might be permitted to express my own narrow opinion, I believe that the Japanese should eat Japanese rice. This, I feel, is ideal, correct, and desirable. If American rice and rice grown in other countries were to enter Japan in large amounts, then this might lead to the abandonment of Japanese-grown rice; there is no question that this presents a major problem for Japan and the Japanese. The better one understands the principle of the unity of the body with the land, the more one cannot help becoming aware of the fact that food is intimately and inextricably connected with people and their environment; although we are all one world, this world is filled with subtle differences depending on where we live. Therefore, it is important that the principle be established that people everywhere on earth must first take as their staple diet the grains cultivated in their own climate and soil, and only then make use of foods grown in different lands, the proportion of these foods being directly related to the proximity to their own land. From the perspective of attaining liberty and freedom for the entire world and all of humanity, the advancing of doctrines based on judgments of relative gain or loss for mere peoples or nations is just blatant egoism. As the markets for rice and other grains are opened up, and as both free and appropriate produce markets and modes of distribution emerge, demand and supply that accords with the principle of unity of the body and land will no doubt establish itself. Naturally, in order for this to happen, it will be necessary to make an effort to enhance the average intelligence and reasoning power of mankind; in fact, I believe this to be one indispensable process toward achieving peace. The reason for this is that peace with and toward others is only possible through a spirit of personal sacrifice and denial, and by putting such a spirit into practice. This is a truth that applies both to individuals and to peoples and nations. Those countries and peoples who pride themselves on being great and advanced should take the initiative by becoming models for the whole world.

## A Revolution in American and Global Life Styles

Everyone knows that the front and the back are both part of one whole. If there is a front, there is invariably a back; where there is a brilliant and showy front, then the back is poor and miserable. Excess luxury begets poverty; sustained gluttony results in illness, after which death awaits; behind joy there is sorrow; coupled with success is hardship. Where there are mountains there are also valleys;

if the mountains are high, then the valleys are low. These things are one of the phenomena of the Universal Order.

I imagine that everyone understands by now that this world is made up of the Universal Principle of Yin and Yang. Behind the visible world there is always an invisible world supporting that visible world, and that visible world is but an infinitesimally small part of the invisible world. I imagine that this much should be clear.

Sacrifice and want lurks in the shadows of prosperity. Another way to put this is that sacrifice and want support prosperity.

After England reigned over the world and enjoyed prosperity, it caught the famous "English disease." Today, it is in the process of recovering, but the experience of the English has sounded a major warning to other affluent nations in today's world.

Yet, in spite of that warning, the United States is coming down with its own "American disease." We humans are animals that always seem to crave luxury. Luxury begets illness. Over and over again we endure suffering, hardships, and pain, only to indulge once more in luxury and extravagance, which plunges us again into illness until ultimately we die a painful, grievous death. Perhaps the desire for extravagance is a disease that cannot be cured except through death. While this may be so for individuals, in some ways things are not so simple for societies and countries. Yet, the same general principle seems to hold.

Today, America is catching the "American disease." America's extravagance is presenting symptoms of a fundamental malaise.

Looking at the current situation in the U.S., former West German Chancellor Schmidt of West Germany recently predicted that if things continue as they presently are, by the end of the twentieth century, America's foreign debts will reach one trillion dollars. Schmidt sketches a broad scenario in which this will result in the adoption of inflationary policies, leading to a drastic fall in the value of the U.S. dollar, and ultimately, chaos in the world economy. According to Schmidt, the only way to prevent this eventuality is to raise taxes which means lowering the standard of living.

The way to treat this "American disease" is to lower the standard of living. Because curing this ailment will also help ward off similar "diseases" elsewhere and will have the effect of curing already debilitated countries, it is absolutely essential that America regain her fiscal health. I too believe that the only way to accomplish this is to lower the standard of living by raising taxes.

Everyone hates the idea of raising taxes. Everyone dislikes the idea of lowering the standard of living. Having to tighten one's belt leaves one with a sentiment of fear and anxiety as if one's life were being threatened.

So the problem is how lowering the living standard is to be achieved. The issue at hand is whether it is possible, while chained and manacled with tax increases, to assure better health and happiness than at present and to live a satisfying life without a decline in the quality of one's life.

To be quite truthful, raising taxes (lowering the standard of living) is a decision that requires extraordinary courage, but I believe doing so would be incredibly effective. This is what is needed most today, and unless the prescription slip is misread, such a therapy will revive the patient. Of course, it is up to the patient's will to recover whether such a valuable therapy shall end as merely symptomatic treatment or whether the effort shall be made to achieve a fundamental cure.

I can provide a way of living whereby people will never become unhappy even if the standard of living is reduced through increased taxes. I can provide a way of living that radically and fundamentally cures people of today's diseases, increases health, restores national finances to a sound footing while leaving budgetary latitude, and enables people to live full lives. The idea is to carry out a revolution in living by using a reduction in living standards as an opportunity. Macrobiotics converts the misfortune of increased taxes into fortune. Rather than being forced from without to grudgingly cut back expenses and live more parsimoniously, by taking things in hand yourself and rising to the challenge of new life through macrobiotics, you can establish your own way of life. Whether America can rid itself of this "American disease" before things get even worse depends on the ability of its people to boldly and correctly lower their own standard of living. The adoption of rice cultivation in many parts of America is due no doubt to God's divine guidance in encouraging people to reexamine their standard of living through an improvement in their eating habits. This is guidance which shows that the only way to restore to a normal condition bodies and minds ailing from carnivorous gluttony, societies and nations ailing from the gluttony of science and industrial technology, and a world ailing from the outpouring of diverse prejudices and arrogance is to make use of rice, that supreme food among the grains.

Fortunately, the U.S. has a sufficiently large rice production for improving people's diet. There is no need whatsoever for the people or the country to fear the decline in living standards that results from a rise in taxes. This need not constitute misfortune at all. On the contrary, it can be the start of a great enterprise by mankind that resuscitates life and sets out to achieve a new and happy world. I pray and urge both the government and the people to devote themselves courageously to improving their diet by the proper eating of rice. This is the only gift I can give.

# Index